How to Think Psychologically

This book discusses the psychological understanding of, and approach to, various central questions and aspects of psychological reality, in each case critically examining under what conditions one's interpretation qualifies as "truly psychological", i.e. fulfilling the criteria of a rigorous notion of psychology in the Jungian tradition.

Providing groundbreaking new insights into psychological theory, Giegerich explores many different topics such as the origin of the notion of the soul (*psychē*), the rise of monotheism, the psychological significance of Christianity in Western history, the inner, above all tautegorical structure of myth, and the soul's relation to external reality, amongst others. Sometimes surprising and at times challenging, but always concretely based and carefully explained and argued, this book will provide readers with an accessible demonstration of the methodological stance of psychology as the discipline of interiority.

This will be of great interest to the Jungian community, psychotherapists and psychoanalysts training in Jungian theory and practice, as well as those interested in psychological, theological, and philosophical issues.

Wolfgang Giegerich is a Jungian psychoanalyst, now living in Berlin, who is a regular speaker at conferences, and teacher at institutions globally. He is the author of numerous publications, including over 20 books, with several books and numerous articles translated into Italian, Japanese, Portuguese, and Spanish.

The Collected English Papers of Wolfgang Giegerich

The Collected English Papers of Wolfgang Giegerich makes the work of one of archetypal psychology's most brilliant theorists available in one place. A practicing Jungian analyst and a long-time contributor to the field, Giegerich is renowned for his dedication to the substance of Jungian thought and for his unparalleled ability to think it through with both rigor and speculative strength.

Titles in this series:

The Neurosis of Psychology
Primary Papers Towards a Critical Psychology *(Volume 1)*

Technology and the Soul
From the Nuclear Bomb to the World Wide Web *(Volume 2)*

Soul-Violence *(Volume 3)*

The Soul Always Thinks *(Volume 4)*

The Flight into the Unconscious
An Analysis of C.G. Jung's Psychology Project *(Volume 5)*

"Dreaming the Myth Onwards"
C.G. Jung on Christianity and on Hegel *(Volume 6)*

How to Think Psychologically
With Jung Beyond Jung *(Volume 7)*

Sharpening Psychology's Concepts
The Spirit of Jungian Psychology and the Danger of Faulty Thinking *(Volume 8)*

For a full list of titles in this series, please visit www.routledge.com/The-Collected-English-Papers-of-Wolfgang-Giegerich/book-series/CEPWG

How to Think Psychologically

With Jung Beyond Jung

Collected English Papers

Volume Seven

Wolfgang Giegerich

Routledge
Taylor & Francis Group

LONDON AND NEW YORK

Designed cover image: Getty Images

First published 2025
by Routledge
4 Park Square, Milton Park, Abingdon, Oxon OX14 4RN

and by Routledge
605 Third Avenue, New York, NY 10158

Routledge is an imprint of the Taylor & Francis Group, an informa business

British Library Cataloguing-in-Publication Data
A catalogue record for this book is available from the British Library

ISBN: 978-1-041-00737-1 (hbk)
ISBN: 978-1-041-00735-7 (pbk)
ISBN: 978-1-003-61140-0 (ebk)

DOI: 10.4324/9781003611400

Typeset in Times New Roman
by Apex CoVantage, LLC

Contents

Acknowledgments

For his always insightful and stimulating feedback and support, from which also this volume benefitted, as well as for his friendship over many years, the author wishes to express his deep gratitude to Greg Mogenson.

Chapter 6, "Love the Questions Themselves: Wolfgang Giegerich at 66, Interviewed by Rob Henderson" first appeared in Robert and Janis Henderson, *"Enterviews" with Jungian Analysts*, vol. 3, New Orleans, Louisiana (Spring Journals Books) 2010, pp. 263–302. It is published here with a few minor changes. I am indebted to Robert Henderson for giving me his gracious permission to do whatever I would like with this text and also to include it in my *Collected English Essays*.

Sources and Abbreviations

For frequently cited sources, the following abbreviations have been used:

CW: Jung. C.G., *Collected Works*. 20 vols. Ed. Herbert Read, Michael Fordham, Gerhard Adler, and William McGuire. Trans. R.F.C. Hull. Princeton: Princeton University Press, 1957–1979. Cited by volume and, unless otherwise noted, by paragraph number.

GW: Jung, C.G., *Gesammelte Werke*. 20 vols., various editors, Olten and Freiburg im Breisgau: Walter-Verlag, 1971–1983. Cited by volume and, unless otherwise noted, by paragraph number.

Letters: Jung. C.G., *Letters*. 2 vols. Ed. Gerhard Adler. Bollingen Series XCV: 2. Princeton: Princeton University Press. 1975.

Briefe: Jung, C.G., *Briefe*. 3 vols. Ed. Aniela Jaffé, in Zusammenarbeit mit Gerhard Adler. Olten and Freiburg i. Br.: Walter-Verlag, 1972–1973.

MDR: Jung, C.G., *Memories, Dreams. Reflections*. Rev. edn., Ed. Aniela Jaffé. Trans. Richard and Clara Winston. New York: Vintage Books, 1989. Cited by page number.

Erinn.:   *Erinnerungen, Träume, Gedanken von C.G. Jung*. Ed. Aniela Jaffé. Zürich and Stuttgart: Rascher, 1967.

CEP: Giegerich, W., *Collected English Papers*. 8 vols. New Orleans, LA: Spring Journal Books, 2006 ff., now London and New York: Routledge, 2020.

Transl. modif: Appearing at the end of a citation, this indicates that I modified the particular quotation from the *Collected Works* or *MDR* in order to bring the English translation a bit closer to the wording and spirit of Jung's original German text.

Introduction

How to Think Psychologically

To some the title of this book, *How to Think Psychologically*, sounds perhaps like that of one of the how-to books with which the book market is flooded. Such books, whatever their particular subject may be, try to present to the reader simple strategies for the reader's acquiring, with as little effort as possible, some skill or knowledge. Their very point is to offer answers to the how-to question and thus they follow the natural course of the general practice of raising questions. For in asking questions, the mind is normally only interested in the answers. The question is no more than a means to an end or a kind of stimulus to elicit the sought-for answer. In itself it is of no importance. The moment it has been answered the question can be forgotten because it has served its purpose and what alone counts and now needs to be kept in mind is the answer.

The title of the present book is different. "How to think psychologically", as a *psychological* question (even if one in statement form), is a *real* question, an open question, a question that cannot find a fixed answer. And this means that it puts psychology itself, i.e., the nature of what psychology is or rather what the psychological approach to phenomena has to be, into question. Thus "How to think psychologically" prevents us from simply following the natural course of immediately rushing forward to possible answers (e.g., answers of the type: To think psychologically one has to do this and this and that). Instead, this question returns us back to itself. It makes us stop and dwell with the question in order, as it were, to try to hatch it out so that in the end it might possibly come home to itself. It may even turn out to be itself the answer.

Upon first hearing the phrase, "How to think psychologically", it does not in any way sound strange, surprising, or unreasonable. It can be spontaneously accepted as a legitimate question. But that it is something special

DOI: 10.4324/9781003611400-1

becomes clear the moment we try to transpose it to other fields: "How to think biologically", "How to think sociologically", "How to think in chemistry / physics / astronomy". These formulations sound weird, maybe even absurd. The reason is that all those fields share the same kind of scientific thinking and any differences in the particular categories to be applied or methodological procedures to be followed are only due to the differences of their particular objects of investigation and not to differences in the mind's thinking-style and thus do not lie on the side of the human subject. That we are not startled by "How to think psychologically" is because psychology, at least as a "psychology with soul" in the tradition of C.G. Jung, is not a discipline of study that has a well-circumscribed object or a clearly delimited field vis-à-vis itself, i.e., vis-à-vis the subject, the psychologist, and distinct from him. Instead of having an object about which, because of this distinctness, positive facts could be established, it is rather a field that consists to a major extent of interpretations by the subject, by the individual psychologists. Psychology is mainly subject-based and for this reason very much dependent on the mental framework and apperception of the persons doing psychology. This inescapably subjective basis is also the reason why there can be and in fact are quite a number of very different, competing disciplines or approaches, all calling themselves and believing to be psychology (by which I refer here only to those psychologies with a therapeutic or human-life interest). This situation gives immediate rise to the question, "How to think psychologically", in the sense of: How do we have to think so that our thinking can rightly be called psychological?

That psychology is special or even unique becomes even more evident when we take into account Jung's thesis, a most essential insight, about the historicity of psychology. I have discussed this thesis several times already in previous texts, but will now take a look at it under a new perspective. As our starting point I present the following three pertinent quotations. Jung wrote:

> Why is psychology the youngest of the empirical sciences? Why had the unconscious not long since been discovered and its treasure of eternal images lifted? Simply because we had a religious formula for all the things of the soul—and one that is far more beautiful and comprehensive than immediate experience. (*CW* 9i § 11)
>
> Whenever there exists externally a conceptual or ritual form in which all the yearnings and hopes of the soul are absorbed and expressed, that

is, for example, a living religion, then the soul is outside and there is no soul problem, just as there is then no unconscious in our sense. It was therefore logical that the discovery of psychology took exclusively place during the last decades, although former centuries possessed enough introspection and intelligence to gain knowledge about psychological facts. (*CW* 10 § 158, transl. modif.)

This problem is new. All ages before us have believed in gods in some form or other. Only an unparalleled impoverishment of symbolism could enable us to rediscover the gods as psychic factors, that is, as archetypes of the unconscious. (*CW* 9i § 50)

Obviously, these quotations are still hampered by Jung's use of the concept of "the unconscious" which is an attempt at reifying psychological reality or the soul and at localizing it in man, in positively existing people, which is an unfortunate leftover of 19th century naturalistic thinking. (The term "the unconscious" in these quoted passages refers, of course, to Jung's "collective unconscious" and not to the unconsciousness of repressed or forgotten or still subliminal personal contents.) But Jung's still working with this term must not pose a problem for us. We can, in our mind, simply ignore the reference to "the unconscious" or substitute for it the idea of the whole of all the autonomous contents of psychological reality. If we do that we can proceed by concentrating, in our context, on the particulars of Jung's historicity thesis and what it says about the status of psychology as a field of study.[1]

All sciences are, of course, historical in the sense that they did not exist from the beginning of human history. The purely *theoretical* relation to reality, which requires rigorous abstraction from all immediate needs of life and without which there cannot be any science, is something entirely new in the history of mankind. And the many individual sciences originated in the course of the continuous self-development of man's theoretical interest in the exploration of reality: The first truly scientific inquiries concerned the most obvious, impressive phenomena of reality and the more the understanding of those advanced, the more the scientific interest could turn to neighboring areas; and the deeper the scientific gaze had penetrated into a particular aspect of reality, the more complicated things became so that

---

1 Just to mention it, another flaw is that Jung still firmly believed in "immediate experience".

each respective science had as a matter of course to multiply into several new specialized sub-disciplines, which in turn could then become sciences in their own right.

According to what Jung says about it, the emergence of psychology cannot be understood in the same way as the natural result of the self-development of man's purely *theoretical interest*. It was not simply so that, after the much earlier scientific exploration of the stars, the physical nature of the world, the human body, etc., in modernity *intellectual curiosity* at long last also turned its attention to a previously neglected and completely different aspect or area of reality, namely, to what goes on inside people, to the causes, functions, and effects of human emotions, impulses, desires, and thoughts. To be sure, this may be the reason why "academic psychology", the psychology that works with experiments and statistical evaluations, could arise. But psychology the way Jung envisioned it originated solely through a fundamental cultural change. The condition of the possibility of psychology was "an unparalleled impoverishment of symbolism", the loss of the belief in "gods in whatever form", the disappearance (not of religion, but) of any really "*living* religion", the loss of a "conceptual or ritual form in which all the yearnings and hopes [we could add: As well as afflictions and conflicts] of the soul are absorbed and expressed" in a form "that is far more beautiful and comprehensive than immediate experience". In other words, the possibility (and actual emergence) of psychology as a discipline depended on an *objective* change in the real history of the soul's life itself.

Chemistry did not originate through a fundamental chemical change in the nature of things. Its origin had nothing whatsoever to do with objective reality. It arose solely on the side of the subject, of *the human mind*, because it at some point in history became seriously interested in this aspect of reality and had mentally and technically become ready to methodically investigate it. The discipline of psychology, however, owes its existence to a radical revolutionary change in the history of the object of this discipline and to be studied by it. Here the serpent is biting its own tail. Psychology is uroboric. It is not a science having that object that it is about objectively vis-à-vis itself. It is itself a product of and inseparable from the soul process to be studied by it. Or, to put it another way, psychology is itself a psychological *phenomenon* (not *also* a psychological phenomenon, i.e., another phenomenon, in addition to the phenomenon to be studied by it, but the psychological studying of the psychological phenomenon is itself phenomenal).

Now it is clear what the difference between the historical origin of the sciences and the historicity of psychology is. For the sciences it is only their origin and their own development that is historical, but their findings, even the most modern, most recent ones, are valid at all times and thus were even valid, e.g., already in prehistoric times. Psychology, by contrast, is *in itself* historical, it exists only as an integral part of the soul's life; it is inextricably contained in the process of the soul's self-manifestation, self-production, that it is studying.

We therefore need to connect Jung's historicity thesis with his thesis about the logical constitution of psychology. Both theses are two sides of the same coin. Concerning the internal logic of psychology Jung wrote:

> . . . it [psychology] lacks the immense advantage of an Archimedean point such as physics enjoys. The latter observes—from the *psychic* standpoint—the *physical* world and can translate this into *psychic* terms. The psyche, on the other hand, observes itself and can only translate its observation again into other psychic terms. (*CW* 8 § 421, transl. modif., my italics.)

As far as physics is concerned, the observation of a physical phenomenon is a mental and thus psychic act, and the knowledge gained about this physical reality through the observation is, again as a mental insight, likewise a psychic reality. In this sense, in the science of physics real physical relations are "translated" into psychic reality (theoretical knowledge). By contrast, psychology is inescapably wrapped up within itself, in its own magic circle. It is dealing only with its own mirror reflections, images, interpretations. One could even say that psychology does nothing else but play its own language game, merely "renaming", "re-imagining" *its own* mental contents, only maybe combining them in new ways. The following quotation expresses this insight even more decisively.

> It [psychology] can only translate itself back into its own language, or fashion itself in its own image. . . . [P]sychology inevitably merges with the psychic process itself. It can no longer be distinguished from the latter, and so turns into it. . . . [I]t is not, in the deeper sense, an explanation of this process, for no explanation of the psychic can be anything other than the living process of the psyche itself. Psychology has to sublate itself as a science and therein precisely it reaches its scientific goal. Every other

science has a point outside of itself; not so psychology, whose object is the very subject that produces all science. (*CW* 8 § 429, transl. modif.)

It follows from this crucial insight into the logical nature of psychology that any endeavor at establishing psychology as an objective science is either illusionary or is not intent upon veritable *psychology* at all, aiming simply for another, entirely different (and yet confusingly like-named) science. To be a *true* psychology, psychology has to comprehend and know itself (and its observations, ideas, and statements) as themselves being an integral part of the psychic process.

This is already one answer to the question of "how to think psychologically".

So far I devoted myself, concerning Jung's historicity thesis, only to the fact that for him psychology was in itself historical and was contained within the soul's own life. I did not pay any attention yet to the particulars of the historical change Jung described. What was it that changed? What was this change actually about?

The change itself is an event of a fundamental loss. Religion[2] as a *living* reality disappeared. Jung speaks of "an unparalleled impoverishment of symbolism". Before the change the soul had the form of "a religious formula for all the things of the soul—and one that is far more beautiful and comprehensive than immediate experience". It was visibly present in lived life in impressive ritual practices. Its "treasures of eternal images" stood in the light of the whole people's consciousness. Thus, what the change brought was simply this lack, emptiness, nothing. Religion was not replaced by a new, different, but fully equivalent soul content, the way, for example, a political revolution might replace a monarchy by a republic, a tyranny by democracy. The loss of religion left only a hole.[3] And though psychology was the successor to religion, that did not mean the end of the lack. On the contrary: If psychology became solely possible through the loss of religion, then psychology's *mother* is loss, lack, and emptiness—and loss and emptiness are psychology's inheritance, its very "genetic makeup".

---

2 I use the term "religion" loosely for what Jung termed "a conceptual or ritual form in which all the yearnings and hopes of the soul are absorbed and expressed, that is, for example, a living religion". In other words, the word "religion" here stands as an abbreviation for mythologies, the practices of the ritualistic cultures, religions in the strict sense, as well as for metaphysics.

3 A hole that of course was filled by numerous surrogates. But surrogates only pretend to fill the hole. The soul remains empty.

This is the crucial implication inherent in Jung's historicity thesis about psychology. The change is a change from the richness, beauty, and fullness of the soul qua religion to its radical poverty ("impoverishment") qua psychology. But on both sides of the revolutionary change is one and the same soul. It was not people who got rid of religion as a living reality, nor was it some external fateful mishap that caused this loss. No, the revolutionary change was the soul's own doing, its own move, indeed its self-transformation, metamorphosis. If we follow (not so much what Jung explicitly says, but) the inner logic of his argument, then the soul had to relinquish its own so impressively rich and beautiful form of "living religion" (in the widest sense) in order to become able to give birth to itself in the absolute poverty form of psychology. It is a real *kénôsis* event[4] in modern history.

We immediately understand what "loss of religion" means. It means that there is for us no God, no beyond, no transcendence, no higher meaning of life. But with this obvious understanding we remain in the mentality of everyday thinking and have not yet comprehended what this loss psychologically means, that is to say, what for the soul is really at stake in this revolutionary change: Psychologically, it is a change from semantics to logical or syntactic form. With the loss of religion, the soul gave up all its contents, its entire inherited semantics. And by giving it up it did not, as already emphasized, only relinquish one particular one (its specific, historically inherited semantics) in order to replace it by an entirely new one. What this change is about is much rather and much more radically that the form of *semantics as such and altogether* was given up, the soul's being defined (or definable) by semantic contents in general. And the poverty it chose instead is not ordinary poverty, but the move to the form *of form*. Form as such, without any semantic content, is utterly empty. The inner telos of the change that Jung described with his thesis about the historicity of psychology is ultimately psychological consciousness's initiation into the logic of emptiness; we could also say: Into negativity as such, absolute negativity. And the psychology that results from this change (from the loss of religion), in other words, psychology proper, is bound to be the discipline of absolute negativity. Alchemically (and thus, *against the grain*, once

4 The paradigmatic model of *kénôsis* is Philippians 2:6–7, where we read about Jesus Christ: "Who, being in the form of God, did not count equality with God something to be grasped. But he emptied [*ekénôsen*] himself, taking the form of a slave, becoming as human beings are; and being in every way like a human being".

more imaginally) speaking, it is the stirring spirit Mercurius that brought about this change because it wanted to free itself from its imprisonment in its semantic shell, the religious (as well as whatever other) imagery, in order to come home to itself as spirit.[5]

Seen in this light, the view that there was a "*loss*" of religion is the apperception of the historical change by a consciousness that is still firmly informed by and clinging to the semantic standpoint, whereas from the Mercurial standpoint the same change appears as a liberation and as an attainment to a higher, much more subtle and refined status. There *is* not really a *loss*. Nothing gets lost. Instead, the seemingly lost contents can get, as it were, distilled so that they come home to themselves. How does this happen? By our *thinking psychologically*, really *thinking* the various semantic contents that, be it history or be it our present, presents us with.

But what is this thinking, this thinking psychologically? It needs to be distinguished from the ordinary reception of the semantic contents, of images or statements. That ordinary or *natural* reception consists in our simply understanding *what they mean to say*, what their intention is, and therefore either in our believing them, abiding by them, drawing conclusions from them, or rejecting, doubting, disputing, contradicting them. It does not matter which, because both, the affirmative and the negative responses, are logically alike, both are conventional. In each case the mind follows as a matter of course the intentionality of the respective statement (and images are also statements, only not in the form of statements). The mind is simply taken with it, we could almost say "seduced" by it. It sort of does the statement's bidding. So much about the ordinary or natural reception. But "thinking it (the statement)" *halts* this one's being taken with the forward movement of its intentionality and returns and applies the statement to itself, reading it as a "speculative sentence".[6] Thinking it is the move,

5 The spirit Mercurius's freeing itself and coming home to itself as spirit is tantamount to its self-sublation, its ceasing to be the spirit Mercurius (to exist in this imaginal, substantiated form). This parallels the history of alchemy itself, of which I showed in my *The Soul's Logical Life*, Frankfurt et al. (Peter Lang) 1998, 5th edition Berlin 2020, pp. 140 and 160, that to fulfill itself it had to sublate itself, to go under and disappear as imaginal discipline.
6 In numerous essays Greg Mogenson has discussed, exemplified, and *practiced* the notion of the speculative sentence. I mention only his books *Notional Practice. The Speculative Turn in Analytical Psychology*, London; Ontario (Dusk Owl Books) 2024 and *Jungian Analysis Post Mortem Dei*, London; Ontario (Dusk Owl Books) 2021.

contra naturam, from what the statement obviously means, from the message that it wants to communicate, to what is *actually (objectively) said* by it.[7] What it means is always the "ego's" (the speaker's, the human person's, the society's, or the cultural tradition's) meaning, which even applies to our understanding of such a decidedly not ordinary meaning as the *archetypal* one of a symbol or image. What utterances or images mean belongs to the sphere of human communication. Psychologically, it takes place within the *unio naturalis*, following as it does the natural course. What *is said* by a statement or image or other psychological content, by contrast, is the soul's own self-expression. In this sense we can see why this move from what something means to what it in truth says can alchemically be expressed as the spirit Mercurius's liberation and coming into his own.

Psychology, I pointed out, is the discipline of absolute negativity. Thinking *psychologically* is logically negative because it is *thinking* psychologically. It does not produce thoughts as entities that one then has as one's possession, but it can only be as the act of actually thinking what in each case needs to be thought. It is fundamentally actuose, performative, but as such also fleeting, transient. It *is* only if and as long as it is in fact being thought. It has the form of form. Psychology cannot come up with semantic contents (not with findings, results, messages, a doctrine or theory, nor with answers to the question of Meaning). It is concerned only with the logic, the syntax, of the real. *As a discipline* it is empty form, just a methodology, and *as the presence of the modern form of soul*, as the successor to and sublation of the ancient mythological and the later metaphysical soul, it is real only in the actual momentary events of spirit and, which is the same thing, in the form of logical negativity.

Jung had the inestimable insight into the birth of true psychology out of loss of mythology, religion, and metaphysics. He had fully understood that what had disappeared was not merely one particular "conceptual or ritual form in which all the yearnings and hopes of the soul are absorbed and expressed,

---

7 "What is said by the statement" can linguistically also be expressed by "what it means *psychologically* (for the soul, or from the soul point of view)". But this latter phrase could easily lead to confusion because of that other "means" in "what it means" and, above all, it is less precise. "What is objectively said" directly requires one's returning to and dwelling with the exact wording of the statement, whereas with "what is meant" we have already left the statement itself—the earth—behind and risen, with our understanding of its *meaning*, above it into the higher sphere of free-floating ideas, our *natural* habitat as human beings.

that is, for example, a living religion", but that such a form (the form of myth, religion, or metaphysics) as such had in the modern situation become impossible, and this means that the condition of the possibility of any *semantic* satisfaction of the soul's "yearnings and hopes" no longer existed. The soul had outlived the time of the *semantic* form of its realization altogether.

But Jung was unfortunately inconsistent in the consequences he drew from this insight. More than that, he refused, or was unable, to abide by the implications of his own insight. On the main, his—ultimately visibly spiteful—reaction followed the pattern: "No, evidently we no longer have any myth. But then what is your myth? The myth in which you do live?" On the main, the whole effort of his psychology was therefore, in the last analysis, devoted to the project of rescuing the outdated level of semantics for the soul. His practical *solution* for the recognized problem of the loss of religion, i.e., of psychological semantics, was his move from "external" to "internal", from "public" to "private", from "general objective *truth*" to "subjective personal felt experience" (*Erlebnis*). If I cannot live in a time in which "there exists *externally* [and this also means objectively] a conceptual or ritual form", then I try to find at least an equivalent in the *psychic* processes inside *people*, in the private inner life of individuals: So one could perhaps describe this his decisively *personalistic* move. For, after all, people in modernity still do dream, still have visions or fantasies; they still have spiritual longings and can be emotionally impressed by dream or visionary images that *formally* are similar to mythic images (a phenomenon that goes in his psychology under the title "numinosity").

The only thing that was still needed for Jung to compensate for the painfully felt deficiency of this personalistic and subjectivist solution was the trick of (a) declaring the personal dreams from the unconscious of people to have been the true (but formerly unknown) origin or source even of the ancient myths and gods, i.e., of the entire externally existing "conceptual or ritual form", and (b) of theoretically underpinning this view with the theory of the "collective unconscious" and the "archetypes-in-themselves". Both moves are logically unconvincing. The private and personal is not intrinsically "collective" and the objective structures of the soul—mythology, religion, and metaphysics—cannot reductively be derived from personal inner experience of individual people.

At any rate, two of his main concerns, the one concerning the individuals, namely the individuation process, on the one hand, and his ideas about what psychologically was necessary for the collective, namely, his speculations about the nature of God and the needed further development of the Christian Trinity into a Quaternity, etc., on the other hand, all remained on and solidified the semantic level. Jung's psychology is characterized by its image-fixation, which in altered and at the same time intensified form continued in Hillman's work.

One can find this tragic. Jung has done so much for a veritable psychology, a psychology with soul, but at least in those few cited areas of his work he remained, like Moses, outside of the Promised Land of how to think psychologically, whose prophet he after all was. He had to remain outside because, according to the implications of his own historicity insight, psychology begins only when the realm of the semantic has been transcended in favor of the syntax and absolute negativity of the soul. What Jung on the main offered was *for the soul* only a toy model of an answer, which, as much as it may satisfy *people*, did not answer the modern soul's real need, similar to how for adults model railroads may satisfy the outlived *child* in them, but are pointless for their real life in the modern world.[8]

So it remains to us to start *living* the question of how to think psychologically, and this concerning each phenomenon, each particular psychological topic.

When I quoted above the passage from Jung, *CW* 8 § 429, that started with: "It [psychology] can only translate itself back into its own language, or fashion itself in its own image. . . . [P]sychology inevitably merges with the psychic process itself. It can no longer be distinguished from the latter, and so turns into it", I replaced Jung's next two and a half sentences by another set of omission marks because they introduce a completely new thought that would have taken away our attention from the immediate issue I wished to discuss at that point. But now I have to make up for this omission and cite this text. It reads:

> But the effect of this [of the merging of psychology with the psychic process] is that the process attains to consciousness. In this way, psychology actualizes the unconscious urge to consciousness. It is, in fact, coming to consciousness of the psychic process, but it is not, in the deeper sense, an explanation of this process. (*CW* 8 § 429)

---

8 This comparison is of course not quite accurate because model railroads are the toy version of the by no means outdated real railroads, whereas semantic images qua images are not the toy version of the sphere of logical or syntactical form and absolute negativity required by the soul in modernity.

Here, where Jung is on the pinnacle of his theoretical insights and where, in his conceptual thought, psychology has truly *arrived* and the soul really come home to itself, here he makes this comment that lets us get a far-reaching idea about what the purpose and benefit of, and thus also the deeper psychological reason for, the historical change from an externally existing "conceptual or ritual form in which all the yearnings and hopes of the soul are absorbed and expressed, that is, for example, a living religion" to psychology in its emptiness (and this means from the semantics of the soul to its syntactical form) is. This purpose and benefit is the need of, as well as the opportunity for, the soul's becoming conscious of *itself*, conscious of itself in its absolute negativity and as sheer process, performance, actuosity, life: The soul's logical life—the life of "how to think psychologically". Psychology, if and where it really happens, if and where it is, like the speculative sentence, the return of the soul's life back into itself, is the presence of the soul itself *in the form of consciousness*, of conscious self-knowing. Mythology, religion, and all semantic-imaginal equivalents of them, on the other hand, are the spirit Mercurius kept imprisoned in "matter" or the soul merely "acted out", as it were, instead of *"erinnert"* (inwardized): The soul in its first-immediacy form of alienation.

Looking back at all the previous volumes of these collected English papers of mine, one could say that the ideas expressed in their different titles, as elucidated in the introductions of each, come together in the title of the present volume or that this title could just as well have been the title of the whole series. Turning to the essays of the present book, the first discusses "interiority" as archaic Man's mode of being-in-the-world, the historical fate of interiority through, at first, the emergence of monotheism and, later, the Christian idea of the incarnation and why modernity had to become the time of externality.

The second chapter shows how "absolute negativity" is the key to understanding the primordial origin of notions of "soul" and "underworld" and what a *psychological* answer to the modern disparagement of them as primitive superstitions has to be.

In the next essay, *"real"* negation refers to the experience of the modern obsolescence of symbols. Jung's comment about his own relation to the Mass reveals that, psychologically thought, this obsolescence amounts to the falling apart of truth into two different truths. The obsolescence turns out not to be a fault, but to have a crucial psychological purpose.

The fourth chapter, starting out from the modern idea of the confrontation of early Man with the fundamentally alien world and that mythology was Man's strategy to gain a distance to the horror of reality, argues that the *human* animal was from the outset in a real *relation* to the world and that this relation is the basis of mythology as well as of all culture. With the help of an in-depth analysis of Jung's experience at the Athi Plaines in East Africa the understanding of what "consciousness of the world" means is unfolded.

Chapter 5, taking issue with Marco Barreto's construal of the myth of Aktaion and Artemis (and of psychology!) as a "Great Hunt" for truth and with his view that the psychology as the discipline of interiority is secretly Kant-based and that it must have more than the status of a pastime in the modern world, namely, that it must have a metaphysical commitment, are due to a stance that is philosophical and not really psychological.

The book ends with an interview that Robert Henderson conducted with me. While also touching on my own development as a Jungian analyst and some personal general views or preferences, on the main it presents some major stances, attitudes, and methodological approaches characteristic of psychology as the discipline of interiority (and thus also of "how to think psychologically") in a more conversational way.

Chapter 1

Interiority and accomplished modernity[1]

The answer to the question of this conference, "Where is Soul?", could be given in the one word: *Nowhere*. And the name of this nowhere is *interiority*. To fill this answer with concrete meaning we have to examine what interiority is, its logical genesis and constitution.

For this purpose a clear criterion is needed that allows us to decide when interiority has truly been achieved and when not. Jung's occasional statement apropos of a particular dream provides us with such a yardstick. Jung said that for a truly psychological dream interpretation "behind the impressions of the daily life—behind the scenes—*another* picture looms up, covered by a thin veil of actual facts".[2] Obviously this statement is at the same time one formulation of the "psychological difference".

From Jung's "two kinds of thinking" to two kinds of seeing

"The impressions of the daily life", "the scenes" and "a thin veil of actual facts" are Jung's designations for the non-psychological or external view. What, by contrast, is beheld from the soul's standpoint of interiority is "the other picture that looms up". The two stances or perspectives that produce these mutually exclusive perceptions could be illustrated by the difference between a modern chemist and a medieval alchemist looking at the same chemical phenomena. For the chemist as modern scientist the

1 Written in 2024. A short version of this essay was presented at the 9th ISPDI conference in Berlin, August 2, 2024.
2 C.G. Jung, *The Visions Seminars*, From the Complete Notes of Mary Foote, Book One (Zürich: Spring Publications, 1976), Book One (Lectures October 30 – November 5, 1930), p. 8.

DOI: 10.4324/9781003611400-2

processes will be nothing but the positive facts of the transformations of chemical substances. The adept, on the other hand, will view the same processes as a spiritual mystery and see in them such things as, for example, the appearance of a green lion, a salamander frolicking in the fire, or the Mercurial serpent devouring itself. One and the same object produces these entirely different perceptions.[3] Jung's early main work began with a chapter entitled, "The two kinds of thinking".[4] The difference *we* have here run into forces us to discriminate between *the two kinds of seeing* as two fundamentally different styles of *relating to reality* or *being-in-the-world*.

The very important concern Jung had in establishing the difference between two kinds of thinking was to demonstrate the legitimacy of mythological images and stories over against the positivistic and rationalistic orientation which exclusively ruled at his time. But his presentation did not really do justice *to his own concern*. Contrasting "directed thinking" with "non-directed thinking" and understanding the latter as fantasizing, mythologizing, and the use of the imagination, his discussion does not go beyond the horizon of the merely *psychic* functions, faculties, and operations of human beings. Thus it perceives only an obvious and itself positivistic (!) surface aspect: Only the fact that what in the second kind of so-called "thinking" *results in* is *images*.[5] What escapes him is the real *ground* of mythological images. They are not due to a different ("non-directed") kind of *thinking* nor to the *imagination*. Rather, they are expressive of a fundamentally different kind of world-experience, an entirely different stance

---

3 The expression "behind the scenes" and the phrases "another picture" and "covered by (a thin veil of)" might invite the misunderstanding as if Jung had here reverted to the Freudian distinction between the "manifest" and the "latent" dream. But as always, so here too, the dream is for Jung not a façade purposely concealing or distorting the dream's actual meaning. No, the dream is for Jung the best possible formulation of what it wants to express; it is "its own interpretation" (CW 11 § 41); and "the image [exactly as it appears in the dream] has everything it needs within itself" (CW 14 § 749). The solution of this little problem that might arise for some persons lies in the observation that when Jung speaks of "another picture" that looms up, he did neither say nor mean "another *image*" (instead of the actual dream image). "Another picture" means: The whole *picture* of the situation in the dream changes for the psychologist looking at the dream; the *light* in which, or the horizon or frame of reference within which, the same actual images of the dream will be perceived and understood, will be a different one.

4 C.G. Jung, *Wandlungen und Symbole der Libido* (1912), also in the completely revised edition *Symbole der Wandlung* 1950. In English in *CW* 5.

5 The term "thinking" is completely misplaced and misleading. What Jung has in mind is nothing else but imagining.

of Man in the world. It is a truly *psychological* difference (rather than the *psychic* difference of Jung's "two kinds of thinking"). Jung's early chapter on the two kinds of thinking, as groundbreaking as it was at the time, foreshadows the image-fixation of the whole Jungian tradition of psychology and its not being truly able to overcome the modern personalistic bias: Psychology's starting out from the isolated individual, which blocks the way to the "objective soul" (Jung's own later discovery!) and thus to a true psychology that deserves its name.[6]

Ordinary as well as scientific seeing is the physical interaction between the human eyes and the object, the gaze of the eyes being arrow-like directed at the object or, the other way around, the rays of light coming from the object to the eyes. What this type of seeing perceives is accordingly nothing but the outside of things, the visual impressions such as the external looks, the shape, color, surface structure, etc. Even if one wishes to see what is behind the outside of something and therefore looks, for example, at an anatomically dissected body, this kind of seeing will again only see what is *now* the external appearance.

But such seeing is not only restricted to the perception of sense data. Real seeing includes one's recognizing *what* it is that one sees. This involves an intellectual function, a mental act of identification or categorizing. Furthermore, if we see a person, we are not only interested in recognizing him or her, but also try to read their facial expression, whether they look happy and friendly or sinister or whatever.

Assessing what this first kind of seeing is, we can make three points.

First, it clearly is in the service of "survival" in its widest sense. Identifying what impression a person makes and who or what it is that we see allows us to distinguish the dangerous, unpleasant, or disgusting from the helpful and desirable. More generally, it is indispensable for our everyday orientation in the world and practical life at large. It is the ego's seeing.

Secondly, it is characterized by a not literal, but subtle "aggressiveness". With its implicit intent upon pinpointing and classifying the object seen, it tries to mentally seize it, take hold of it. Indeed, it has logically always already construed it as *object* for the subject and as empirical *fact*, even if the object is a human being.

---

6 Cf. W.G., "The Opposition of 'Individual' and 'Collective' – Psychology's Basic Fault. Reflections On Today's Magnum Opus of the Soul", now chapter **8** in *CEP VI*.

Thirdly, this kind of seeing can only perceive the familiar. There cannot be anything truly new for it. Of course, semantically, this seeing can encounter something utterly new and surprising. But syntactically or logically, even what in actuality is truly new can with this kind of seeing inevitably only be apperceived *in terms of* the familiar concepts, experiences, images available to consciousness, and if not in terms of them then at least in terms of the Kantian categories of the understanding.

It is essential to understand that we psychologists, too, inevitably approach dreams with this kind of seeing, at least initially. The dream story appears to us as if it were a real-life story in empirical reality. As Jungian analysts we of course know that dream images are to be taken as symbolic or imaginal, not literally. So we tend to *identify* the specific images in a concrete dream with general psychological concepts such as the anima, the shadow, the nigredo, or some archetype, thus subsuming them under a category. The point here is that even with the most mythological and mysterious sounding concepts we do by no means arrive at "the other picture" and in interiority, but still remain with the first type of seeing and the "impressions of the daily life", since for Jungians, concepts like that of anima or the archetypes are part of their daily life and all-too-familiar intellectual tools in their tool chest.

The second kind of seeing

What is the other kind of seeing that really gives us "the other picture" and takes us into interiority? And how can this type of seeing come about? As a particularly striking and illumining paradigm from which we can read the answers to these questions, I choose a very special real-life event, the event of a person's, say, a man's, suddenly falling in love at first sight with a woman; but we could just as well exchange their roles.

When this event happens, the man is catapulted out of his ordinary sense of life. In this moment he does not just, with the first kind of seeing, see this woman's external looks, her possibly existing beauty and erotic attractiveness. Such an external observation could not suddenly disrupt the conventionality of ordinary life for him. Rather, what happens to him is that he is struck by the flash that comes to him from her unveiled soul or innermost essential being. Indeed, we must here not shy away from admitting that what really flashes up for him is nothing less than the other person's *divinity*, nor must we, out of embarrassment, sort of euphemistically play down the outrageous sense of this word by, for example, claiming that this is "*of course* only a manner of speaking". The divinity has been *seen* by him, although probably unbeknownst to him, because consciously he in all likelihood merely feels its emotional effect.

The *seen divinity* is what gives to the experience of falling in love its absolutely overwhelming, mind-shattering power. The radiating shine coming from the woman's ultimately divine soul penetrates the man. Being hit and penetrated by this shine or gaze, he knows himself as seen through and through by her soul, and at the same time he has ipso facto also seen *her* innermost truth. By having been struck by this flash he has been flung out of his everyday existence into the status of interiority or the land of soul. He and she are empirically two. And yet for him they are not two because psychologically, in his status of interiority, they are in one another. It is the factual (although *subliminally* occurring) revelation of the divinity of the other person, as her ultimate truth, that represents for us the supreme paradigm for what Jung called the looming up of "the other picture".[7]

Usually we view experiences of love as emotional happenings and attribute them to desire. The *word* "love" covers, of course, a variety of quite distinct realities. But at any rate, the love I am here concerned with is *in itself* by no means an emotional event. It *is* a strictly *cognitive* event. He sees and *knows* her soul in its unveiled truth. But since this cognitive event is such a mind-shattering one, it is, of course, also accompanied by and results in powerful emotions. As cognitive, falling in love at first sight is an event of a *true meeting*. When speaking here of a "true meeting", I do not mean the *psychic* meeting of the *two persons*, him and her. Because then an unrequited love could not be a true meeting. What I mean by the phrase "true meeting" is, by contrast, the *psychological, "diagonal"* meeting of the one *person* with the *divine truth* of the other person (even if his love should be unrequited), which means that in the case of a mutual falling in love there would be, as we must say, two "true meetings" at the same time.

But now we have to add that this the man's own cognition, his own *seeing*, really *comes* exclusively as his *being* seen, we could even say as

---

7 As one sees, I am not starting out from the human person's faculty of the imagination. The seen divinity (or the divine image) is for me originally not a fantasy-product. It has its basis in the Real, *is* a reality.

his being the "victim" of the penetrating shine or gaze radiating from the other soul. The second kind of seeing is in itself self-contradictory. To be sure, as in the case of the first kind of seeing, this seeing, too, is clearly directed forward at the other person. But in the second kind of seeing, one's forward-looking gaze is *contra naturam* not allowed to live itself out, not allowed to find its natural fulfillment by one's simply recognizing what is objectively there and positive-factually to be seen. Instead, it is within itself *checked, halted*. This astounding possibility of the *self-inhibition* on the part of a person's impulse, instinctual desire, or general outward orientation[8] against its natural course, here the self-inhibition of the first kind of seeing, is the human animal's singular distinction. Through it the forward-looking gaze is, as it were, dammed up and thus driven back deeper and deeper into *itself* so that its *nature* changes: It turns into a *recursive* forward looking. What this change of its nature, this its becoming in itself recursive, amounts to is that the second kind of seeing has now become *pure receptivity*, free of any volition or desire. It is fundamental *openness* precisely for the inner *unknownness* of what is before one's eyes, for the object's or person's innermost essential being or soul, for its internal *infinity*, in other words, for what according to Jung is "behind the scenes".

Another example, cited by Jung, of the second kind of seeing, in addition to that of falling in love, can give support to the notion of the "true meeting".

When Ludwig the Saint once visited incognito Saint Aegidius, and when both, who did not know each other, caught sight of each other, they both fell on their knees before each other, embraced and kissed each other— and *spoke no word with each other*. Their gods recognized each other, and their human parts followed suit.[9]

"Their *gods* recognized each other"! Not: *They* recognized each other (with the first kind of seeing). To be more exact I would even reformulate the quoted sentence and say: They were each struck and pierced by the flash of the radiating shine coming from the divinity of the respective other. And

8 Self-inhibition means nature's (i.e., *human* nature's) own *opus contra naturam*! It is *not the human being's* act of inhibition, *his* checking the natural course.
9 C.G. Jung, *Briefe I*, p. 54, to Hans Schmid-Guisan, 6 Nov. 1915. My translation. *Letters I*, p. 32.

it was not really they either who fell on their knees before each other; the phrase "their human parts followed suit" much rather indicates that falling on their knees was the divine gaze's doing that so to speak automatically made them (their human parts) prostrate themselves before the Holy. It was not *their* reaction, *their* answer. Once they had been struck by the gaze of the divine, they, in their ordinary human-all-too-humanness, had no choice but to worship.

Ludwig the Saint and Saint Aegidius did not recognize each other in the personalistic, human-interrelation sense and did not take focus on and discern each other's (their human part's) looks. Instead, we have here again a recognition as a true "diagonal" meeting and, as in the case of *two* people falling in love with each other, one to be formally represented by *two* crossing diagonal lines X, each starting from the "the god" of each and going to the respective other's "human part". Jung adds, "We must understand the divinity within us, but not the other, so far as he is able to go by himself and understand himself".[10] As the a priori *checked* "first kind of seeing" and thus as a seeing that has become in itself recursive, cognition here is pure receptivity for "the other picture", the soul truth of the other. Furthermore, this cognition means for the person to be the *victim* of an intruding "insight".

We cannot decide to use the second kind of seeing. It is not a method or technique, not an ego achievement. The pure receptivity is not just an abstractly empty form of openness ready and waiting for something, for anything, to fill it. *If* it is there, it *has* always already been filled. Because it only comes into being in the moment of, and by, the gaze that hits consciousness like a flash, just as conversely this gaze can only happen to this in-itself-*checked* seeing that has become pure receptivity. Both are equiprimordial, or two sides of one coin. They happen—or they do not happen.

---

10 Apart from the fact that (1) it would be better to say "the divinity in the other person" than "the divinity within us", that (2) in this context there cannot be a "must" for us, and that (3) it is, on the contrary, even impossible *for us* "to understand" this divinity inasmuch as it would have to be the other way around: *It* would have to gaze into us of its own accord—apart from these necessary qualifications, Jung's rejection of the idea of our understanding *the other*, i.e., of a humanistic-personalistic approach (which is perfectly in tune with "the first kind of seeing"), is a bold and essential insight! That, on the other hand, "so far as he is *not* able to go by himself" we as therapists should try to understand *him* as the person he is, is the psychic, human-all-too-human task of therapy, but has *in itself* nothing to do with psychology in the sense of soul-making.

The only thing that may be possible for us to indeed do in this regard is to create conditions and fortify attitudes in ourselves that do not *exclude* such happenings from occurring.

It is essential to comprehend that it is not the *semantic character* of being utterly different from ordinary reality, that it is not really its perhaps being mysterious, archaic, mythological, that makes the *otherness* of "the other picture", but exclusively the syntactical reversal: That instead of being the seen appearance (the looks) and thus the impressions of the daily life, it is the soul "behind the scenes" that is seen and that instead of being the object of *our* looking, it is a veritable *subject* that piercingly gazes at and into us, calling us into question.

I spoke of the beloved person's divinity. By this I do not wish to divinize this person as the human being that she is, as if this divinity were a kind of hidden personality trait or her property, something permanent, upon which she could pride herself. Her divinity only *arises* in its flashing up and only exists for the duration of its impact. It is not an empirical fact, not a psychic truth, but a transcendental or psychological truth. Soul truths are not like facts, they have to be *made* or they make themselves. They are *contra naturam*. And this divinity also arises exclusively for that person for whom it flashes up, not for everybody. For it flashes up "behind the scenes", so much so behind them that even the very person *whose* divinity it is remains utterly ignorant about it.

Another crucial point. This divinity is only (only?) the felt impact of the abstract conceptual quality of a literally "adorable presence", but it does not show itself as an *image*, the image, for example, of a goddess or god. **There cannot be an *image* of a god or goddess because the true image of the seen divinity *is already there*: The *real person is* the existing, living *image* of the presence of the divine for the lover.** The divinity is nothing additional to, nothing behind or above, the beloved. If it were otherwise, it would not be the experience of love, this type of love, and it would not be a moment of realized interiority. In general, historically the original images were not mental contents, nothing "imagined" or "imaginal", not image in the poetic sense. The primordial form of images in the psychological sense, the form of the only images that there were, were quite literally the real things or phenomena in their physical concreteness existing out there in the natural world, and, a little later, they were man-made idols or statues or paintings. The soul always begins out there and with the concretely real, not in the alleged unconscious, this modern fiction.

This is why I have to decisively contradict Jung's statement, which was very dear to Hillman, too, that "The psyche creates reality every day. The only expression I can use for this activity is *fantasy*" (*CW* 6 § 78). This is a modernistic, subjectivistic fallacy, at least if it is supposed to express the true relation of Man and world. (That for the modern worldless, atomic individual Jung's statement has some validity, is quite another thing: What the psyche indeed creates every day [or at least in every new situation] is only such *particular* things as the neurotic's neurosis.)

The very special event of falling in love at first sight was chosen by me only as a most suitable paradigm for the second kind of seeing. But this seeing is neither restricted to cases of love nor to interpersonal relations in general, but can also happen in any human encounter with a thing or event or situation that belongs to the natural world. It is a general potential of man's world-relation. And as we have seen, in order to explain such an event of love we don't need to have recourse to archetypes, in our example, to an Aphrodite or any other god or goddess of love, as an additional third factor. Nothing from outside the event itself, from a kind of metaphysical back world, is needed. Being human, a person has within himself everything needed for an ordinary meeting (be it of two *this-worldly* persons, or be it of a person with a this-worldly thing, or event) suddenly to turn into *the true, the absolute meeting*[11] and thereby to raise the experience to the "outrageous" level of the interiority of the soul. It is simply the *situation-immanent* move from the impressions of the daily life to "the other picture" that "looms up behind the scenes".

To return from here to the alchemist looking into his retort or the psychologist looking at a dream and thus to move from an experience in the immediacy of real life (my example of falling in love) to an already reflected and more theoretical sphere, we can say now that as far as the "looming up" of "the other picture" is concerned, the alchemist and the psychologist are entirely dependent on *their being gazed at* from within the retort or the dream. If the dream interpreter were to insist on his own seeing and his own understanding the meaning of the dream images, the switch from "the impressions of the daily life" to "the other picture" or from the first to the second kind of seeing would not have a chance. Why? Because this type of

---

11 In the case of two persons for the one person only or for both at once, but "diagonally" in either case.

attitude has the very purpose of preventing such a thing as an experience of being struck by the gaze that flashes out from the dream itself. The best thing a psychologist can indeed do is to resist letting himself get seduced by whatever looks familiar and instead to tentatively assign the quality of unknownness and not-understoodness to the dream, even more than that: To accept precisely the darkness of the dream images *as his teacher*. This attitude does not *produce* "the other picture", but at least it does not obstruct a possible self-manifestation of it, or perhaps, it even prepares a favorable condition of the possibility for such a self-manifestation.

Having used an event belonging to the range of possible personal experiences of individuals, an event that can still happen in modern times, as example in order to demonstrate what interiority in itself is, we can turn to interiority in the *opus magnum*, in the course of the history of the objective soul. But before we get to history, we still need to clarify the nature of the human part in the human world-relation.

The human animal and its humanness

The moment *Homo sapiens* appeared on the stage of the world, he was the *existing* psychological difference, an identity that is in itself different, namely, animal *and* human, or biological organism endowed with psychic faculties *and* soul. That he is animal and has a psyche is a naturally given empirical fact. But that he is truly human, that he is soul and that therefore he is fundamentally *more* than an animal is not an empirical fact. His being human, being soul, is given by nature only as an empty logical form without semantic filling and empirical representation, only as a mere promise or *calling*. *Homo sapiens* is by nature in himself incomplete. It is he who has to fulfill this "promise", he who has to slowly acquire, nay, *create* his own humanness individually in his lifetime as well as collectively in the course of history and thereby bring about his missing completeness.

His humanness is not even *in him* as a kind of seed. What we call the human soul is also not something comparable to how our genes are given by nature. It is not a kind of organ of the human organism. A seed is an actual potential, not empty form, not mere promise. The seed would only have to develop and unfold its existing germinal disposition according to its innate law. *Homo sapiens*'s essential second half of his constitution, in fact, precisely that which constitutes his very human distinction, is, however, still completely up in the air, fundamentally unknown and lying in future.

What it will be like once it is realized is unpredictable and in part also contingent. It is only a *transcendental* reality: Real only in the idea, not real in or as empirical reality.[12] From the outset it is, *as this emptiness or absolute negativity*, nevertheless absolutely real.

What this means is that precisely through his having his human essence "up in the air" and outside himself in the open future, *Homo sapiens* logically *extends a priori beyond himself*, outside of himself. In other words, he *within himself* transcends himself, he exists as self-transcendence. And this his self-transcending nature is precisely his essential being as human. But where could this extending beyond himself go? It could only go to what there is beside himself, in other words, to the natural world. With his, to begin with not existing, soul or essential being, that is, with his empty logical form of soul, the human animal has *logically, psychologically*, a priori reached out over the external reality and therefore overarches it (although *empirically* or psychically the natural world, with which Man is confronted, is and remains an Other for him, initially unknown and possibly threatening). No, not the human animal, not Man, has reached out over the world; he is born into this arch encompassing himself and nature. In his humanness, *Homo sapiens* exists *as a relation: As* Man-world relation (which must not be confused with: Existing as an animal or [human] being *who relates*!).

The *human* animal and nature out there are consequently from the outset mediated with each other; they both have their place within this mediation. This in-ness in the mediation is what constitutes interiority. Animals, by contrast, are from birth complete in themselves, because they have their whole nature in themselves. Therefore, much like things, they exist (live) in the "environment" and not in what we call the "world". For the human animal, by contrast, there is a *world* because, existing as relation, the empty form of its own soul has from the outset already encompassed what for animals is the natural environment and this is why the *human* animal has never lived in the environment. The environment exists for Man only as an abstraction. The world is a priori his own. It is his home in the full sense of "home". Nature is for him nature in the strict sense of Mother Nature.

Only from outside of himself, from his experience of and interaction with the world, can Man's empty form of soul in the course of time receive

---

12 Cf. Kant: Transcendental: Soul as *"Substanz in der Idee, aber nicht in der Realität", nicht in der Erfahrung* (KrV A351).

its semantic filling and precisely not from within *himself*, not, for example, from his so-called unconscious. The spelling out of his own essential being, of his own humanness, has to *come* to him. The converse to this is that the empty second half of Man, i.e., the emptiness in Man, is Man's a priori existing pure receptivity or fundamental openness for such a thing as the essential being coming to him from nature. Man's self-transcendence, essential incompleteness, and his overarching the natural world, on the one hand, and the fact mentioned in my discussion above of the second kind of seeing, namely, that in Man instinctual desires, impulses or purposes can check themselves and inhibit their own natural course, on the other hand, are two sides of the same coin, just as, the other way around, it is evident that animals's being from birth complete in themselves and their having their whole nature in themselves is the reason why in them instinct cannot inhibit *itself*. It can only be inhibited from outside, either by another more powerful instinct or by external reality. The drive's potential self-inhibition allows for reflection, for an a priori reflected experience of the world.[13]

The real human distinction does not lie in Man's greater intelligence, in his having a larger brain and similar attributes. It lies solely in the fact that being human is in its deepest essence *counternatural* and amounts to an absolute *reversal* over against the animal situation as well as over against the everyday understanding of the relation to the world. The reversal is absolute because it is not only that Man's innermost essential being or soul is out there like a treasure to be found in nature vis-à-vis him. No, in addition, nature or the world, having been overarched by Man's soul, has ipso facto also so to speak turned around so that it ceases to be nothing but *object* and instead *faces* Man, *presents* to him *its innermost essential being, its soul* (above and beyond its own empirical-factual appearance that Man's

---

13 In my paper, "C.G. Jung's Psychology Project as a Response to the Condition of the World" in: *CEP VI*, pp. 1–20, here p. 7, I discussed, using a concrete example, how on the ontogenetic level it can be observed how small "children slowly learn to restrain their natural impulse to interact directly with an image. Through curbing their impulses, they become capable of *simply looking*, and only when they can simply look at the depicted object has an image become *image* for them, whereas before it was confused with its referent." As indicated before, it is not really their, the children's, curbing their impulses. The latter curb themselves. Seeing an image *as image* is, as "simply looking", already in itself reflected seeing, but of course not yet "the second kind of seeing", which would require a second self-inhibition. Reflected seeing can still allow for "the first kind of seeing".

eyes can see by themselves). Nature, now not only a priori *reflected* (i.e., no longer immediate) but also *animated* nature,[14] has become a veritable *subject* that speaks to him and sends its gazes into him.

But the whole relation is still a bit more complicated. I said that Man *is* relation and has his place within the Man-world-mediation. He cannot get out. However, although he cannot, he *is* always already—*within* the mediation!—out of the mediation. This is the difficulty: That the "out of it" can exclusively be "within it" and that both are necessary.

It is easy to see that the a priori *mediated* relation between the human animal and nature out there is the very condition of the possibility of language and conceptual thinking. It is the world that gave to Man the semantic concretizations of his soul and that taught Man to speak as well as to acquire concepts. It is precisely not so that Man arbitrarily invented the words of language all by himself, as, for example, in the *Old Testament* (Gen. 2:19), where God brought all sorts of creatures "unto Adam to see *what he would call them*: and whatsoever Adam called every living creature, that was the name thereof".[15]

Furthermore, it is also the described a priori mediatedness of Man and world that makes it possible that words spoken by Man *in fact mean* the real thing they refer to.

The archaic mode of being-in-the-world

With all this in mind I claim that from the outset Man's entire mode of being-in-the-world was that of "the true meeting", as we have got to know it through the example of the special event of love at first sight. Having the form of his innermost essential being out there in the world, early Man could not help looking into the world with what I called "the second kind of seeing", that is, with a looking from the stance of pure receptivity, the stance of openness precisely for the fundamentally *unknown* essence "inside" the things of the world he was faced with, the inescapable openness for their soul, their inner *infinity*. And because Man's soul has a priori overarched the world as such and the latter is at the same time an *inverted* nature that *faces* him, the things of nature are not mute for him, not mere

14 "Reflected": First inhibition, "animated": Second inhibition.
15 Just as above I had to contradict the idea that "The psyche creates reality every day".

objects. They have soul in them and can at any moment "speak" to him and gaze at him, so that he would find himself struck by "the other picture": The things' inner divinity gazing at and into him. Thus, during those ages, Man inevitably experienced numerous gods, demons, and nature spirits indwelling in the trees, rivers, mountains, winds, the sun and moon, etc., as their own ultimate truth. The whole world and everything in it was ensouled and enwrapped in meaning. Reality *as empirical reality* was a priori transposed from the status of empirical reality into the status of *transcendentality*, and its nevertheless existing empirical-practical aspect was thus only an always already sublated aspect within reality's transcendental truth.

Since the primordial condition was that of the interiority in the true meeting of Man and world, we could say that archaic Man directly faced the "thing-in-itself" (Kant), because he was hit by the divine soul of the real things. As illumining as this sentence is *for us moderns* in some way, we should *not* say it because the term "thing-in-itself" belongs to the first kind of seeing and its *epistemological* concerns (Kant: "What can I know?") and it inevitably brings with it the split between itself and its counterpart, the "appearance". As such it is incompatible with the archaic situation, in which Kant's question would be absurd. For, in the archaic situation, the truth follows the simple, i.e., *identical* form: "The sun is god. Everyone can see that", as Jung's chief of the Tao pueblos put it (*MDR* p. 251).

What I said does therefore not mean that archaic Man did not take seriously the sober and strictly pragmatic or utilitarian first kind of seeing and was not also rationally dealing with the empirical reality of things.[16] What it means is that even daily chores and utensils that received his full and practically necessary attention were nevertheless *implicitly* enwrapped in a divine shine and had their authenticity in their having their metaphysical origin in the fact that they had primordially—*in illo tempore*—been founded by some god or mythological culture-hero.

---

16 The problem that many have with Lévy-Bruhl's hotly debated thesis of the "pre-logical mentality" of the primitives could in my opinion be resolved if one were willing to understand that Lévy-Bruhl's phrase "pre-logical mentality" was his name for what I termed "the second kind of seeing" as the dominant relation to reality. It does not refer to the *psychic* mental functions and intellectual capabilities of early Man. Lévy-Bruhl wanted to say that for the primitives, to put it my way, "the first kind of thinking" was not their supreme mode of being-in-the-world.

Originally, gods were, however, not permanently existing other-worldly beings, persons, or subjects who *sent* these gazes. Originally they were only momentary flashes coming from within the earthly things and events *themselves*. As Kerényi has shown, the ancient Greek word for god, *theós*, was only a predicate, not a (sentence) subject: Originally nothing was predicated of *theós*, but *theós* was predicated of other things. Even more important is the fact that according to linguistic evidence, the original semantic content of the *name* "Zeus" seems to have referred to the event or phenomenon of a momentary *flaring up of a light*. Only later did this name take on the meaning of the permanently existing originator of and behind this flashing up.[17] Similarly, Jung, discussing the East African ceremony he witnessed, of greeting the sun in the morning, stated: "The *moment* in which light comes *is* God. . . . To say that the *sun* is God is to blur and forget the archetypal experience of that moment" (*MDR* pp. 266–269). And Heidegger, connecting etymologically Greek *theós* (god) with *theáomai* (to gaze at, behold), viewed the gods generally as *die Hereinblickenden*, the ones who gaze into our ordinary life,[18] which, after what I just explained, I would like to change into *das Hereinblicken*, the gazing pure and simple as momentary happenings without a subject that does this gazing.

Animals as exclusively *natural* beings know only the first kind of seeing. They look at what they encounter exclusively with such questions as, "is it a possible prey and food or an enemy? Is it useful or dangerous?" and completely ignore what is neither. Animals, as I pointed out, live only in their factual environment, in empirical reality, but not in what we call the *world*. During a thunderstorm they may certainly witness flashes of lightning and possibly be startled or scared. But nothing *gazes* at them *from within* these empirical flashes; there is for them no "flaring up of a light" from within the physical lightning that could *open* their eyes,[19] let alone a Zeus. And there cannot possibly be a divine "flaring up of a light", which is already the first

---

17 Karl Kerényi, "*Theós*: 'Gott' auf Griechisch". In: *Idem*, *Antike Religion* (München: Albert Langen, 1971), pp. 207–217, here pp. 210–214.

18 Martin Heidegger, *Heraklit*, Gesamtausgabe vol. 55 (Frankfurt a.M.: Klostermann, 1979), p. 8. See also *idem.*, *Parmenides*, GA vol. 54, ibid. 1982, pp. 152 ff.

19 The Kena-Upanishad's equivalent to my first kind and second kind of seeing as well as Jung's contrast between "the impressions of the daily life" and "the other picture" is: "Not what the eyes can see, but what opens to eyes".

immediacy of a *concept*, since being complete in themselves and lacking the solely human gift of nature's potential self-inhibition, animals cannot have and do not need concepts.

Because of what we learned from Kerényi, the use of the words "gods" and "nature spirits" for the earliest, at least somewhat accessible, period of cultural history is anachronistic. More appropriate to the real character of the experience are, for example, the concepts of "numinosity" in its image-less abstractness and the likewise abstract "the holy" (Rudolf Otto). In fact, Otto's "holy" is decisively conceived as what corresponds to my "second kind of seeing" and the flashes that can strike Man. Only at a later time, when after generations of such experiences by numerous individuals man had become a bit more accustomed to them and ipso facto had gained a certain mental distance to them, could these experiences congeal into images, lead to the production of idols or statues of gods and was it, still later, even possible for consciousness to unfold the internal complexities of the images into the form of whole narratives, the myths, about them. The transformation of an occurrence into a divine being causing the occurrence amounted already to the original experience's having been processed by the human mind as well as to the mind's partial appropriation of the former awe-inspiring flashing-up as the mind's own image, so that it received a certain permanence as well as a partial independence from actual experience. Here we can recall Jung's insight ("the great truth") "that every spiritual truth gradually reifies itself turning into something material or a tool in the hands of man" (*CW* 13 § 302[20]).[21] In cultural history, the flashes slowly turn into images, the images slowly become independent of the experienced reality that once gave rise to it. Thus they become properties of the human mind that the now stand-alone mind can at long last freely use of its own accord and for its own purpose: The birth of Man's own imagination or fantasy life. Nevertheless, even for the early imagination, these gods continued to have

20 Translation modified according to the original.
21 The other side of the gradual interiorization and appropriation of the primordial "flashes" by the human mind as its mental property is the other important insight of Jung's into the character of our modern dream images as *sunken, sedimented cultural assets*: "What, with us, is a subterranean [i.e., unconscious] fantasy was once open to the light of day. What in our case crops up in dreams and fantasies [i.e., any archetypal, mythological images] was formerly a conscious custom or general conviction" (*CW* 5 § 35, transl. modif.).

their authentic and only residence in the respective things or events of the natural world.

What I described allows us, and forces us, to leave behind two favorite ideas of psychology. The first idea is the belief in the priority of *image* and that soul *is* image. In the last analysis, the deepest nature of what Jung called "the other picture" is not at all its being a picture or an image. Picture as well as image imply their being seen by us and thus our seeing them. But "the other picture" is other only because it, conversely, gazes at us, actively pierces, strikes us. "Image", as ordinarily used in psychology, is already the castrated, objectified divine gaze and psychology's "numinous images" are the already castrated "holy" of Rudolf Otto.

By this I do not wish to imply that dream images, poetic images, and images in the sense of statues of a god could not at times perhaps gaze at and into us, possibly striking us with a flash. My point is only that psychology's criterion has to be whether or not the respective image has indeed *gazed, struck, and pierced*. It *cannot* be the image as such. "Image" always implies that we are the agents, be it the "seeing" or be it, as Hillman thought, the "sensing" ones. This assessment remains of course also true if you believe that "an image is not what you see but the way you see" (Edward Casey, with Hillman concurring).[22] Here I must refer back to my earlier discussion about the divinity of a beloved, where I showed that "There cannot be an *image* of a god or goddess because the true image of the seen divinity *is already there*: The *real person is* the existing, living *image* of the presence of the divine for the lover".

The other idea is the belief that the unconscious is the original source of the gods and archetypes and that the psyche creates reality.[23] The thesis of the unconscious of Man as the true place of origin of the gods (cf. *CW* 9i § 5; 18 § 1366) does not only give to the gods a false parentage, but also no more than one single parent, thus letting them be the result of a kind of virgin birth. Neither Man, the human psyche, Man's unconscious, on the

---

22 Cf. James Hillman, "Image Sense", in: *Spring 74*, 1979, p. 134. Earlier in this article, on p. 130, Hillman had written: "We do not literally see images or hear metaphors; we perform an operation of insight which is a seeing-through or hearing-into". Apart from the fact that it is again we who have to perform this "operation of insight", I wonder how you can see through an image without first having seen it, seen it quite literally, *and without keeping sticking to* the literally seen image while performing these operations.

23 I already mentioned this idea above in the section "On the second kind of seeing".

one side, nor the world, nature, on the other, are the place of origin. My thesis is that the gods (as well as the flashing gazes as their forerunners) are the product of the *true meeting of Man and world*, a meeting, however, that, other than in the case of falling in love, is their always already having met and irrevocably from the outset *being* in an intimate connection, logically being intricately entwined, being in one another. (Above I have similarly claimed: The "true meeting" is from the outset Man's entire mode of being-in-the-world.) This invisible, unimaginable a-priori entwinement of Man and natural world is the *nowhere* I spoke of at the very beginning, that nowhere that is the place where the soul is.

Because our discussion circles around the gazes coming from the inner divinity of things or events as well as around the divine idols and mythological gods of a somewhat later phase, we might be tempted to classify this whole topic of the archaic experience of "the other picture" under the rubric of "religion". But then we would literalize; we would fall for "the impressions of the daily life" and "the thin veil of facts". No doubt, *for the people* of this stage of development and for their felt experience all this had a quality that from our modern Western perspective is at least equivalent to religion. But for us as psychologists, it is obligatory to see "the other picture" even behind this "religious" surface appearance, namely, to see what the archaic subjective experience of the world objectively means from the soul perspective and for the soul.

Sandplay therapy as a model for understanding the history of the objective soul

At this point it might be helpful to adduce the concept of sandplay therapy. By completely spontaneously, without reflection, shaping the sand in a sandtray and selecting and positioning toy figures in it, patients create a picture of a particular scene that can be understood as a visualization and concrete representation of an otherwise invisible soul (or psychic) situation. Psychology is of course not interested in the sand and toy figures as such nor in the created picture as such. It goes without saying that what psychology is interested in is "the other picture that looms up" from within this sandplay picture. The created picture *is* not "the other picture". It cannot *be* that because the latter, just as the soul itself, always remains transcendental. The finished sandplay picture in its material reality is only a *visual aid*, a kind of *foothold in sensual reality, for* the elusive, always fleeting soul to—wittingly *or unwittingly*—concretely unfold its own unrealized potential, to possibly even reflect itself and to become objectively aware of itself. Furthermore, in this way, namely through the soul's gaining self-awareness by means of the sandplay picture, psychology can *realize* itself in the first place: The empty form of soul obtaining a semantically concrete (*psychological*) body.

At the same time the finished sandplay picture does not only rest in itself. Having given to the soul or consciousness a solid visual articulation of a previously not accessible soul situation, it is at the same time also a possible stepping stone for consciousness's or the soul's potential further-development, for its pushing-off to a new, more differentiated and sophisticated stage of itself.

What needs to be noted is that the patient in the sandplay-production process is not the only active, or not even the real, producer of the sandplay picture. In fact, in the beginning the patient may not have any idea of what image to produce at all. Looking with his empty mind at the sand and the whole range of available toy figures, these begin to play an essential role. There is something in this or that one of all these figures available that evokes, invites, excites certain feelings or associations or ideas in the mind and in this way influences the direction that the production of the picture takes; or they even themselves produce in the person the very idea for the image to be shaped. So these material objects are co-authors, if not at times the decisive authors, of a sandplay picture.

With such ideas in mind, we can comprehend mythology as a whole and the ritual practices, indeed Man's entire *productive* world-relation and mode of being-in-the-world, as the unwitting production of "sandplay pictures" and, through them, as the creation, discovery and semantically spelling out of Man's own other transcendental half, the, to begin with, completely *empty form* of soul. Furthermore, we can comprehend the whole historical development of Man's mode of being-in-the-world as an ongoing sequence of sandplay-picture production. Step by step ever new and more visual and concrete "semantic presence in reality" is given to the soul, and this without Man's having a blueprint (which is why I said before that the actual form that the semantic filling of the empty transcendental half will take in reality is in part contingent). The process is thus, on the one hand, simply an immanent self-development following solely its own logic, while, on the other hand, being dependent on the affordances of the happenstance condition of the world at a given historical time. The world and the different world situations function like the sand and the things or events in the world as the toy figures of the sandplay.

Does not John Keats' statement, so important to Hillman: "Call the world if you please, 'The vale of Soul-making.' Then you will find out the use of the world"[24] sound just like another formulation for the sandplay-like work of the semantic spelling out of Man's own other transcendental half? We call the ongoing production of Man's "sandplay pictures" the history of *culture*. The cultural process is a building of "castles in the air" in the *non-existing* sphere of the soul's logical life, the sphere of interiority and the dimension of meanings, *but*—and this is what makes it sandplay-like— with a *foothold or anchor in the empirical reality of the natural world*. For, after all, culture produces empirically real rituals, temples, societal institutions, poetry and works of art, etc.

That in olden times the result of this soul-making appears as religion (or something like religion) merely reveals how deficient and absolute unworthy the empirically real half of Man felt during those ages vis-à-vis *his own* transcendental half, which, when it showed itself, appeared as absolutely holy, as the Wholly Other. He could not meet it on an equal footing. He had to prostrate himself before it as before something completely out of his reach, above his head, and absolutely awe-inspiring. But this does not change the fact that this "Wholly Other" (including all the later *specific* gods, demons, and spirits as well as the one God) was psychologically, but unbeknownst to Man, the first immediacy of his becoming aware of *his own* essential being.

It follows that for a true psychology, a psychology *with* soul, the *true meeting* of Man and World has to be its supreme theoretical starting point, not the *Two* who *are* conjoined in their meeting, and least of all only the one of the Two, the human individual, as I suggested already at the end of the previous section when criticizing the idea of the unconscious as the true place of origin of the gods. Only then has psychology truly taken its place in *interiority*. And only then is the disastrous personalistic fallacy and underlying dissociated scheme of all traditional psychology (including Jung's)—its *prôton pseûdos*—overcome and has the notion of the *objective*

---

24 James Hillman, *Re-Visioning Psychology*, New York et al. (Harper & Row) 1975. p. IX, quoting H. B. Forman, ed., *The Letters of John Keats*, London (Reeves & Turner) 1895, p. 326.

soul, and even the very term *soul* (in contrast to psyche) become theoretically justified.[25]

Other than presented above in the context of one's falling in love at first sight, "the true meeting" is in reality not only something that at times *happens*. It is much rather, and more fundamentally, the a-priori logic or truth of human existence as such. True interiority is therefore not at all something inside the individual, not itself *in* "the inner". It is precisely above the heads of people in the height of the transcendental point of the a priori mutual entwinement of Man and world. Man by himself does not carry his essential being, the soul, in *himself*, especially not in himself as *individual* person. Man has the soul in the experience of and interaction with the world (where "world" includes all the other human beings and peoples). **The soul has *two* parents, the human mind and the nature of the world**.

The concrete form of soul must be comprehended as the *resultant* of Man's world-relation, the relation to the always specific *local* world in the respective particular geographical region of the globe and at each respective time in history. Man receives the specific semantic contents or soul truths from outside, from the gazes flashing forth to him from the things and events in the world. The real things and events in the world with its historical and geographic concreteness supplies for Man the semantic filling of his empty form of soul. But *which* gazes reach him and to which extent and how clearly and intensively and deeply he is able to perceive them depends, conversely, on the degree reached of the human mind's "pure receptivity" and "openness to the inner infinity of what he sees" as well as also of the mind's "finer intelligence" and depth of personality.

In this essay I purposely speak generally of Man, the archetypal *Anthropos* or the psychological Concept of Man, Man as species being, because the topic of true psychology is the logic and life of the transcendental soul and not empirical reality, not actual people, who each exist as private individuals and as part of a collective community. But if we nevertheless leave for the moment the strictly psychological level and turn to empirical reality

25 Jung had a deep *intuition* of the "autonomous, objective soul" and frequently thought in terms of it and with it. But "the objective soul" remained theoretically *unfounded*, because at bottom Jung's psychology never overcame the standpoint of the individual and thus of the dissociated half of the whole relation. His constructs of the "*collective unconscious*" and the archetypes were rather helpless attempts to provide a basis for the idea of the objective soul.

in order to ask who on the level of actual *people* concretely received the "semantic filling" of Man's "empty form of soul" and who possessed the pure receptivity, finer intelligence and depth of personality necessary for receiving it, we must avoid naive, simple answers. If, in our imagination, we go back to the earliest times of human history when the "empty form of soul" was really empty, the gazes flashing from out of the world were, I suppose, not right away received and experienced in their full reality. I rather imagine that initially there were in individuals (a) only completely vague and dull, hardly felt experiences that remained to a large extent subliminal and because of their vagueness and newness could not yet be articulated in words; that (b) in the course of time numerous different individuals had the same type of experience; (c) when after a long time of incubation and germination, maybe even for several generations, a large number of persons carried these felt experiences tacitly and unwittingly or dimly wittingly in them, the mute presence of this vaguely felt content created in the community as a whole a pregnant atmosphere on the basis of which (d) a particularly gifted person may have given explicit articulation to the experienced particular reality, be it in words or as some artistic product.

My point here is twofold. First, I reject the idea of a direct and fully conscious experience (revelation) in these early times. Secondly, I believe that at all times even the great individual that Jung at times spoke of, the great artist, thinker, shaman, does not get what Jung called his "big (or great) dream" out of *himself* or that he creates a great work *as the solitary creative individual* that he is. No, he is dependent on, and precisely open, deeply sensitive, to the hidden presence in society of the mute, undifferentiated experience by all the nameless individuals, as well as dependent on the long time of incubation and germination that these contents silently and invisibly underwent in his community. This does, however, not take anything away from the greatness of the great individual. It lies in his being this "pure receptivity" and in his capability to give true, deep, articulated expression to the respective content.

Analogies or metaphors may be as revealing as they can be, in some way they nevertheless do not work. This is also true for my sandplay example. In sandplay therapy, we have the duality of the patient and the sandtray. Empirically speaking, the patient produces the sandplay in the sandtray in front of himself and his producing a sandplay picture serves as a deliberate method used for a specific purpose and only at a particular time, namely in a therapy session of limited duration. By contrast, in what I used the sandplay image for, Man does not have the world as a sandtray vis-à-vis himself. He cannot freely select "toy figures" from it. Nor is this sandplay performed in the safe *temenos* of a consulting room. On the contrary, it happens in absolute earnest. It is inescapable. This sandplay is human life itself, lived life as a whole, and it is lived as Man's very mode of being-in-the-world. Whether he will or not, Man finds himself as "a figure" *in* the sandplay picture, both as subjected to what is going on in it and as active subject in it.[26] This his inescapable in-ness in the "sandplay"—that is to say, *his* being contained in the "true meeting" of Man and world and *their* being intricately in one another—highlights once more the sense of absolute interiority that prevailed in the archaic situation.

Now I want to highlight a few major stations of the fate of interiority in the history of the soul's *opus magnum* in the West.

The revolution of monotheism

The first epochal change that I want to discuss[27] is the rise of monotheism in ancient Israel. Again, as psychologists, we must here not simply fall for "the impressions of the daily life" by taking over the believers' self-understanding and feeling and thus see the appearance of monotheism as a *religious* phenomenon.[28] As Jung told us, in its images the soul is speaking about *itself*

---

26 I mentioned before that Man "*is* always already—*within* the mediation!—out of the mediation".

27 By this wording I wish to indicate that this epochal change is not the *first one in general*. There were several other previous ones, I just remind you of the one example hinted at by me earlier, the change from the simple experience of the happening of a "gaze" coming from a phenomenon to the later imagination of a god or goddess as the actor behind the appearance.

28 It was James Hillman's terrible mistake to declare his archetypal psychology to be a "Psychology with Gods", a "Polytheistic Psychology", a "theistic" psychology (*Re-Visioning Psychology*, New York et al. [Harper & Row] 1975, p. 167), and to raise the question, "Psychology: Monotheistic or Polytheistic?" (in: *Spring 1971*, pp.193ff.). It is a both psychological and methodological or *wissenschaftstheoretisch* mistake. Gods are *psychological phenomena*, and as such subject to the soul's history as well as cultural geography. Phenomena cannot be raised to a discipline's principles or axioms. Rigorous psychology can only be a "psychology *with* soul", not "with gods". Of course, Hillman goes to great lengths to emphasize that his psychology with Gods or polytheistic psychology is *not a religion*. Apart from the fact that this does not heal the methodological mistake, it also deprives the resulting "Gods" of their being veritable gods, for whom it is essential to be *holy* and to require piety and worship from people. Hillman states:

(and thus not about the images *telles quelles*), and the soul's process (i.e., according to my model presented above, the process of its production of "sandplay pictures") is one of "formation, transformation". According to a poem by Nikolaus Lenau, it is by using its own colorful songs (so to speak as its "ladder"), that the lark blissfully climbs up into the air.[29] Likewise it is for the Siberian shaman his drum that serves him as his eight-legged horse[30] which through its sound transports him into ecstasy and makes the soul's journey into the beyond possible. In the same vein I say that by means of creating such a fantastic idea as that of a monotheistic God the soul *does* something to *itself*. The idea of the monotheistic God must *psychologically* not be read as a theoretical assertion, a truth claim, but rather as the soul's formulation of a *program* for its future.

Also, concerning the emergence of monotheism we should not let ourselves get ensnared in the numeric "the One versus the many" topic. That is only a side issue. The crucial point of the emergence of the monotheistic God is much rather that he is the soul's invention of an absolutely world-*external* creator of the *world*. This amounts to a revolution. It is a truly unheard of and also a self-contradictory thought. The world is of course the whole, everything, all-inclusive. But now the soul has all of a sudden dared to *think* a point outside of the whole, outside of everything, outside of its own containment within itself. This point out there exists only in a literal nowhere. The monotheistic God is the imagination, or at least the first dawning, of the concept of an Archimedean point, an Archimedean point imagined in personified form. As such it not only serves as a stable, absolutely fixed point, a Pole Star or, more theoretically, as first principle

---

"In archetypal psychology Gods are *imagined*" (in explicit contrast to religious "ritual, prayer, sacrifice, worship, creed", *Re-Visioning* p. 169). But Gods that are *imagined* are castrated gods, "gods" already taken prisoner for "the first kind of seeing" (despite the fact that gods by themselves are the foremost example of what appears to "the second kind of seeing"). This makes them also fake gods: One gets the advantage of the most eminent rhetoric while in reality one simply uses them as nothing but *our* imaginal tools of psychological understanding.

29 Cf. W.G., "By its Colorful Tunes the Lark Blissfully Climbs Up Into the Air", in: *idem*, *The Soul Always Thinks*, CEP IV, New Orleans, LA (Spring Journal Books) 2010, now: London and New York (Routledge) 2020, pp. 379–385.

30 Odin's horse Sleipnir, too, has eight legs. The shaman's horse is eight-legged because the top of the shaman's drum had often a picture of the cosmos painted on it which represented the cosmos with its eight cardinal points. S. also H. Findeisen and H. Gehrts, *Die Schamanen*, Köln (Diederichs) 1983, p. 134.

to orient oneself by amidst the unreliability of the flux of life in reality. But by virtue of the idea that God *created* the world, this Archimedean point has also the sense of that active practical potency implied by the dictum attributed to Archimedes, "Give me a place to stand on, and I will *move* (i.e., unhinge) the Earth". I spoke of the soul's program that it pursued with the monotheistic God. Now we see what this program was: The soul wishes to rise above itself, to catapult itself out of its original status of interiority.

Coming from my model of sandplay production to this new situation, what emerges for us is (1) that this new God, being a pure *thought* without worldly substrate, on principle bursts the very rules of the soul's sandplay production. There cannot be any "sand" nor any "toy figure" to represent this pure thought of God in the sandplay picture. Indeed, this God comes, absolutely consistently and indispensably, with the explicit prohibition to make a graven image of him, any physical representation. Such an image would be visibly present in the world, it would have a material, natural presence in empirical reality and thus undermine his own essential distinction: his natural-world-external or pure-thought character. This God is "the other picture" in absolute purity *without* its counterpart of any "impressions of the daily life", "behind the scenes" of which he would need to be discovered. (2) Formally, the revolution amounts to a kind of explosion of the self-enclosed absolute interiority of the archaic "sandplay", in which humans only to that extent actively shaped the "sandplay-picture" to which they were on their part shaped and conditioned by it. Now human life as sandplay-picture production has been given an external producer of the sandplay, the cosmos-*external* Creator of the universe who is fundamentally out of reach, so that now for the first time, we get a clear duality that corresponds exactly to that in our modern literal sandplay therapy of patient and literal sandtray vis-à-vis him. Or it corresponds to the duality of alchemist and hermetic vessel, which, as Jung emphasized, "was meant to represent the cosmos [*das Weltall*], in which the earth was created" (*CW* 13 § 245). The previous interiority as the intricate in-one-another of Man and world is in principle over.

This means two things. First, *from God's point of view*, the former natural world is now logically on principle encapsulated and thus in a certain sense "pocketed", sublated, we could even say it is now no more than a toy version of the world. Nature as "Mother nature" has been rendered obsolete. Man does no longer receive his soul or essential being directly from his world-relation, from the divine gazes coming horizontally from the real things and events of the natural world. The gazes of the natural phenomena have, as it were, all been abstracted and absorbed by the supercelestial God. The all-seeing God is now the only source of metaphysical gazes and revelations. The things of this earth, by contrast, do no longer gaze, they now only have their looks that are seen by us.

But the term "gazes" in connection with God is no longer quite appropriate. Through their removal out of this world, the former direct gazes striking Man like flashes have turned into the blunt *seeing* or *watching* of the all-seeing God, on account of which Man knows himself to be constantly and inescapably observed. And the equivalent of the former *flashing* gazes now comes in the form of the revelations from the invisible, sensually not accessible extraterrestrial God. Man finds his soul in his vertical relation of obedience and faithfulness to the transcendent God who is Man's highest principle or essence and soul treasure.

The second point is that *from an innerworldly perspective*, the Creator-God represents the first immediacy, or the very first hunch, of the possibility of an independent reflecting consciousness, a consciousness that is not, as all *psychic* functions (including mere awareness) are, of natural origin.

A further and major psychological acquisition inherent in the emergence of the monotheistic God is implicit in the fact that there is no place anywhere for God to have his place. This "nowhere" (or, which is the same, this "everywhere") of God amounts to an anticipation of the psychological reality of the sphere or dimension of *spirit* as a reality in its own right, in other words, spirit not in the old naturalistic sense of a ghost or a wind or of a fairy or nature spirit. It is spirit as the *explicit* reality of absolute negativity, of the *reality* of the bodiless, invisible and intangible. The monotheistic God is already implicitly *meta*-physical.

Having described all these features inherent in the monotheistic revolution, I have to modify my statements a bit. As radical and momentous as this change *in principle* was, practically, *for Man* living in the first centuries after it, the changes were mostly only *semantic*, just a new belief-system. The syntax or logic of life in the world did not really change much, and so also the interiority of the original situation was not yet broken in reality, in people's experience of life, but broken only in the explicit contents of the new belief system.

So, as far as the people were concerned, I have to stress the implicit, anticipatory or first-hunch character of the new acquisitions. Logically, they had not come home to Man right away. It was rather the instalment of a germinal predisposition and, at the same time, the soul's tentative formulation of its inkling of a future project and assignment for itself. So here I can repeat my earlier statement: The revolutionary change to the monotheistic God must *psychologically* not be read as a kind of ontological statement, a theoretical claim, but is in reality, but unwittingly, the soul's formulation of a *program* for its future. A program not set by people, but by the soul for *its* further-development. In this sense, the monotheistic God is the still utterly remote, externalized, and transcendent precursor of the early-modern[31] ego or I. This God is, so to speak, *the discovery of the blueprint of the I.*

Another version of the "same" revolution

A corresponding revolution happened in ancient Greece. But here it did not take the form of the fate of the divine and, thus, was not a revolution in the area of religion as the domain of a compelling force and origin of powerful emotions that claim the whole man for themselves. The other version happened in the calm area of theoretical thought. I mention only in passing four, let me say, "symptoms", that reveal this change, without discussing them in detail.

(1) Anaximander (550 BC) and Heketaios (around 500 BC), both of Miletus, designed or improved respectively a map of the world. This is a sign that in them the soul had *mentally* taken off from the earth and their interiority in the earthly world and now looked at the earth from a standpoint above it and from outside it, much like our modern remote sensing satellites do in actuality.

(2) The rise of Pre-Socratic Philosophy amounted to the radical move away from mythological thinking to *reflection*, to Logos and reason. Xenophanes even criticized the anthropomorphic mythological gods and introduced instead the idea of the One God.

(3) In inscriptions on ceramic vessels of the earlier period, the vessel is speaking in the first person ("I"), while referring to the maker of the

---

31 The term "early-modern" is a makeshift name for a historical period for which English, just as French, does not have a separate word. In German we have the noun *Neuzeit* and the adjective *neuzeitlich* in contradistinction to *die Moderne* and *modern*. The problem of "early-modern" is that linguistically it contains "modern" in itself, thus inevitably suggesting a closeness to modernity, whereas in reality one of the most decisive logical gaps or ruptures in history separates the "early-modern" period from modernity.

vessel in the third person. Thus the vessel says, for example: "So-and-So made *me*". Since it is the craftsman or artist who composed the inscription, this surprising wording of the inscription reveals that the maker of the vessel himself, who for us would be the subject and the one entitled to say "I", did precisely not feel as subject. He felt, conversely, the vessel to be the real subject that speaks to and about him.[32] Similarly, in the older period statues of the ruler of a *polis* used to gaze directly at and into an onlooker and demanded respect (just as still today statues of Christ or the Virgin Mary demand of the Catholic believer their making the sign of the cross or bending their knees). This was likewise reflected in the inscriptions on such older statues. They read, for example: "*I am* Chares, the ruler of Teichiussa". But then in Athens the inscriptions read, "I am the *statue, the gravestone, the memorial of* So-and-So".[33] This is a wonderful example of the change from immediate interiority in the world (as one's being exposed to the gazes) to *reflection*, to a now reflected world-relation.[34] It is also the first indication of a historical process that could almost be imagined as a "peeling off" of the former *gazes* from the respective things, as if the gazes were decals or transfer pictures. The result was that these now abstracted and independently existing "gazes" become a reality in its own right, the reality of images and art in contradistinction to the 'real' reality of things. From this we learn again that image qua image is psychologically secondary, a product of history. The described severance of image[35] from thing is of course also one form of the ending of the primordial interiority in the world.

(4) Plato's Parable of the Cave. Existence as "interiority in nature" is denounced as cave-dwelling. Likewise, the experience of nature is

---

32 Jesper Svenbro, *Phrasikleia. Anthropologie des Lesens im alten Griechenland*, Paderborn / München (Brill | Fink) 2005.

33 Bruno Snell, *Die Entdeckung des Geistes. Studien zur Entstehung des europäischen Denkens bei den Griechen*, Göttingen (Vandenhoeck & Ruprecht) 1975, p. 101.

34 Harking back to my statement about the inner dialectic of interiority or mediation that Man "*is* always already—*within* the mediation!—out of the mediation", we can comprehend the emergence of reflection as the shift *within* this dialectic from a situation of dominant in-ness in interiority in which Man's also being (within it) out of it remained completely implicit and subliminal, to a situation in which the "out of it" becomes fully explicit and dominant.

35 To be more exact: What used to be gaze and is now, on account of this severance, nothing but image.

denounced as a world of appearance and mere shadows. The cave is, formally, the equivalent of the alchemical retort and the sandtray and it is thus the sign that, as mere appearance, the world is fundamentally encapsulated and superseded. Although the beginning in the parable is the in-ness in interiority and one of the cave-dwellers has to painfully and step by step make his way out of the cave and into the sunlight, the parable itself is from the outset told from the absolutely higher and fundamentally external standpoint from which it looks down upon the cave existence and thus the natural world that it has already once and for all left. The *real* world, the truth, is outside the cave, and the sun is in this parable the imaginal representation of the highest principle and is clearly the analogue of the absolutely extra-terrestrial monotheistic Creator God. Furthermore, the people in the cave are clearly conceived as the *seeing* ones; they are like movie or TV watchers. This, as well as two of Plato's key terms, *idéa* and *eîdos* (both meaning "seen form or shape"), show that Man has taken over the seeing or gazing and feels no longer as the one who *is being hit* by the gazes coming from the things of the world.

As before with the monotheistic God, I claim here too that by letting Plato invent this Parable of the Cave, the soul did not, as of course Plato himself did, make a philosophical (ontological or epistemological) statement, but formulated a program for the future.[36]

Because it remained to a large extent *semantic*, the change to monotheism in ancient Israel is much more gripping, of more psychic, emotional impact, than the sober, intellectual Greek move to reflection. The other side of the coin is that for the people of that age, the monotheistic move was simply an exchange of one religious content by another, whereas the *logic* of their being-in-the-world as well as much of people's concrete religious practice remained unchanged. Therefore, as radical as the invention of the world-external Creator of the world was as (semantic) *idea*, it did for a long time not bring about a fundamental psychological change, a change in the inner constitution of Man's consciousness or mode of being-in-the-world. The much more quiet mental move to reflection in Greece, on the other hand, had a much deeper *psychological*

---

36 Cf. Wolfgang Giegerich, "The Occidental Soul's Self-Immurement in Plato's Cave", in: *idem, Technology and the Soul*, (Collected English Papers, vol. 2) New Orleans (Spring Journal Books) 2007, now: London and New York (Routledge) 2020, pp. 213–279.

significance because it imperceptibly revolutionized the syntax or logic of Man's actual world-relation.

A *semantic* further-development of the soul's monotheistic revolution

From here we can go over to the second epochal change with respect to interiority that I choose to highlight, the appearance of Christianity on the stage of history. In Christianity the oriental (Near-Eastern) *passionate* religious concern and the occidental (Greek) *sophistication* of thought joined forces.

Christianity introduced two main revolutionary thoughts. First, the thought that the world-external God, while as Father still staying up there, as Son has come down from his supercelestial height into this earthly world. His coming down did not have the external sense of merely appearing on the earth the way mythological gods used to do who at times wandered on the earth by taking on the guise of humans. He came down in the absolute sense of: Himself without reserve becoming man, a finite, mortal being.

The second revolutionary innovation is that God himself changed his very nature. Instead of being a divine *being*, he became *spirit*. "God is spirit" (John 4:24). With this change the logical consequence is at long last drawn from the fact that the monotheistic God had from the very start been a pure *thought* without worldly substrate, as I put it above, although he was for a long time still *imagined* in his former form as substantial being. What else, but spirit, *pneûma*, *Geist*, could such a God in its true understanding be? We have, in a text, probably a later insert into *Kings 19* (verses 11–12), a precious piece of documentary evidence of how the inadequacy of this naturalistic form, at some time, made itself felt and how the soul attempted to come closer to a concept of God in his appropriate form as spirit, without, however, as yet being able to truly reach it, because it remained still stuck in the mode of imagining. The text describes an epiphany of God: Elijah is told:

"Go out and stand on the mountain before Yahweh." For at that moment Yahweh was going by. A mighty hurricane split the mountains and shattered the rocks before Yahweh. But Yahweh was not in the hurricane. And after the hurricane, an earthquake. But Yahweh was not in the earthquake. And after the earthquake, fire. But Yahweh was not in the fire. And after the fire, a light murmuring sound. (New Jerusalem Bible)

The last expression has alternately been translated as "a still small voice", "a sound of a gentle blowing", and "a sound of sheer silence". This text lists the traditional main forms of Yahweh's manifestation in the sensible, absolutely impressive and terrible spectacles of nature, namely hurricane, earthquake, and fire, only in order to be able to negate them. What is obviously sought but not yet fully reached is the absolute negativity of spirit. This last categorically different step to absolute negativity was finally taken by Christianity. God's having become spirit found its separate explicit expression in the notion of the third person of the Trinity, the Holy Ghost.

As far as the incarnation, God's having become man, is concerned, we need to understand that it did by no means imply a retraction from God's extramundaneness. It meant much rather that it was precisely *the absolute world-externality* that came home to itself and became real *in the world.*

Concerning the previous epochal change, the revolution of monotheism, I stated that for the people it was, *qua religion* (belief-system), on the main only a semantic change that did not syntactically really change Man's mode of being-in-the-world, namely, his interiority in the natural world. The idea of the absolutely transcendent God was at first only a program or blueprint the soul had set up for itself. That the soul now came up with the idea of the incarnation indicates that the world-externality that came with the monotheistic God had meanwhile already been inwardized into the logic or syntax of the mode of being-in-the-world. It had ceased being only *a semantic idea* and ceased being up there. It had come down into the reality of this world as people's own inner orientation and real feeling. This meant that the natural world and the interiority in it were now *also for the people*, and thus explicitly, sublated, severely downgraded.

But it also meant that an unbearable distance to God, a fundamental gap between Man and God had arisen through this inwardization, a gap that was felt like an open wound and gave rise to a desperate longing for salvation and redemption in Hellenistic times. The soul's invention of the idea of the incarnation, together with the move from substantial being to spirit, had the function of closing this gap and promising salvation.

Again, as with the invention of the monotheistic God, Christianity's absolutely new idea of the incarnation (as well as the idea of God as spirit) amounted, when it arrived, to a merely semantic change, a new belief, but did not penetrate the logic of Man's existence. These new ideas were again only the formulation of the soul's *program* for the future.

And so we have to distinguish two phases within the history of the Christian epoch (instead of "phases" some might perhaps prefer to speak of two separate epochal changes). The first, medieval, phase is characterized by a rather external reception of the new semantic message, by acting it out *as religion*, which meant that instead of the actual *happening* (realization) of the incarnation precisely the opposite, its transcendent, world-external character was celebrated in the pious way of life of people. Religious life was merely the practical reformulation in people's lived life of the soul's Christian *program* and the confirmation of people's faith in this *program*, but not the progressive fulfillment of the program. (The latter only became the task of the second, early-modern phase of the Christian epoch.)

Thus the main and *deepest* concern of people was now the beyond, the afterlife, and the worry about their possibly not being good enough to be able to pass through the Last Judgement and achieve final salvation. The world, and life in this world, by contrast, had now become *logically* negated: Only a temporary world, a merely transitional stage, and mainly nothing but a time of trial. *Psychologically* Man had left the interiority in the natural world behind (in contrast to the Old Testament situation, in which it still survived). People had their soul or essential being in the beyond, with Christ up in Heaven as well as in the future of afterlife. In this way, the interiority in this world was now ended in a very real psychic sense, and its logical supersededness became explicitly acted out in the form of asceticism which renounced the world, above all in monastic and in eremitic life.

With this we approach already the area of the second gift of Christianity, the notion of spirit. It likewise received a presence only in the form of being acted out. *Negatively* it was acted out in the form of acts of penance, of the mortification of the flesh, i.e., the mortification of Man's natural sensuality, above all of his sexual desire, which at the same time is a literal attempt to overcome nature and the interiority in the natural world. It was, further, *positively* acted out in the practice of contemplation and meditation, which is a merely *psychic* or literal inwardness of spirit.

That during the medieval phase the reception of the Christian truths remained external comes also out in the fact that for their salvation, people were dependent on the Church as external institution and supreme authority concerning the Christian teachings.

The *syntactic* further-development of the monotheistic revolution

The second phase of the Western development of Christianity, comprising the early-modern period, very roughly speaking, from the 15th century up to the time of Hegel and Schelling, is characterized by the fact that both the incarnation and the spirit came finally home to themselves by being absolute-negatively interiorized into themselves.[37]

As early as with the late-medieval movement of the *Devotio moderna*, faith made itself independent of the institutional bonds of the Church. Faith had now its own certainty in the inwardness of the believer, which also shows that the individual, too, had acquired a self-certainty of his own. Now, the person having this faith can say: "Here I stand, I cannot do otherwise". Similarly, natural reason, which for Thomas Aquinas had still been under the primacy of sensibility, made itself during this phase independent, autonomous. Before, the human being had been "the substance" who does the thinking. But now, instead of man the human mind or spirit, the *mens humana*, has become the real substance, a reality in its own right. It is defined as *res cogitans*, the *thinking*-substance that subsists in itself (i.e., thinking, thought, *as* substance in its own right). It is the presence in Man of the third divine person, the *spiritus sanctus*. The spirit or the *thinking*-substance realizes itself not only in the early-modern autonomous inwardness of faith but also as the early-modern autonomous thinking and in the early-modern I (*ego cogito*), which is natural reason's own self-consciousness and self-certainty. This I is historically an absolute novelty. It must not be confused with the everyday sense of I.

The thinking I's thought has the form of *repraesentatio*, representation, which literally means "placing whatever it may be before one's mental eye". It goes without saying that with all this the soul's basic standpoint has now fully come down to earth after the first Christian period's fundamental orientation to the beyond.

What in our context emerges is that with the *mens humana* as substance and early-modern I, the incarnation as God's becoming man has at long last become real. For, this I is now itself truly the Archimedean point that before had been established with the idea of the world-external monotheistic God.

---

37 For this whole section I am deeply indebted to insights gained from the writings and lectures of the philosopher Claus-Artur Scheier.

The I is the pure *thought* that we have seen formerly this God to have been, now, however, *as really existing* (and not only as being thought). The I really *exists* down here in the world in human beings, and this without having regressed to the form of natural existence, namely, as "graven image" that God formerly still needed to absolutely forbid. Existing as the *thought* of I, of pure *res cogitans*, the *thinking*-substance, it is nothing natural. And at the same time the I is, as the world-*external* Archimedean point's having come home to itself, the world-externality's having, *as world-externality*, become world-immanent.

Before I said that Christianity introduced two absolutely novel ideas, that of the incarnation and that of God as spirit. Now we have to realize that they are not really two, but rather only two sides of the same coin. The incarnation could only become real in the spirit and as spirit. Only the spirit was able to cross the gap between Man and God. God's incarnation in man as a literal event, his incarnation as a separate physically existing individual would remain an isolated case, an absolutely erratic event of no *real* significance for all the other humans. People could make it only secondarily significant for themselves by turning it into a subjective religious belief-system for themselves (together with a corresponding pious practice). But that would always remain their human doing. Psychological *reality*, *objective* reality,[38] the incarnation could only receive if it occurred in and as spirit, that is, in the very *definition* of Man as such.

"Incarnation" literally means, of course, "becoming flesh", and John 1:14 explicitly states: "The word was made flesh". But such a dictum needs to be read as a "speculative sentence" and thus what it says is tantamount to my earlier statement that the world-externality has, *as world-externality*, become world-immanent. The "flesh" as such, that is, Man (as *really existing human beings* in this world), is the living reality, the real and only abode, of the word, the logos, the spirit. With literal "flesh", "body" in contradistinction to spirit, mind, intellect, this saying has nothing to do. Does not the New Testament itself suggest this way of understanding? "I am telling you the truth: It is for your own good that I am going, because unless I go, the Paraclete will not come to you; but if I go, I will send him

---

38 This is a reality that simply exists independently of any subjective faith or attitude and regardless of whether it is conscious or unconscious, wanted or scorned, embraced or condemned.

to you" (John 16:7).[39] Christ, the representation of the *literalized* incarnation in the form of the one individual Jesus of Nazareth existing in the flesh, has to disappear and this his *disappearance*, his negation, the negation of this preliminary *literal* conception of the incarnation *is* in itself the arrival of the spirit. And this, Christ himself says, is the truth. To put it in terms of the Christian Trinity, God the Father, as pure thought, could only become real in God the Son, and the Son could only become real in "the flesh", i.e., in Man living on this earth, and the flesh, Man, could become the real embodiment of the word, the logos, only through and *in the form of* the Holy Spirit.

The I is I because it is the abstraction from all semantic signifiers; it has been stripped of all natural imaginal attributes that used to come to Man through his world-relation as the gazes that shone into him from the things in the world. Much earlier in this paper I stated that Man has his humanness *beyond himself* merely as an empty form. This his self-transcendence had meant that the logic of human existence was such that it has a priori reached out over the world, so that step by step in Man's world experience the world could sandplay-picture-like present concrete semantic aspects of his humanness to him. But now it turns out that what had in the end needed to come home to Man and thus come into *real existence* in him was not at all the richness of all the semantic signifiers, the images and concepts, received through his world-relation during the course of the soul's history. On the contrary, it was precisely nothing but the *empty form itself*, the I, its autonomy, its *repraesentatio in abstracto*. In other words, the imaginal semantics, the filling of the empty form, was not the goal. It was only *the way through which* the goal was to be reached. And this goal was the actual acquisition by the human *animal* of its self-comprehension as truly *human* animal, the comprehension that it has its essential being not by virtue of nature and as something natural, but in the autonomous I as existing concept. The human distinction lies in Man's freedom (i.e., in his "being-free"[40]).

The fact that the I has the faculty of *repraesentatio* as its "placing (whatever) before its mental eye" shows that the I has become the Lord of the gaze.

---

39 Greg Mogenson kindly reminded me of this Biblical verse.
40 *"Being*-free" in contradistinction to freedom as licentiousness ("anything goes").

Nevertheless, throughout this period the self-certainty of the early-modern I logically still hinged on the transcendent God, which is why, for example, Descartes needed to provide a proof of the existence of God to supply his thought with its keystone or logical ground. God was indispensable as guarantor of the *mediation* of Man and world. By the same token, the *mens humana* was only the earthly "copy" of the *divine* reason. It was, to be sure, infinite spontaneity, but synthetized with finite sensuality or receptivity (Kant). It could be productive, but not creative like God. All this means that despite all these revolutionary changes the logic of Man's containment in interiority still stayed intact, namely, as the relation between autonomous self and the Absolute, the *ground* of Man's transcendental essential being. "God" is the producing source and ground of Man's "being-free" within the fully determined natural process of the universe. As Schelling put it: "freedom is our and the Godhead's highest good".[41] But of course, this logic stayed intact only inwardly, spiritually, only in *distilled* form, in which the former semantic form of a literally religious Church practice had been sublated.

This diagnosis is also corroborated by what takes place at the very end of this period in Hegel's philosophy. In it, the semantics of the entire *repraesentatio* of Western metaphysics (i.e., all its teachings about the soul, the world, and God) becomes, so to speak, alchemically dissolved into its pure logical syntax. As such it has become perspicuous to itself, sheer fluidity, in other words, become truly distilled, pure spirit. This in turn means that in Hegel's work metaphysics itself has, as it were, seen through itself, seen through to its very ground, to the syntax that *produced* it. And thereby metaphysics has concluded and completed itself, and thus also exhausted itself. It had no task or job anymore. It is a little bit like with a primer at a time when the pupils have mastered the skill of reading and writing.

What happens in Hegel's philosophy is a real and momentous *event* in the history of the soul, just as the ancient rise to monotheism had been an earth-shaking happening. We must not confuse Hegel's philosophy with nothing but a personal theory of his. To be sure, Hegel was the place of manifestation for this thought, but the producing subject of this thought was the soul of the West or, more concretely, the immanent logic of Western

---

41 F. W. J. Schelling, *Urfassung der Philosophie der Offenbarung*, ed. by Walter E. Ehrhardt, vol. 1, Hamburg (Meiner) 1992, 13. Vorlesung, p. 79, my translation.

metaphysics itself that pressed for its own conclusion and fulfillment. So my point is not at all that *Hegel* concluded metaphysics. Such a conclusion is not, could not be, *a human individual's* work and achievement. No, my point is that Hegel's *Phenomenology of the Spirit* is something like the "symptom" of the fact that by his time metaphysics had objectively come to its end.[42]

The conclusion of the soul's monotheistic program *as its own about-face*

The second phase of the Christian epochal change was not simply *followed* by a new period. It had itself explicitly brought about its own *conclusion* by bringing about the fulfillment of the project or program that the soul had established with the second epochal change, nay, even with the earlier one

---

42   Those who insist that metaphysics is by no means over are able to do so only because as scholars or philosophers they view (apperceive) metaphysics in its numerous historical varieties only as intellectual *theories* in the history of ideas and human thought. One can do that. It is certainly conceivable that individual *people* in the 21st century might come up with a metaphysical theory. But a psychologist cannot apperceive metaphysics as a theory. For psychology, metaphysics is a *psychological reality*, namely as (the philosophical articulation of) the in fact prevailing logic of being-in-the-world at a given historical time, just as mythology and ritual life were analogously a form in which the ruling logic of another mode of being-in-the-world expressed itself. An additional, but very different problem of the thesis that metaphysics is nowadays *not* obsolete can be that one chooses to define metaphysics only abstractly-intellectually, only in semantic terms, e.g. as a person's belief in verticality or transcendence. Of course there is no limit to what *people* can believe in or what theories they can come up with. But again, for a psychologist the decisive factor is not whether there still are cases of theories characterized by verticality, but (a) whether the internal "syntax" or logic of the thought backs up this its own propounded verticality or transcendence and (b) whether this theory of transcendence expresses the *objective* spirit of the respective age or not. Psychology as discipline in the Jungian tradition is committed to the objective soul. And in the objective soul, as Jung put it so clearly and decisively, "The value of life now lies wholly in this world. . ." (*MDR* p. 265, transl. modif.). "The otherworldliness, transcendence of the Christian myth [and thus the foundation of any sense of verticality] was lost . . ." (*MDR* p. 328). Repurposing a formulation of Jung's from a different context (*GW* 16 § 449), we could say that "the numen has of late immigrated into" the sphere of this-worldliness and "the whole weight of the critical issues of human existence as such (*Menschheitsproblematik*) has shifted to" this sphere. This is the modern soul *reality* according to Jung. In Africa, seeing a medicine man's metaphysical obsolescence, it had become clear to him that the former world of a vertical orientation (and thus implicitly metaphysics in modernity) was an "outdated and *never recurring* world . . ." (*MDR* p. 265, my italics).

of the first invention of the idea of the monotheistic God. Such a conclusion *is*, however, *in itself* the next epochal change: The change to modernity.

Having arrived at its goal and brought to conclusion a project encompassing millennia, the soul could at the end of the early-modern period feel absolutely elated. But then, when it woke up the next morning and had to *face* the coming day, standing now on the high standpoint acquired through history, it found itself thrust into modernity, into the modern world, and felt in a hole.[43] Why? I list four reasons.

(1) Having as modern I at long last irrevocably *become* and thus itself now simply *being* the Archimedean point, modern Man had lost his *having* a Polar Star for himself to orient himself by in life.

(2) Man's transcendental essence having actually arrived in him, he or the soul had lost its *purpose and direction*. It could no longer expect anything higher and essential, any metaphysical fulfillment, to come to it from anywhere and so it stood there empty-handed without any metaphysical hope, completely thrown back on itself as man for himself.

(3) By the same token, as having come home to him, Man's transcendental truth did no longer reach out over the world; his former in-ness in the mediation overarching Man and world had ended, with the consequence that now *fundamental otherness* ruled.[44] For although empirically the I was of course world-immanent, as the Archimedean point it logically was world-*external*; and for a world-external I the natural world evidently had to be radically other; nature had now logically turned into the realm of positivistically apperceived physical facts in their naked materiality and as such, again logically, was now open to uninhibited dissecting analysis and unrestrained exploitation. A continuation of the "sandplay" that had been going on all this time had once and for all become impossible, since Man had already integrated his essential being as his "being-free" into himself

---

43 This idea can also be expressed in logical terms in the following way, to put it in the words of Greg Mogenson (email comment on this passage, June 2, 2024): "After so, so many second-order negations throughout the millennia of its Christian history the soul's restored Position has the character of alienation."

44 This "fundamental otherness" is something totally different from the "Wholly Other" as the Holy in the sense of Rudolf Otto. The otherness of the Wholly Other consists in its being the absolute reversal from the first kind of seeing to the second kind of seeing as one's being hit and pierced by the "gaze" of the Holy. The "fundamental otherness" in modernity means logical separation, lack of connection, the exclusion of any idea of a possible real relation.

and had ipso facto himself become the Lord of all gazing. Along with the interiority of his previous mode of being-in-the-world he had lost his a priori *containment in meaning*.

(4) Furthermore, the monotheistic God had not only semantically been established as the Archimedean point. As it turned out, he had also had a practical function for the soul itself. God as the Archimedean point had syntactically to serve as a lever to lift Man out of his archaic containment in the interiority of his world-relation and install him in the new *modern* world-relation of fundamental otherness. But by now, God had done this his work, so God could go—in fact, logically, he had already gone.[45] No longer: *Vocatus atque non vocatus deus aderit.* The loss of God, however, means that existence had lost its metaphysical *ground*.

On account of all this (loss of ground, orientation, purpose, containment in meaning) a gaping abyss had opened up for *modern* Man. The 19th century called it nihilism.

This gaping abyss is, however, not a simple perception of the prevailing truth, but rather the result of a dissociation, the dissociation between ego and soul. For in truth, this abyss exists only for a consciousness that is *not adapted* to the new reality. Although *de facto* and as soul, Man was already *in* modernity, he nevertheless, as ego, apperceived the world with the old consciousness that kept clinging to the values and expectations stemming from the pre-modern period, a discrepancy that led to the powerful, but completely inappropriate *feelings* of disappointment, loss, and of his feeling confronted with an abyss.

In itself, however, the epochal change to modernity is simply *the flip-flop-like switch from interiority to externality* and from the primacy of the second kind of seeing to that of the first kind of seeing.[46] It is the revolutionary change to Man's new world-relation in terms of positivism.

But what is this externality? It must not be confused with the outwards orientation of animals, with *their* harmless form of the first kind of seeing.

---

45 Cf. what I said above about the conclusion of metaphysics, that it had no task or job anymore.

46 Rather than how people experienced it, namely as the flip-flop switch from the early-modern elated feeling of fulfillment to the modern feeling of loss, emptiness, and of an abyss. On the other hand, from the point of view of the traditional consciousness, the feeling and idea of an abyss is also a correct description of this change. The switch character is in both versions adequately perceived.

In their perceiving the environment, animals are not *interested* in what is around them as such (in fact, they are not really "interested" in anything at all). In pre-modern times, Man, too, was not really "interested" in the empirical nature of things,[47] although, being soul, he was by nature an interested being. But his real interest went to inner infinity or divinity of reality as reflected in the myths, religions, and the metaphysical tradition. These satisfied the needs of the pre-modern soul. The fundamental interest in the natural world as something worth investigating in its own right, by contrast, is due partly to the early-modern and then to full extent to the modern situation, on the one hand, and to the workings of man's self-transcendence under the conditions of the modern situation, on the other hand. In this situation the way to the second kind of seeing was once and for all closed as the dominant relation to reality. Only the first kind of seeing was now available and it inevitably led to Man's being directly confronted with naked nature in its radical Otherness. This means that his inescapable *transcendental* need to reach out beyond himself could now only make itself felt within the narrow *empirical* confines of this direct focus upon things, with the consequence that this his empirical first kind of seeing became unwittingly "inflated" with a transcendental surplus, i.e., with an urgency and *dynamic* stemming from Man's being driven to logically reach out beyond his own biological nature. And this inner drivenness of his first kind of seeing shows as his *interest* in empirical nature as such. It shows as pure inquisitiveness about, or rather as the intellectual assault upon, the Other. So we see that the modern externality also leads to an openness for the *unknownness* of things, but now of course to an "openness" not for the things' divine mystery, but to the things' *hidden innermost technical makeup*. And whereas the second kind of seeing of old was rewarded by the flashing-up of a gaze coming from the real things, a gaze in which the *vertical* innermost truth of the things (associated with *eternity*) revealed itself once and for all, the internal dynamic of the modern first kind of seeing never *arrives* at a truth as the logical end of its inquisitiveness with respect to any particular phenomenon. Under the conditions of the *horizontality* of its approach to reality, what used to be *arrival* is inevitably translated into the *temporality* of an endless succession of uncovering layers of preliminary "truths" of the same

47 Of course, with the exception of a select group of intellectuals in ancient Greece and in later times.

phenomenon, one layer after the other, comparable in some way to an infinite progress or process of unpacking Russian Matryoshka dolls.

After this clarification about the nature of externality we can return to the discussion of the soul-historical switch from interiority to externality. Contrary to the initial feeling of having lost all direction and purpose through this switch, the *opus magnum* that the soul pursues in modernity is still determined by a clear goal-directedness and purposiveness, merely a different one from before. In fact, modern Man is even propelled forward by an enormously powerful, irresistible force in the direction of externality, much more so than it was ever driven forward during any of the previous ages under the aegis of interiority. Today, all love and passion of the soul flow to the physical world in its materiality and positive facticity. We could perhaps even speak of a deep *devotion* in the religious sense, but one of which Man is systematically kept unwitting.

Devotion might here even be seen as having again in some remote sense the decidedly downwards direction of the archaic *devotio* ritual (in which a Roman consul, before a battle, consecrated himself, together with the whole enemy army, to the underworld and thus to his and their death in this battle, thereby explicitly renouncing for himself all personal bliss and happiness on earth as well as any higher aspiration to ideal spheres, to the upper gods, to spirit and freedom, so that through this sacrifice his own army might prove victorious). Keeping this in mind, the motto, taken from Virgil, under which Freud at the very beginning of the 20th century placed his *Interpretation of Dreams* could with some justification be said to be the secret motto of the soul's program in modernity: *Flectere si nequeo superos, Acheronta movebo*. This quotation, stripped of its mythologizing *façon de parler* and the way Freud used it, clearly expresses the resolute switch away from the commitment to higher spiritual ideas and divine powers (a commitment which according to this dictum has been experienced as being no longer possible) to the new devotion to naturalistic causes and mechanisms or to externality in general.

There is in the modern world indeed such a passionate downwards orientation, namely, an ever deeper immersion in the material world, in physical reality, above all through physics, biochemistry, and nano-technology, down to the smallest particles and even beyond all particles. With constantly accelerating speed, science and technology are swept forward by an immanent will that wants to get to the end. The end, the ultimate goal, seems to be for the mind to become able to synthetically produce life and to understand (or even go back behind) the big bang—and in this way to bring about, in empirical Man, an approximation of the knowledge and technical skill that would, at least in principle, enable him to re-create the world. In other words, the goal would be to achieve a psychological realization and empirical *Wahrmachung* (veri-fication) of the old idea of the Creator God.

So that this program could be executed, the gaze, whose owner the modern I has become, had to come decidedly and exclusively under the sway of what I called the first kind of seeing, in explicit disdain of any interest in such things as the essence or divine ground of things.[48] In its character this seeing has, so to speak, become X-ray-like, the "aggressive" will *to see through*, to detect and uncover, to penetrate deeper and deeper into the material world in order to get wise to the hidden mechanisms and ultimate tricks of nature, including the mechanisms of the psyche, and so take *intellectual* possession of the Real. By the same token, the former *mens humana*, the *spirit* in the highest sense in Man, had to turn into calculating intellect,[49] into formalistic, technical, rationalistic thinking devoted to the sole interest in the *functionality* of things ("how things work") as *its* ruling spirit. Even the very logic has in modernity turned into the logic of the function (Frege).

The same passionate downwards drive is also at work in Man's self-relation. Man nowadays feels the strong need to view and define himself as (higher) *animal*, as biological organism and individual body, as naked ape, as in two thirds of his DNA-sequence being closer to chimpanzees than to gorillas. His deepest effort goes to his understanding himself from beneath, in terms of biological evolution and physiological processes, and to explain all his higher functions (such as empathy, consciousness, language, thinking) strictly naturalistically, be it neurobiologically from the brain, or be it as the evolutionary further-development of rudimentary functions existing in animal precursors, or be it as natural results of early Man's social behaviors in response to practical necessities.

Externality as radical otherness of man and world or of subject and object even surpasses itself, namely in Man's *outsourcing* some of *his own* most precious distinctively human faculties. In remote sensing, the modern I delegates its own "being the observer-standpoint" to satellites and

---

48 Although it is utterly free of the self-curbing constitutive of the second kind of seeing, it is not a totally unchecked, uninhibited seeing, because it is scientific seeing and thus methodically, i.e., externally, by the human mind, controlled seeing.

49 Heidegger's *rechnendes Denken*.

their sensors, and in the automation of processes and in robots it delegates its own "being subject" and "being self-determined, self-responsible", to external machines. Photography and people's obsessive picture-taking is the objective reification and mechanization of the modern I's "being the Lord of the gaze" and at the same time the blind celebration of the first kind of seeing. Through "Artificial Intelligence" apps Man unburdens himself of his own faculties of thinking and being artistically creative, a tendency that amounts to a kind of de-selfing on the part of Man and to a celebration of externality *per se*. Even the self as such of Man is logically externalized into the ephemeral, utterly superficial selfies (or the phenomenon of selfies is one visible symptom of the self's externalization).

While *semantically* seeing himself more and more as decidedly earth-born, Man has *psychologically* already left the earth. Psychologically he has now his real home in Virtual Realities[50] and in outer space,[51] although according to "the impressions of the daily life" he is obviously still living on this planet. By the same token, he longs to be swept away by strong emotions, to drown his alert consciousness in loud music, to lose his self in mass events, to follow fads, trends, and influencers, and to get into an altered state of consciousness—in short to find self-oblivion. Even in practical reality, in everyday experience, the natural world is increasingly becoming replaced by a technically produced artificial world and translated into a more and more digitalized, ultimately a virtual reality, into the Metaverse, including the genetic reprogramming of living things. It is as if the Biblical predictions, "Behold, all things are become new" (2 Corinthians 5:17) and "And I saw a new heaven and a new earth: For the first heaven and the first

---

50 The difference of Virtual Reality from the world of the mind and the imagination is that Virtual Reality aims for *experiences by the senses* and thus depends on physical devices like Head-Mounted-Displays. It also involves the bodily interactions of the experiencing person. The mind, however, although dependent on the audible or silent sounds of language, uses the sounds only as a kind of springboard to push off from, and, negating them, frees itself precisely from this sensory basis so as to enter and exist as the dimension of spirit and meanings.

51 Through his fascination with space flights and numerous popular science-fiction novels and movies, such as *ET*, *Stars Wars*, or *Star Trek*, as well as through his fantasies about Martians and intelligent life in different galaxies, modern Man *celebrates*, even if in a veiled way and without acknowledgment, his own already being an Extra-Terrestrial. Psychologically, the point of these mighty fantasies is by no means that they betray a longing for journeys into outer space, but that, in the image of space travel, they attest Man's unwitting already *having left* the Earth.

earth were passed away; and there was no more sea" (Revelation 21:1) were being empirically realized.

* * *

I started this presentation with the assertion that the answer to the question, "Where is soul?", could be: "Nowhere", and that the name of this "nowhere" is interiority. Now I must modify this statement by adding that it is only true for the bygone past. In modernity, *the soul* is precisely present in the "nowhere" or absolute negativity of the force that drives human existence ever deeper into externality and the sensory.

No doubt, there is also one exception: The discipline of interiority. But this interiority is a methodically produced one, not an interiority as a mode of being-in-the-world prevailing as a matter of course. That nowadays interiority has to be methodically produced confirms that the discipline of interiority is itself under the rule of externality.[52]

And then of course, modernity is also a time and a fertile field that lets sprout up numerous political, religious, spiritual, and psychological movements promising deeper meaning or salvation. Formally, some of them may perhaps give a place to interiority. But they are not in the service of the soul. As varied as they may be, they are all clearly the ego's response to the challenges presented by the modern reality of the objective soul and cater to the subjective emotional needs or longings of people's psyche.

Coda

This ends my analysis of "Interiority and Accomplished Modernity" as my contribution to the discussion of the question "Where is Soul?". But I feel that it is appropriate, if not necessary, not to end with this ending, but to still attach two psychotherapeutic warnings to this essay. The first concerns a possible error or confusion. The description and analysis of the internal

---

52 Here we might remember Jung's crucial insight that psychology as a scientific field became only possible as well as necessary as a consequence of the disappearance of religion or metaphysics as a living and lived reality. We could in our context also say, the disappearance in the Western world of interiority as Man's mode of being-in-the-world. Jung's insight holds true for all three types of psychology, 1. the scientific (positivistic) and technically oriented psychologies, 2. psychologies as ersatz religion and consolation for the loss of meaning, and 3. psychology as the discipline of interiority.

telos of the *modern* soul's *opus magnum* might lead us to faultily conclude that developments, simply on account of their being modern, must ipso facto also be an authentic expression of the modern *soul* and its *opus magnum*. But as at any age, the soul today is only what is "behind the scenes". It is not what the eyes can see. Among what is accessible to the "impressions of the daily life" in present-day reality, there is so much that is superficial, childish, simply silly, crap or even destructive, and sometimes downright pathological; and there are so many headless people susceptible to any fad or trend or to the suggestions of influencers. The warning is: "Believe not every spirit, but try the spirits whether they are of God" (1 John 4:1), which for us means: Whether they are of the soul. Much discrimination is needed, which in turn requires in each of us the distinguishing power of a well-differentiated feeling function (Jung) or of the faculty of judgement (Kant).

The second warning concerns our own humanness, both in the sense of our individuality together with our sense of agency and self-responsibility *and* in the higher sense of the "transcendental half" or the heart of our humanness.

If we take to heart the insights gained about the direction of the modern soul's *opus magnum*, we might, as psychologists committed to the soul, believe that it is our duty to wholeheartedly support this the soul's dynamic. But as well-meant as it is and as deeply psychological as it sounds, this belief would be the same mistake that during the 19th century led people to experience modernity as nothing but a loss and as the opening up of an abyss, namely: It would be one's clinging to the values and expectations stemming from the pre-modern period. However, with the modern soul's flip-flop-like shift from interiority to externality, the very sense of being faithful to the soul has also radically changed. In part 4 of my book *What is Soul?* I distinguished two directly opposite intentionalities or purposes that the soul in general can have for us.[53] The one I called "initiation" or "soul-making", the other "emancipation from the soul". In that book I discussed these two possibilities of what the soul wants to bring about in us humans mainly in the context of psychotherapy, but also pointed already out that they are relevant for the nature of soul as such and its *opus magnum*. What in the present context needs to be stated is that simultaneously with the

---

53 W. Giegerich, *What Is Soul?* New Orleans, LA (Spring Journal Books) 2012, now: London and New York (Routledge) 2020.

flip-flop-like switch from interiority to externality, Man's psychological task also suddenly reversed from what I called "initiation" or "soul-making" to "emancipation from the soul".

It seems completely paradoxical, if not downright crazy, to have to realize that under the conditions of its modern *opus magnum*, which is rigorously devoted to externality, *to serve the soul* requires precisely the *modern individuals'* emancipation from the soul. But it is absolutely consistent and indispensable. Such a radical turn as the one from interiority to externality must have similarly drastic consequences for psychological economy, for Man's relation towards and stance vis-à-vis the soul. Of course, in the old, traditional world, that of ritual, myth and religion, the private family rituals (*opus parvum*) had harmoniously their place within the larger framework of the public cult life (*opus magnum*). They had the same purpose and direction. The nature of modernity, of the world after religion and metaphysics have become completely pointless for the soul, entails *the radical falling apart of the opus magnum and the opus parvum*, even their becoming oppositional. This is why emancipation from the soul becomes necessary today *for the individual*.

There simply had to be a reversal into the opposite. It cannot possible be in the interest of the soul for us to get absorbed by and to completely identify with the *modern* soul's powerful rush deeper and deeper into a totally technological civilization and externality.

That is the one aspect. The other is that it can also not be in the soul's interest that all its achievements reached in the human development during the past thousands of years up to the point of "the autonomous I" get lost through, and get overwritten by, our letting ourselves *psychologically* be sucked into the modern soul's powerful movement towards externality, positivism, and automatic processes.

But what precisely and in detail does emancipation from the soul mean? It means

1. that we must retain our psychological independence and standpoint clearly vis-à-vis it so as to be able to serve the soul as objective observers and critical consciousness of its cultural process: To serve it as *its* possibility to become conscious of itself (in and through us). "Initiation" had meant (in some way) merging with the soul's process, in the depths of one's being entering the soul's mysteries. As such, even if it empirically led to "higher knowledge", *psychologically* it amounted to becoming unconscious, to be identified with this higher knowledge. But what

is now needed is becoming truly *conscious* of the soul, seeing it for what it is and seeing this precisely *from* our own *human* standpoint, *with* our *human* values.

2. And, the psychological reason why we have to emancipate ourselves from the soul is that we *each* have the *personal* (ego!) duty as conscious modern individuals to protect and preserve our *humanness*, our individuality, self-responsibility, the sense of selfhood, mineness and eachness.[54] It is our duty to protect them *against* the many often powerful forces in the modern world that fundamentally threaten all this, such as the whole abstractness dominating so much of our present-day life, the prevailing one-sidedly utilitarian and efficiency-directed attitude, the quantifying, statistical approaches together with the social as well as political tendencies trying to enforce conformity and standardization, the influence of social media, the self-stultification through trivial and thrilling entertainment, the mighty longing for self-narcotization through the drug[55] culture, and so on.

In view of all this, we have the task of being the guardians of the treasure of our individuality. In this context a dream image of Jung's has always seemed helpful for me.[56] It reads (*MDR* p. 87f.):

> It was night in some unknown place, and I was making slow and painful headway against a mighty wind. Dense fog was flying along everywhere. I had my hands cupped around a tiny light which threatened to go out at any moment. Everything depended on my keeping this little light alive. Suddenly I had the feeling that something was coming up behind me. I looked back, and saw a gigantic black figure following me. But at the same moment I was conscious, in spite of my terror, that I must keep my little light going through night and wind, regardless of all dangers.

In a similar way we each might protect the little light of our individuality and humanness from the mighty wind of history blowing in accomplished modernity that threatens to put it out.

---

54 Cf. what I wrote on pp. 368f. of my "The Opposition of 'Individual' and 'Collective'—Psychology's Basic Fault", in: W.G., *CEP V*, pp. 327–369.

55 Not only literal drugs.

56 See also my "A Little Light, to Be Carried Through Night and Storm", in: W.G., *CEP II*, pp. 333–336.

By the same token, we are also, each according to his abilities, appointed guardians of all the intellectual, spiritual, and material treasures that the soul in its entire pre-modern history from the earliest times onwards achieved or acquired, by taking heed of them in *Mnemosyne*, so that these treasures can in this way still have a *historical* presence in modern life, although they are admittedly no longer a present *reality*.

The in modernity so much more difficult task of preserving our humanness concerns our *existence* AS *self-transcendence*. One might perhaps think that because, as I showed, Man's transcendental essence had at the end of the early-modern period actually arrived in him in the form of Man's now being autonomous I, the issue of our being *more* than we literally are was once and for all taken care of. But this would be a grave error. The "empty second half" of our human nature I spoke of is not like an empty box that through what I termed "its semantic filling" would get literally filled. Not at all. No matter how much it gets filled, the *structure* of humanness (humanness as having an empty second half) remains, or rather, it always *restores* itself on each new level that human consciousness has attained in its historical development. It might only be that we are not aware of it because we let ourselves be blinded by the impressions that the *previous* arrival of the transcendental essence in the form of the I makes. It was Jung's merit to have understood this and have stood up for it.

> It is not ethical principles, however lofty, or creeds, however ortho-dox, that lay the foundations for the freedom and autonomy of the individual, but simply and solely the empirical awareness, the incontrovertible experience of an intensely personal, reciprocal relationship between man and an extramundane authority which acts as a counterpoise to the "world" and its "reason". (*CW* 10 § 509)

The issue of "a counterpoise to the 'world' and its 'reason'" is indeed crucial, because it is what human self-transcendence is ultimately about. And certainly, it is not ethical principles, all our noble, but idle talk about "our values", about "human rights" and "human dignity", that lay the foundation for the freedom, autonomy, and humanness of the individual. But the fact that all this is not essential, that something completely different is needed, this is also where the difficulty I hinted at lies. The great problem is that in modernity the possibility is no longer available to us that Man's self-transcendence, *Homo sapiens's* logically *reaching a priori out beyond himself,* still had in archaic and pre-modern times. His overarching the natural world, his having gods or God as *"an extramundane authority"* in the cosmos (or, in the case of the world-external God, beyond the cosmos, but even then nevertheless within an imagination that starts out from the cosmos), became impossible the moment Man had logically himself become the world-*external* Archimedean point. This means that now his *transcendental* reaching out beyond himself is, as shown above, forced down into the form of his *empirical* inquisitiveness concerning the material things' hidden technical makeup and thus exactly into what Jung called "the 'world' and its 'reason'" and thus precisely not to their counterpoise.

On the other hand, the fact that nature or the cosmos (just as Man himself) has been released from the bond of interiority and mediation (of Man and world) and become absolutely other, the fact, furthermore, that accordingly modernity is totally devoted to externality is, surprisingly, in this connection even helpful, "therapeutic", because it is precisely the *emptiness* of the empty second half of the constitution of Man that in this way will be expressly experienced and might in this way become explicitly conscious, just as it might compel modern Man to stop looking outwards for something to which his psychological necessity to extend beyond himself could go. Instead the fact that a return to what else there is beside himself has become impossible could throw this his logical necessity of transcending himself back solely upon *itself,* or, rather, force it explicitly and irrevocably into *absolute negativity,* and thereby—possibly— onto an altogether new level, the level of spirit.[57] We may here cite Paul

---

57 In response to his analysis of modernity ("We are confronted with the darkness of our soul . . . It hollows out and hacks up the shapes of our culture and its historical dominants. We have no dominants any more . . . Our hitherto believed values decay accordingly and our only certain[t]y is that the new world will be something different from what we were used to", *Letters 2,* p. 590, to Read, 2 September 1960), Jung entertained the fantasy of the coming of an "awe-inspiring guest who knocks at our door portentously", a guest who, qua guest, would obviously have to be hospitably received by modern Man. This fantasy of Jung's clearly shows the logic of "the second kind of seeing" to be at work in his mind and the semantic content of his fantasy, the idea of a *guest* emerging from something as unlikely as the advanced technological civilization is structurally the intuition or imaginal anticipation of the (possible) "other picture that looms up". Nevertheless, I wonder whether with such a fantasy Jung's thinking does not perhaps stay

Valéry: "L'humain n'est humain que par ce qu'il suggère de surhumain, et celui-là n'est vraiment homme qui ne se transforme d'homme en plus qu'homme" (The human is human only through what it intimates of the superhuman, and that person is not truly human who does not transform himself from human into more than human).[58]

But all that is merely a kind of signpost, not a real solution. One thing, however, is clear: the solution of Man's self-transcendence in modernity and thus of a possible counterpoise to the "world" and its "reason" in our days cannot have the form of a cultural, collective truth. Each individual has to find this counterpoise to the "world" and its "reason" for himself and all by himself and in his very own way. (The solution Jung offered with his idea of an individuation process within a Jungian analysis and thus mainly through dreams from the unconscious is not convincing. It still clings to the hope for a merely semantic answer, as in times past.) So for most of us what the solution could be will remain an open question.

When I talked above about our task to protect and preserve our individuality, I also stated that this was an *ego* duty. By contrast, one's transforming oneself from human into more than human is a task that cannot be performed by us as ego-personalities. It calls the *whole man (homo totus)* to the fore and forces him to show his colors, the depth and greatness of his humanity.

3. My insistence on emancipation from the soul and its *opus magnum* in modernity could be misunderstood as having the active sense of suggesting that we should be against the modern soul's *opus magnum* and resist or even fight it. On the contrary, emancipation from the soul in order to *psychically* (as individuals and ego-personalities) protect our own must go along with the insight that *psychologically* we need to *adapt* to the new situation. The soul's ever faster move into the transformation of the natural world into a thoroughly technological one must also transform

---

too much enthralled by the no longer possible mythological, personifying, and above all semantic mode of thinking and may with such a decidedly *positive* answer not miss the unique feature of the soul of the modern world: Its requiring the mind's openness to and initiation into absolute negativity, into the logic of emptiness. Would this not be the real truth of Man's self-transcendence? Is not perhaps the real "awe-inspiring guest", to stay with this mythologizing parlance, or what really wants to come home to consciousness *in some distant future* (!), precisely (logical) *negativity as such*, negativity as Man's real essential being and distinction? Whatever this may practically mean?

58   Paul Valéry, *Cahiers II (Bibliothèque de la Pléiade*, Gallimard) 1974, p. 539.

the very constitution of our consciousness, our inherited categories of understanding and our expectations. More than that. The new artificial world even needs us, needs our human feeling (precisely also our suffering under it). It needs to ultimately[59] find a place in our heart and to be received in (and with) our rigorous thought so that eventually it may cease being dissociated from us, cease being nothing but dead fact, but can at long last again become *our own*, our *human* world.

59 I say "ultimately" because our giving it a place in our heart cannot be imposed on us as an obligation, a duty. It must be spontaneous, honest—i.e., come directly and freely from our own heart itself. This means that the time for such a thing to happen must have come of its own accord. We must have become ripe for it.

Chapter 2

Negativity and the soul

On the genesis and history of the soul[1]

Absolute-negative phenomena

"Absolute" here means being freed ("absolved") from the opposition of *either* positive *or* negative. It means being both at once, rather than being the one and having the other outside of itself.

I begin with the example of neurotic symptoms such as hysterical blindness or paralysis, compulsive hand-washing, agoraphobia or dog phobia. They are actually nothing, just hot air, fantastic. What is feared in a dog phobia is precisely not aggressive, dangerous dogs (if that were the case it would be *Realangst*, realistic fear and not a phobia), but something in the dog that nobody but the phobic person can see or sense. It is a strange *idea* or *fantasy* of "dog". And yet it is not nothing, because this idea is an extremely powerful reality that can paralyze the phobic person.

My next example is life. If I take away $500 from somebody, I have the $500 in addition to all my other possessions and the other person has lost them. But if I take somebody's life, I do not have his life in addition to my life and he has not lost anything either, because he simply ceases to exist; he is gone. Life is not an entity or substance, not even a vapor, that is added to a body or could be taken away from it. It is really nothing. By contrast, let us take the example of body organs. Organs can be demonstrated, seen, and touched. They can even be transplanted. The heart exists. But the life of a body cannot be seen or touched. You cannot demonstrate it. In this sense it is nothing. You could only demonstrate that a person or animal *is alive*. But life as such does not exist. And yet life is an undeniable powerful reality. It makes a real difference whether you are alive or not.

1 This essay was written in 2017.

DOI: 10.4324/9781003611400-3

Just like life, the soul does not exist. It also cannot be demonstrated. Even less than life. For since one can show that animals or people are either indeed alive or dead, there is in the case of life at least indirect evidence, while there is no empirical evidence for the soul at all. The soul is only negativity, a logical nothing, which is why in modernity, in modern psychology, and thus also in Freudian psychoanalysis, the term is simply not used anymore, and "soul" is considered to be merely an ancient superstition.

In what follows, I want to discuss this "ancient superstition" a little more: How it first originated and what it involves or entails and can teach us.

The historical emergence of negativity

In my book *What Is Soul?* I pointed out on the basis of the research of several scholars that for Homer the *psychê* comes into play only after a person's death. And I claimed that what originally gave birth to the notion of soul and to the notion of the living dead in the underworld, to the idea of the ancestors, was the very real sight of a *corpse*.

But how and why could the sight of the corpse give rise to the notion of soul? To discuss this question I start out from new research about the etymology of the Greek word *psychê*.[2] The authors of this study begin with the observation that, to be sure, it is generally accepted knowledge that the *psychê* is the soul of the deceased, the "free soul". But then they go on to show that another still generally accepted idea is not tenable, namely the idea that *psychê* etymologically originally meant "breath" (in German "*Atem, Hauch*") and that therefore *psychê* was a "breath soul" and referred to the living persons' breathing. The authors convincingly demonstrate that the verb *psýchô* (from which *psychê* is derived) does not at all mean "breathe" and that *psychê* itself is *not connected with any life function*. It is much rather the "shade soul" or "soul of the dead". By contrast, the real meaning of the verb *psýchô* is "to blow, to cool". From this it follows according to them that the original etymological meaning of *psychê* was *das Kaltwerden*, (the process of) "growing cold", and, derived from that, (the state of) "having grown cold", i.e., the "coldness" of the (deceased) human being. *Psychê*

---

2 Peter-Arnold Mumm und Susanne Richter, "Die Etymologie von griechisch ψυχή", in: *International Journal of Diachronic Linguistics and Linguistic Reconstruction* 5 (2008), S. 33–108.

was originally—in prehistoric times—the Greek word or name for the *corpse*!

This is a momentous insight. What it means is that here we do not at all begin with the pair "body and *soul*", but with the totally different pair "*living, warm* body and *cold, dead* body", in other words, two times body! *But*: The cold, dead body IS here, in this early situation, itself precisely *psychê*, a term which only later came to mean soul. At first, when *psychê* was the name of the corpse, there apparently was as yet nothing mysterious, spiritual, otherworldly connected with it, no idea of Hades, of underworld or yonder and therefore also not yet any soul. In this situation we were dealing very concretely, realistically only with visible, tangible positive facts: The living person and the cold corpse. Completely this-worldly and empirical.

Of course, there is here already a sense of negation: The corpse is the negation of the warm living body or person. But it is not absolute negativity. The corpse is something positive, totally positive, since it no longer has the logically negative and mysterious quality of "life" in itself that the living body had. The corpse is purified of all the negativity that the living person still had. The corpse is precisely nothing but positivity, paradigmatic positivity. And yet it is *psychê*! This is paradoxical, just as the fact that we begin with two positive facts, living body and corpse, and not with one positivity (body) and one negativity (soul).

In this early situation, there was no fantasy of a breath-soul leaving the living body and through its leaving causing the death of the person. In medieval paintings we sometimes see the death of a person depicted as a tiny homunculus or angel, representing the soul, coming out of the mouth of the dying person. But here, in this early situation, nothing of the sort is imagined.

The question therefore arises how the notion of "soul", how the transition from *psychê* as positive-factual corpse to *psychê* as logically negative underworldly soul came about. Where does such an idea as "underworldly soul" come from in the first place? What is the origin of absolute negativity as a dimension of human thought and experience? How would people come to imagine that there is such a thing as a soul and along with a soul an underworld, a realm of the dead ancestors, although there is not the least evidence for it? How did such ideas as the soul and underworld, that is, the dimension of absolute negativity, become possible?

Before I come to these questions I need to introduce a necessary insight on which I will rely.

Before substantiation

There are cultures for which the sun is god *only* at the moment of rising, but not during the rest of the day or night. Jung experienced this very concretely when he was in East Africa. The natives with whom he was staying performed a ceremony every morning when the sun appeared. They went out of the house, spit into their hands, and held them up to the sun. Only then was the sun *mungu*, god. Jung adds to this the following important comment: "The *moment* in which light comes *is* God. . . . To say that the *sun* is God is to blur and forget the archetypal experience of that moment" (*MDR* pp. 266–269). This notion of god is very surprising, completely strange, because it is in total contrast to a consciousness familiar with all the sun gods or goddesses in other cultures, Atum of the Egyptians, Helios of the Greeks, Amaterasu of the Japanese, to mention only these. If not the sun, but rather the moment of rising is god, then god is not an existing entity, a being, or person, but a happening, an event. God comes into being each time afresh when such a moment occurs and he lasts only for as long as that moment lasts. He is not immortal, not a supreme being, but temporal, even ephemeral.

Similarly, Karl Kerényi explained that the original content of the *name* "Zeus" meant, according to its linguistic properties, *das Aufleuchten*, the flaring-up of light, the flash as event, and that it only much later took on the meaning of *"he* who illumines", the light-bringer, *he* who sends the flashes of lightning. What happened to this one name in early history is probably just one single example for a fundamental and general shift in the history of consciousness from a prehistoric, archaic logic of event or happening, a logic of momentary *phainómena*, to a later logic of subject, person, entity, of thing or substance. What originally was a momentary happening turned later into an existing divine agent *producing* such happenings at times, an invisible, mysterious subject behind the event. Now there are two (agent and event, subject and verb); before there was only one, the real event.

Originally, *the real phenomena* were all there was. Zeus was nothing behind or outside of them. When the particular happening of a flaring-up of light was over, there was no Zeus anymore, just as before the event there had also not been a Zeus. Zeus was a concrete and always particular experience in actual reality. As a happening *in* sensible reality (contained and enclosed in the sensible event itself) he was not a "he", let alone the "Father of gods and men" who dwelled on Mount Olympus.[3] Grammatically speaking we could say that Zeus was, as it were, a "verb" and not a "noun". He was neither ontological nor imaginal, and not an immortal being behind the scenes. *The original Zeus predates mythology and the imagination.* And when the East Africans greeted the moment in which the light came as god, this god was of course also unimaginal. It was the *moment* of the coming of light and a moment cannot be an image. Before it could be an image it is already gone.

I pointed out that at a later time what originally had been a momentary phenomenon and as such ONE event *was divided into two*: subject and event, the doer behind the deed and the deed. *Now*, when this division has happened, one can rightly speak of epiphanies. But the thus arising *horizontal* duality of doer and deed has a second *essential* aspect. It is at the same time the *vertical* duality of the sphere of the temporal, the temporality of each actual Now, of each occurring epiphany, on the one hand, and the immortal god himself as imagined subject or person, on the other hand, who is above the temporal and lives in eternal bliss.

But why is the moment in which light comes *god*, and why is the flaring-up of light *Zeus*? Why are they not simply the empirical facts that they are? Why this going beyond the empirical, positive-factual significance of these events? Millions of animals also experience the rising of the sun, and to many it is also important, just think of the dependence of cold-blooded animals on the coming of the sun and its warmth. But there is neither a sense of "god" nor is the moment of rising emphatic. And higher animals probably react emotionally to such alarming events as flashes of lightning, but they do not experience anything like "Zeus" in them. How does the surplus significance of the divine come about in *human* experience?

Animals have no sense of the divine. They see only with their eyes. The fact that humans actually experienced a "god" or "Zeus" in the very natural, ordinary moment in which light comes or in the flash of lightning is evidence of the fact that for humans there is *not* only "what the eyes can

---

3 We therefore must in our context clearly distinguish *phainómena* from "epiphanies". As a real happening, the very nature or essence of Zeus was not really an epiphany but strictly *phenomenal*, that is to say, he was enclosed within this particular kind of event; he was not manifesting or revealing *himself in* or *through* the events (which would give them the status of "epiphanies"), and they were not *his* epiphanies in the sense of epiphanies *of him* in the first place. Zeus was nothing else but the real *phainómenon* itself.

see, but" also "what opens the eyes" (Kena-Upanishad). That is, humans see *more*. They see *also* what can *not* be seen with the eyes, what is *not* empirically given, what is *not* positively there. The fact that in archaic times "god" was experienced in natural phenomena such as the moment in which light comes or as the flash of lightning makes it evident that humans are more complex, that they are *not* primarily animals, but rather, as Aristotle said, animals that have *logos*. From the beginning, i.e., by nature, humans are, as Jung put it in somewhat flowery mythological language, "more than autochthonous animalia sprung from the earth, but as *twice-born* ones have *their roots* in the deity itself" (cf. *MDR* p. 333).

This reversal, this twice-bornness, this internal duality and reflectedness of man's essence, is the human distinction and expresses itself also in the *internal twofoldness of his seeing*, in his being open not only to what the eyes can see, but also to what opens the eyes. In man, logos, mind, *Geist*, thought, language are therefore not a secondary addition, a kind of super-structure added on top of animal existence. On the contrary, man has from the outset his home in language and thought. And the fact that the saying from the Kena-Upanishad speaks of "opening the eyes" shows that it is not another mysterious *sense organ* besides the eyes (a higher, religious or metaphysical sense in man) that is required. No, the saying stays with the same eyes. The move from ordinary seeing to seeing with *opened* eyes comes solely about through the seeing's self-negation, self-reflection, i.e., through a logical move.

When we talk about what the eyes can see, the eyes are the *instruments* for one's seeing, and the gaze of the eyes goes straight forward to what lies out there in front of the eyes. What we see in this way we see as human animals, and need to see in this way for our being able to survive in the world. It is pragmatic seeing. But when we hear of "what *opens* the eyes", the direction is all of a sudden turned around. Our concern is now no longer with what is in front of the eyes, with the object of our seeing, but with the eyes themselves, or rather: With *their* being opened.

It is crucial to understand that this reflection, this bending backwards, this turning around, is neither a literal turning around (a U-turn, so to speak), nor one's now looking at the literal eyes as physical organs by means of a mirror, nor is it a move to introspection. The seeing does not really return to the eyes, it returns to *itself*. *It* becomes reflected. This is what "opening the eyes" means. The bending backwards is therefore not an empirical behavior in space, but a *logical move* that leads to a new *form* of seeing, namely, an *in itself reflected* seeing. If it would have been a literal turning around or if it used a mirror, the gaze of the eyes would still go straight forward to what lies out there in front of the eyes. The only difference would be that the object *at which* one looks would be a different one, namely the eyes and not a tree, animal, thing or person. But the eyes would not have been "opened". The eyes have become opened when they still look forward *at real phenomena* such as the moment in which light comes, but are able to see in them what the eyes can *not* see, namely god, in other words, when the seeing has become *in-itself-reflected* seeing, in-itself-opened-up seeing—the soul's or mind's seeing.

It is a seeing characterized by the fact that into it, negation ("*not* what the eyes can see") is a priori integrated, indeed, we could even say: That *death* is integrated into it, which in our context of corpse and "*psychê*" is of course especially relevant. Ultimately it is death that opens the eyes, man's a priori being informed by the knowledge of death. And *opening* the eyes means opening-up the fundamentally "new" dimension of spirit, logos, soul—through pushing off from the ordinary sensory perception of the eyes. When one's eyes have been opened, one's seeing has "death" within itself.

This in-itself-reflected seeing means, in the case of our two examples, that the moment in which light comes, the event of an *Aufleuchten*, the flaring-up of a flash of lightning, do not just pointlessly happen and exhaust themselves in momentarily illumining the things of nature for our practical purposes in the pragmatic context of daily life. No, each of these events also returns to itself, is applied to itself and thus comes home to itself. The twice-bornness of man informs also his seeing and also that which is seen. The flash of lightning, so to speak, also strikes *itself*, thereby breaking *itself* (the flash) open and illumining the *natural* light-experience from within. The flaring-up happens a second time, this time by focusing upon itself rather than upon the environment. The light experience is duplicated; a bright light *within* the experience of the natural light is ignited, a no longer natural light. Now the momentary light is no longer, so to speak, "wasted" upon merely illumining the things that the eyes can see, but it opens the mind and, which is the same thing, opens a "clearance" (Heidegger's *Lichtung*) within the seen phenomenon. And the seeing of the resulting second-level light is the experience of "mungu", "god", or "Zeus"; or, maybe even more adequately, Rudolf Otto's abstract term: The experience of "the holy".

So what the people of the African tribe ceremonially greeted was by no means the moment of the plain, indifferent *natural* coming of light, simply the *literal* sunrise as positive fact, not that coming of light that animals also see. If it had been that, their idea of god would have been a superstition and their ceremony would have been idolatry.[4] No, it was much rather a seeing of the bright shine flaring up *within* the literal coming of light, the flaring-up of the light that reveals itself to the soul, the spirit, *Geist*—in contrast to the eyes as organs of sense perception.

Of course, there is not, as I presented it here, *first* the empirical event of a flash of lightning and *then* as a second happening the self-application of the flash to the flash itself. Rather, the primordial *human* experience of "the moment in which the light comes" *begins* as *in itself reflected* experience, as self-illumined by its own inner light, the inner *divine essence* of the particular experience. The flash as a *human* experience has always already come home to (returned to) *itself*. This is why the god could immediately and truly be *seen in* natural phenomena. It was real *seeing*, not a belief, not an opinion about the phenomena. And the god was really seen *in the phenomena* as *their* inner truth and not a projection upon them,[5] let alone an illusion or superstition in the subjective mind.

This is also why on this stage of cultural development there was neither need for, nor possibility of, what in archetypal psychology is called "seeing through". The seeing was in itself complete, fulfilled. It was *in itself* the seeing of the god. As seeing, it had everything it needed within itself, everything that needed to be seen, the whole soul truth of the *phainómenon* in question.

What is it that dawned on man in the primordial experience of a body's "growing cold"?

Having gained the insight into this *in-itself-reflected seeing*, a seeing that has negativity within it, we are ready to approach our topic of the corpse as *psychê* and the emergence of the ideas of soul, underworld, and ancestors. To

---

4 But superstition and idolatry cannot be original, primordial. They cannot be used as explanations for the coming about of seeming experiences and ideas of "*mungu*", god, "*psychê*". For their becoming possible they conversely already presuppose a situation in which the mind is already explicitly informed by a seeing that opens the eyes. Animals are never superstitious or idolatrous.
5 Cf. Jung's insight: "The word 'projection' is not really appropriate, for nothing has been cast out of the psyche; rather, the psyche has attained its present complexity by a series of acts of introjection" (*CW* 9i § 54).

understand the original transition from *corpse* as "psychê" to *psychê* as soul or shade in the underworld we need to go back to the archaic logic of momentary happening or phenomenality and see that—analogously to what Jung had shown about the East African's greeting the rising sun—"the *moment* in which the living body that just a minute ago was warm suddenly grows cold IS 'psychê'. To say that the *corpse* as 'positive fact' is 'psychê' is to blur and forget the original experience of that moment". *Psychê*, so to speak as a "verb" and not as "noun", namely as the experience of the shine that flares up within the sensory feeling of the body's growing cold. For as the striking *essential* experience that it is, "psychê" does not come as the *natural* experience of any empirical and trivial "growing cold" the way, e.g., a cup of tea may become cold, or the way that animals might notice the coldness of the dead body of a member of their own species. As a truly human experience, it comes as a priori reflected, returned to itself, opened up. The coldness is duplicated. It comes home to itself as a chilling experience. It illumines itself, so that its *inner essence* is the foremost content of the experience.

The experience of the human body's "growing cold" is obviously not a "moment in which *light* comes". It is conversely much rather a moment in which the *flame* of life is extinguished. It is nevertheless *also* a moment of a flaring-up of an inner light. In other words, the flaring up of an essential inner light does not depend on literal light phenomena like a sunrise or flash of lightning.

The question is: *What* light does this in-itself-reflected and illumined coldness bring? The experience of the body growing cold has two different aspects. It is (1) the experience of the *negation* of the warmth of life, and together with it (2) the experience of the *negation* of the living person. This twofold negation is the reason why it is a fundamentally *chilling* experience, an experience *piercing* the heart of the experiencing subject (rather than only an experience of a fact). Concerning the first aspect, I submit that what flared up for prehistoric man in the alarming experience of "growing cold" was the notion or feeling of *absolute negativity as such*. What does that mean?

When the East Africans greeted the *rising sun*, their seeing was, to be sure, in-itself reflected, in-itself negated seeing, but *what* they saw was god and not negativity as such. By contrast, the light or insight that flares up within the chilling experience of the "*growing cold*" is not something concrete like "god", but something much more general and fundamental. It is the "light" of that negativity itself. This negativity has in the case of the awareness of the "growing cold" become a direct experience. But it is also at work within *all* in-itself-reflected seeing and is the condition of the possibility of such experiences as that of "god" in the rising sun. But the difference is that in those experiences it is not the specific content or "topic" of these experiences, since what is experienced in them is a specific god. What is experienced through the "growing cold" is, however, negativity pure and simple, in its own right, negativity in its abstractness, coldness, ghostliness, in its sheer logicity, and as the very principle *of human nature* as such. In this sense this event was the awakening of (the first immediacy of) an awareness of man's *primarily* not being an animal and not a piece of nature, not having his true home in nature, but on the contrary of having his *roots* and true inner essence in *absolute negativity*, in logos, soul, *Geist*. The event could pierce the heart of the experiencing subject because it had an immediate echo in the slumbering absolute negativity as which man exists from the outset. It is this reverberation in the experiencing subject that brought about an (of course still only "implicit") "awakening" or (merely) dawning awareness of man's rootedness in absolute negativity.[6]

The word "absolute" is essential. For the fact that death as empirical event is the experience of a negation is trivial. It probably is that even for animals in a superficial sense. This negation is a simple negation and means no more than "over", "passé", "bygone". The primordial experience of "psychê", i.e., of "growing cold", inasmuch as it is a *human* experience and *in-itself-reflected seeing*, negates the first simple negation once more, and as negation *of* the negation it is absolute negativity: Clearly a negativity, not an empirically present entity, nothing positive, nothing visible or tangible—and yet also *not nothing*, but something most essential, the innermost ground and nature of man's humanness. It is self-contradictory.

In the primordial experience of the event of "growing cold" a most general and rudimentary sense of absolute negativity as a kind of dimension "dawned" on man (I say "dawned" with particular reference to the East African's celebrating the daily *emergence* of the sun). It was not yet a concept, let alone a clear one, nor a conscious awareness. In fact, it was nothing psychic, not an idea, feeling or intuition, not a subjective mental state *in people*, nothing in their "inner",[7] their mind, because it was still

---

6 The experiencing subject's heart being *pierced* by the experience of the body's "growing cold" and thereby *awakened* to the still slumbering inner essence of human nature is the passive counterpart to what I termed, in the context of my psychological analysis of archaic rituals of sacrificial slaughter, "the soul's killing itself into being".

7 An inner did not exist as yet. Even at fundamentally later stages of cultural development, there was not yet an inner, as Jung pointed out: "[. . .] everything I have observed lies *in*

completely outside, *in* the real object out there, *in* the objective event. And it was totally immersed in this objective happening as *its* quality, namely, as *its* (the object's or event's) own internal luminosity, not as people's awareness. People had, so we could say, *their* (implicit) consciousness or (initial) awareness only as (and in) their really seeing *the object's* luminosity.

This luminosity as the light that flared up from within a *real phenomenon* was completely worldly and by no means other-worldly or transcendent (just as the god in the *natural* moment in which light comes had not been anything transcendent; this god was on the contrary very much down to earth). Nevertheless, as the rudimentary sense of absolute negativity, even though it was still objectified, quasi materialized, and resided out there in the objective event, it was the first immediacy, the nucleus and precursor, of what, historically much later, became the sphere or dimension of *logos*, thought, *Geist*, mind, and people's consciousness.

Even if what dawned on man had originally its true place out there in the real event and did at first not yet have the form of mental concept or idea, it was nevertheless a human experience and therefore it involved, fundamentally affected, and deeply touched man. The experience was, as I said, "chilling"; it came as a shock, it pierced, as I said, the heart. It is to be assumed that the primordial way in which this impact of the event was concretely *reflected* in the experiencing persons was that it spontaneously erupted and expressed itself in *exclamations*, as the precursor, first immediacy, and/or first origin of later *words*, words like: "Mungu!", "Zeus!", "psychê!". When I speak of "exclamations", I want to suggest that they were not yet full-fledged linguistic words, inasmuch as they predated concept or idea as the meaning aspect of words.

So far I have discussed the first aspect of the primordial experience of "growing cold", the experience of absolute negativity in the most general sense. Now I come to the second aspect, namely, that the event of the body's "growing cold" amounted to the negation of "person". "Psychê" was historically thought of precisely as *each person's individual soul*.

The transition from warm to cold body means that the formerly living person is stripped of the whole colorful richness of all his or her various

---

the soul; everything, so to speak, on the *side of the inner*. I must, however, add at once that this is something peculiar, inasmuch as the soul is not always and everywhere on the inside. There are peoples and epochs where it is outside, peoples and epochs that are unpsychological, as, for example, all ancient cultures, [. . .]" (*GW* 10 § 158, my transl.). The inner is only the late result of a long history of interiorizations.

specific qualities and characteristics, his or her movements, activities, changing moods, emotions and affections, desires, interests. The former person is reduced to the abstractness, bodilessness, and paleness of a shade. The event of the person's growing cold freezes the person, fixates him or her much like a snapshot does, or rather precisely not like a snapshot that eternalizes the *accidental, contingent* looks of a person that he or she shows at one single particular moment. Rather, at death all the particular contingent details and along with it the sense of his or her physical presence are removed and compacted (contracted, condensed) into the cold, abstract *concept* of the person, who he or she *typically* or *in essence* was, his or her characteristic *Gestalt*, as the only thing that remains: The soul, shade, or spirit, ghost (in more modern times: The memory image).

The person's life is finished, *vollendet*. He or she has irrevocably vanished. Nevertheless in and through the experience of the body's "growing cold" qua "psychê" something remains. *What* remains is of course not his or her present reality in its concreteness. Rather it is his or her having-been-ness (*Gewesenheit*), the perfect tense of *who* he or she in essence *was*. But this indeed *remains*. And it remains because as what "who he or she in essence *was*", it cannot change anymore. As the pale, bodiless, lifeless abstractness of his *concept* or, as the Greeks said, "shade", it is supertemporal, exempt from the transience of natural life. *From within* the concrete sensory feeling of the coldness, something not-natural, chillingly cold, and abstract flared up for prehistoric man, the reality of the "concept" of the former person—and along with it a sense of something that lives on after death and is indestructible, timeless. The coldness IS thus the primordial *presence* of the wholly other (namely logically negative and fundamentally *absent*) reality of "that which *has* been and *therefore* lasts even after life", even when the dead person as present reality has vanished. It is the precursor of what *later* would be called the souls in the underworld, Hades, afterlife.

From primordial experience to mythological or philosophical idea

But of course all this, the person's concept and his timeless, indestructible life, remained at this primordial stage subjectively still unconscious. Nevertheless it was fully real. But it was still completely immersed in the real *event* of the body's growing cold (and thereafter resided *in* the cold corpse itself), rather than in people's minds.[8] This is why impressive, costly burials according to strict ritual rules as well as mighty graves or tombs and perhaps even embalmments became extremely important in prehistoric cultures.

What I said about the experienced inner divine light of events, namely that it was nothing psychic, not an idea, feeling, or intuition in people, but was completely immersed in the real events themselves, applies also to the ceremonial burials and the graves as well as to all ceremonial objects. They were *not* symbolic, not carriers or representatives of some higher meaning! Rather, they were themselves the real thing. They *were* the "higher meaning": Sacred.

Only later did the inner essence of the momentary experience become extracted from the experienced reality itself (*as whose* own inner essence it had existed) and thus detached from it. It was *substantiated* (hypostatized) as an independent and therefore now also *imaginable* reality. Now mythology had become possible. And now the difference originated between the mere corpse (Greek *sôma*), on the one hand, and, on the other hand, the *psychê*—*psychê* now in the sense of the soul of the dead and as a shade *in the underworld*. As strictly disconnected from life and residing in the underworld as a place inaccessible to the living, the *psychê* is now transcendent. But of course, as a *mythological transcendence* it is still, just as before, world-immanent, inasmuch as the underworld is itself located either in the depth of the earth or somewhere in the extreme West where the sun sets.

What also remains is that it is still "out there", not subjective, not in man's inner, not in the mind. Owing to this externality the form of culture had to be ritualistic, cultic. Cult and ritual are forms of acting-out (in a non-clinical sense). Truth resides here in the doing itself, in the ritual act or performance, not in people's thoughts or feelings. Mythology is also a form of externality. To be sure, it is about figures, events, and places that all have the logical status of absolute negativity. However, since mythology's logical form is imaginal or pictorial and since it therefore presents all those negative contents in the form of images or narratives, absolute negativity *itself* has here inevitably become "positivized" in a certain, of

---

8 In people it only led to the type of "exclamations" I mentioned earlier, where "exclamation" with its "ex-" clearly reveals an outward movement, rather than pointing to the interiority of the mind.

course fundamentally pre-modern, sense: (Imaginally) Substantiated. Ritual and imagination are modes of externality. We can say that imagining (hypostatizing, substantiating) is the already *inwardized* equivalent (almost "*theoretical*" equivalent) of ritual performance (acting out, deed), just as linguistically full-fledged words as "names" of things and events are the original "exclamations" interiorized into themselves.

The moment that mythology and the imagination come upon the scene and the soul as well as gods become substantiated as imaginable realities, is also the moment of the birth of the symbolic. Only now may ceremonies, ritual objects, and events take on a *symbolic* function. The symbolic depends on the simultaneity (or better identity) of mythological transcendence and world-immanent empirical presence.

Still later, with Aristotelian philosophy, the *psychê* or soul was, as it were, interiorized into *man*, into each *living* individual, as the organism's life principle. It still stayed logically negative, but was again wholly world-immanent. On the other hand, it has become a philosophical concept, that is to say, it can no longer be imagined, but needs to be thought, and, as far as its practice is concerned, it no longer requires ritual, but moral behavior.

In Christian metaphysics it stays located in each human individual, but since it is now the eternal part of man it has its true home in the beyond, in transcendence. Nevertheless it needs each person's taking care of his or her soul during their lifetime on this earth, and this care for the soul needs to be founded in true *faith*. As such, it is the first immediacy of "the inner", which still later, after the demise of metaphysics and religion, came home to itself in introspective psychology, whose form of practice is the ritual of psychotherapy.

The phases in the historical development of soul truths

Earlier I stressed that from the beginning, i.e., by nature, humans are "more than autochthonous animalia sprung from the earth, but as *twice-born* ones have *their roots* in the deity itself" (as Jung had put it, cf. *MDR* p. 333). What Jung expresses refers (in spirit, not in detail) to the same reality that "dawned" on prehistoric man in the experience of the human body's "growing cold" at death. In early man's first experience of "absolute negativity" hidden in the alarming sensation of ghostly coldness and in the first faint awareness of an indestructible supertemporal dimension, prehistoric man did not, as it of course appeared to *him*, learn something new about an objective dimension of the *natural world* out there, but he in truth, but completely unwittingly, discovered a knowledge about *himself*, about the inner logic of *his own* deepest essence. In the light that flared up for the East Africans in the moment in which the light comes, they no doubt greeted and worshiped, according to their own understanding, the emerging sun as god, but in truth, though completely unwittingly, they celebrated *their own* having by nature their true existence in the light of consciousness, their own being twice-born and, as twice-born, their own being in-themselves reflected and illumined. They revered their own potential of a suddenly rising awareness. What for them was a relation to something out there in the real world, was in truth their self-knowledge *avant la lettre* and their express affirmation of it.

There seems to be a paradox here, indeed a double paradox. Firstly, if, as I insisted, humans are *by nature* and thus a priori rooted in absolute negativity, why did this absolute negativity, a negativity that was after all a priori inherent in the essence of humanness, originally nevertheless need to be *discovered* at certain points in prehistoric times and at first appeared only in its first immediacy, in dim and rudimentary form? And secondly, when it was in fact discovered, why did it not right away appear as man's subjective self-knowledge, but instead as Other, as objective, cosmic realities out there (such as an afterlife, an underworldly soul, the ancestors, or a god)? Why did it remain completely unconscious to mythological man that mythology was the soul's self-explication, the self-representation of the logic of *his* innermost essence, in other words, that in mythology he was talking about himself, his own soul, and not about the cosmos? Why this *self*-explication *in the form of otherness*?

One would expect that what is already inherent in man as his true nature would be fully accessible and conscious to him in total clarity from the outset, *if* he is, as was claimed after all, twice-born and as such a priori in-himself reflected and illumined. But now we have to realize that this so obvious expectation does not really comprehend what "twice-born" implies and absolute negativity involves.

Man exists as internal duality, as reflectedness. Logically he is from the outset both autochthonous animal sprung from the earth AND spirit, *Geist*, absolute negativity. However, with his physical birth, man's double nature is itself immersed into and submerged in the realm of nature and temporality, and this has the result of a second doubleness, that of "implicit" versus "explicit". The latter two concepts seem to be a new pair of opposites, but in reality they are nothing else but the projection (in the sense of geometry) and transposition of the first-mentioned logical duality into the medium of extension and temporality. With his birth, only the animal-side of man becomes "explicit", empirically present in the world, a positive reality, whereas his true inner nature as *human* being, despite being already inherent in this "animal", is inherent in him only implicitly, *an sich*.

As such, by existing *as the duality of "implicit" and "explicit"*, man has to live *uroborically*. His twice-bornness means that he has to catch up with himself. He has to be the "tail-eater, which is said to beget, kill, and devour itself", which implies that he is not from the start in possession of the true essential nature that he *is* from the outset, but, on the contrary, has to *discover*, in the course of time, what he has logically already been rooted in all along. He has to *find out* what his true inner essence is. He has to gradually, in many small steps during a long course of human history, conquer for himself that still implicit *essential* reality that he is and has been from the outset. Soul needs to be *made*. From the point of view of psychology, this "making" of soul is the purpose and task of human existence, of human history.

His true essence (or particular aspects of it), which actually lies "behind" or hidden "inside" him, in empirical life comes to man from outside, from what he sees before him. From within some real natural event or phenomenon the "face" of his own inner essence suddenly seems to gaze at him and deeply impresses him. In this way the "psyche" appeared to prehistoric man in the coldness of the corpse, the quality "god" or "Zeus" struck man from within the flash of lightning. Such events evoked a first dawning awareness of his nature,[9] however, as we have seen, an awareness still completely immersed in and identical with objective events out there and therefore one that has still the fundamental form of *otherness* (and not that of self-knowledge), such as the form of separately existing gods, demons, and spirits in nature, or in the form of the dead souls or ancestors in the underworld.

This dawning awareness needs to be strengthened and given a certain permanence by being explicitly treasured, worshiped, and celebrated through

---

9 In German we say still today things like this: "*An dem und dem Beispiel (oder Erlebnis) ist mir die Idee des Tragischen aufgegangen*" (Through such and such an example [or in such and such an experience] the real understanding of what "tragic" means suddenly dawned on me). Particular events or experiences may have a *maieutic* function.

regular cultic practice over a long time. In this practice, too, the so-called dawning awareness was not yet "inside" people, not a mental content or idea or a conscious awareness in people's subjective minds. Rather, the soul truth was decidedly objective, completely immersed in the symbol-laden utensils used in the cultic practice and in the actual deed, the ritual acting out. It is just as Jung said: "I am inclined to think that things were generally done first and that only a long time afterwards somebody asked a question about them, and then eventually discovered why they were done. . . . Faust aptly says: 'Im Anfang war die Tat' (in the beginning was the deed)" (*CW* 18 § 540 and 553).[10]

But then, after a long time, what is still out there, enclosed and dormant in the ritual acts, needs slowly to come home to man so that he can acquire a first clear concept and conscious subjective awareness of it and, in a further step, at long last recognize *his own* innermost nature (or particular aspects of it) in what used to appear to him as "others", as the underworldly soul, as otherworldly divine beings, as a religious or metaphysical beyond, etc. All this means that these soul truths become inwardized into himself.[11] And finally, by fully inwardizing and integrating them into consciousness, by making them truly his own, this acquired understanding becomes *explicit* and *objective*: An integral part of his real existence in empirical life, his simple unreflected mode of being-in-the-world. In other words, it becomes released from his subjective conscious control and sinks into his real *mode of being* or the *objective constitution* of consciousness, so that it is independent of *his* subjective conscious awareness, his reflection and decision, and so

10 Of course, if my hypothesis is correct that the first dawning awareness erupted, in the experiencing people, into *exclamations* of what later became *words*, we might in some way have to go back precisely to that saying that Faust, in order to prioritize the deed, rejected, i.e., to the dictum "In the beginning was the word".

11 In the quote just cited, for Jung the development goes from performed deed (a deed performed without conscious understanding of what it means) to asking questions *about* it and *explaining* it. I think that is a psychologically wrong sequence. The truly psychological development is from externally performed act to interiorization into the mind. Rational questions about it and its purpose or justification ("Why?") and explanations are a sign that the respective soul truth has become obsolete and that such a consciousness has simply fallen out of this soul truth so that it is now in the mode of external reflection and thus outside the sphere of the soul's life. The real soul move is—in Freudian terms, but not in Freud's sense—from "*Agieren*" to "*Erinnern*": from acting out to inwardizing.

that it simply *rules*: Unquestionably, quasi automatically.[12] When this new status is reached the respective soul truth has become what we are used to call "second nature" (although in this case it is actually his first nature). At this point one can say that the *making* of soul has attained its completion.

What I outlined is not, the way I represented it, one single linear process in the history of the soul, but happens repeatedly on many different levels of development as well as in different areas, each relating to different aspects of the essential nature of humanness. And it is a process both in the history of man ("man" in the psychological sense of *purusha*, *anthropos*, homo maximus) and—in abbreviated form—in the history of an individual life.

But there is a further step. What has been fully integrated into the objective logical form of consciousness slowly spills over into external reality; it becomes "reified", "materialized": Objectively represented. In this sense Jung already expressed the view "that every spiritual truth gradually turns into something material, becoming an object or tool in the hand of man" (*CW* 13 § 302, transl. modif.). When this happens, the old truth has become stale and matter of course, to the extent that it loses its character of self-knowledge, indeed its connection with self, with the human subject, and thus its being of soul-significance. It emigrates from the living self and disappears instead into the status of *positive fact* and into *externality*. A particular project of the history of the soul has then exhausted itself, come to an end. When this has happened, the time is ripe for something totally new to start, for a new chapter in the book of the soul's logical life.

The modern reductive explanation of the origin of the idea of an afterlife of the soul

When in modernity modern man hears that the experience of the coldness of death and the negation of life is the dawning consciousness of man's inner spiritual (*geistige*) essence that lasts beyond his death, he is perhaps inclined to resort to the explanation that this amounts to a case of a denial of the irrevocable nature of death and a compensatory wish fulfillment. The unbearable experience of death, so the idea may go, leads to the counter-factual, superstitious consoling *invention* in the mind of an invisible essence that continues after life and is supertemporal.

---

12 Similarly to how in us prejudices function.

But this explanation is fallacious. The experience of death is by no means in itself unbearable. For, the necessity of dying is inherent in life itself. It is not anything alien happening to it from outside as a nasty fate. Death is life's very own determination. We have to see this very clearly: It is the very nature of the life of living creatures from within itself to be heading for its end. For millions of years all kinds of forms of life have had to go through the experience of death, without finding it unbearable, unnatural, or outrageous.

It is precisely the other way around. Modern man can only experience literal death as on principle unbearable because what in prehistoric times had been no more than the very first immediacy of the timeless and super-natural nature of humanness has in modernity become so completely interi-orized and integrated into the very form of consciousness and man himself has become so secure in this superior stance that he has lost his immediate contact with the natural physical side of his existence, his being at one with it. Man having in his *objective* (not private, personal) self-definition become identical with what we call "the ego", the natural bodily process of life with all its vicissitudes (above all life's irrevocable transience) is no longer self-evidently and intimately his very own, but on account of his sta-tus as atemporal ego appears to him as something alien, an external mishap. Death is no longer *felt* as his innate necessity. It is felt as something wrong, something that should decidedly *not* be. Instead of a "Sickness *unto* Death" death *as* the very sickness. And this is why modern man can emotionally experience death and man's mortality in general as a narcissistic blow to his ego and as unbearable imposition.

The theory that the prehistoric emergence of the idea of the under-worldly soul was a defense against a narcissistic wound that the experi-ence of death dealt man and his flight into a counterfactual fiction amounts therefore to a retrojection of the modern situation into ancient times. The idea of the ever-lasting essence of man and, as a consequence, of an after-life, rather than being a defensive reaction to death, on the contrary origi-nated as human nature's first attempt at a self-expression and actualization of the inner nature of man or the *existing concept* that he is, of the fact that humans are "more than autochthonous animalia sprung from the earth, but as *twice-born* ones have *their roots* in the deity itself". It is the inner truth of humanness that this humanness is from the outset negated and reversed, in-itself-reflected, and thus in itself different, opened up: "Cleared", illumined (*gelichtet*). It is man's *nature* to always already be distanced from *nature*.

Man is, as it were, "extra-terrestrial", or, more correctly: As twice-born a *terrestrial* extra-terrestrial: Conscious.

Consciousness is extra-terrestriality. Logically, man looks, *within him-self*, so to speak from a kind of outer-space position upon the world and upon himself. This is why he does not simply "experience" and "live" his life, live it out like the higher animals, but has inevitably a *relation to* what happens, as well as to himself. He is the animal that has *logos*. He *knows* about himself. He can only know about himself because he *is* not simply what he is, but looks at himself from outside of himself. Everything he experiences therefore comes to him as already *viewed in some way*, wrapped in an inter-pretation, opinion or theory. This is why Jung said: "All that I experience is psychic. . . . We are in truth so wrapped about by psychic images that we cannot penetrate at all to the essence of things external to ourselves. Every-thing we can possibly know consists of psychic stuff" (*CW* 8 § 680, transl. modif.). Or: ". . . as though there were anything that is *not* psychic. . . . The presence of objects is entirely dependent on our powers of representation, and 'representation' is a psychic act. . . . Nobody seems to have noticed that without a reflecting psyche the world might as well not exist . . ." (*Letters 2*, p. 487, to Tanner, 12 Feb 1959).

With the ideas of an afterlife, the underworld, or the Christian heaven, this fundamental internal (logical) extra-terrestriality that is the human dis-tinction over against the animals was in no way in conflict with the mortal nature of man, but on the contrary confirmed and affirmed death as the necessary gateway to an otherworldly life. Rather than having lost inti-mate contact with the natural physical side of his existence, early man *gave expression* to its inner truth, the truth that man's real nature is that of an animal that has intrinsically been twice-born.

This changed explicitly with modern man, with the moment that he became logically constituted as "the ego".[13] With this status man had indeed become alienated from his natural side, and the extra-terrestriality had,

---

13 It is important to keep in mind that "the ego" in this paper and in many of my writings does not mean the "ego-complex" as the center of *a person's* field of consciousness (Jung) or as the one pole of Erich Neumann's ego-self axis. Rather, following the spirit of other statements of Jung's ("the ego—that is, the empirical man—", *MDR* p. 346; cf. "man—that is, his ego" *MDR* p. 337; "the ego, i.e., the empirical, ordinary man as he has been up to now" *CW* 11 § 233, transl. modif.), this term means here the logical constitu-tion of modern man as such.

as it were, been duplicated: Become not only positivized and literal, but also absolutized and appropriated by the *empirical* human being (as the status of each individual) in contrast to man as such. As "the ego", man had—*logically, psychologically* (of course not totally in empirical-practical regards)—become immured in utter abstractness.

The origin of the modern definition of man as "the ego"

One question is how the new psychological status of man as "the ego" is to be understood and how this revolutionary change came about, what made it possible in the first place. A second question is what this new situation entails. I will first turn to the question of the derivation of the status of modern abstractness.

In the section above about the phases in the historical development of soul truths, we saw that the psychological historical development had a clear direction. What originally had first appeared as the flaring-up of a soul truth became an object of cultic practice lasting for ages. Both the truth of the primordial flaring-up and the later object had the form of otherness, and the worshiped objects (the souls of the dead, the gods and spirits) were located in some kind of beyond (afterlife, underworld, heaven). At a still later stage, this soul truth was gradually inwardized into people. In a further stage, the former "other" became interiorized and integrated into the very form of consciousness to such an extent that it became "matter of fact" and consciousness's "second nature"; consciousness had become objectively permeated and satiated by whatever the respective soul truth had been so that it was the resulting and now simply prevailing logic of man's being-in-the-world.

With this result, a reverse movement set in: This now prevailing logic "seeped out", as it were, from the interiority of the constitution of the subjective mind and objectified itself again—namely, in everything that was produced by man at this particular level of consciousness and cultural development. In all the products produced, in the way man shaped his life, his surroundings, and his society according to the new standards, *this logic* slowly gave itself an independent material existence as an external reality with its own inherent dynamic, a reality in which man lived and to which he was *exposed*.

My description so far gives the impression that this process of history was one *linear* development. But in reality it is more complicated. The alchemists used a particular vessel called a "pelican" that had the function of feeding the result of a distilling operation back to the body of the vessel, there to be subjected to the same operation all over again. In a similar way the overall historical process took place as a sequence of numerous larger or smaller processes in which each time the result of the previous process was the starting point of the next higher-level process, whereby each process followed the described pattern of development. Each time a new "chapter" in the book of the soul's life began.

But when "new chapter" is applied to what began with modernity, the expression all of a sudden has a fundamentally more radical sense. Inasmuch as, according to my thesis, the one ages-overarching process which began with the discovery of the "psychê" seems to have been concluded, all the earlier individual processes and levels of this development ("chapters") appear from this perspective as chapters of one single "volume". What thereafter, with modernity, follows is, however, the beginning of an entirely new and different "volume" of the book of the soul's life with its own chapters. The radicalness of the difference lies in the fact that the objectification or materialization of the logic of consciousness reached through the final interiorization that preceded the modern situation was a translation of this inner logic into *technical reality* (or into the reality of *modern technological civilization*). The inner logical constitution of consciousness exists now out there in an independent physical form, in the form of *positivity*, hard facts.

It is necessary to add another step to the previously given sequence of: 1) initial flaring-up of a truth; 2) prolonged cultic practice; 3) interiorization and integration into the form of consciousness; and 4) objective representation. What has spilled over from the inner constitution of consciousness into external reality and has thus taken on the form of objective material existence does not have the status of a dead object, let alone a waste product, that could psychologically be ignored or rejected. I already mentioned that man is *exposed* to the external reality he himself produced, or better: *Exposed* to the objective logic invested and materialized in this created reality. This reality, even if it has the nature of hard facts, is not dead, but it has effects. From within it, the logic congealed and manifested in it not only stares man in the face, but it also imperceptibly rubs off on him; it becomes reflected in and determines the subject.

Man always defines himself, or rather *finds* himself objectively *defined*, in the image and likeness of the objective reality he created. And this definition is one in depth and truth, not merely "definition" as his (as people's) subjective intellectual opinion about himself (or maybe the term opinion is inappropriate from the outset, since this "definition" is something completely unwitting). Man is not the master over, but the recipient of, the definition of his nature. He receives it from his own products, from their logical constitution. There is no choice in the matter.

At this point one could of course think that since the logic invested in the produced *objective reality* is nothing else but consciousness's own inner logic anyway, man's exposure to his self-produced external reality cannot make much of a difference to consciousness. Same meets same. But this is not so. Leaving aside the fact that there is an enormous difference between subjectively knowing a certain truth about oneself, on the one hand, and being confronted with the same truth from outside, objectively, on the other hand,[14] the logic inherent in the objective representations is not really the *same* anymore that it was when it was the objective form of consciousness, especially in the case of modern technological civilization. In technological civilization, the logic is immersed in the rigid, positivistic form of positivity. And it is precisely this positivity that imparts itself to the subject.

(In addition, there is the other aspect of the succession of *generations*, which is essential for the development of cultural history. For the generation that produced its share of the new objective reality on the basis of the logical form of consciousness resulting from an inwardization process, this logical form had become "second nature", as I said. But for the new generation that is exposed to this objective reality, the latter is not at all "new", because its members have been born into it; they never experienced anything else, any "prior" situation. The logic invested in the new reality is for them matter-of-course; it is precisely "first nature", so to speak, and thus it is for this new generation the *starting point* to push off from to its own further processes).

The decisive quality of the logic of modern technological civilization that imparts itself to the definition of modern man is its positivity. Now it is of course clear that at all times in past history all the products in which the particular status of the soul's logical life had become *materialized* or

14 One may think here of the psychology of subjectively *known* guilt or shadow aspects and the common fear that they might escape from this safe privacy of one's knowing into other people's knowing, which would entail one's having to *face* them as facts and thereby having to release them from the safety of one's inner into the uncontrollable *fierceness of their truth.*

otherwise objectified had been logically positive. All the symbolic expressions, the performances of cultic rituals and the sacred objects used in them, the masks, the statues of gods or demons, the religious paintings, but also the non-religious artifacts used in daily life, etc. were as a matter of course positivities. However, theirs was an innocent positivity: Because it was in itself soulful, it "spoke" to man, came in the last analysis imbued with a mythological meaning. This is so because, as we said, the twice-bornness of man informed also his seeing and ipso facto that which is seen. The latter was in-itself-reflected, illumined. Man saw himself, his own innermost truth, reflected in his own products. There was an intimate unity between man and them.

When we come to the term positivity in the context of modern technological civilization, positivity takes on a fundamentally different, much more radical meaning. Machines and apparatuses, but also the commodities mass-produced by means of them are experienced as definitely alien (despite their ultimately human origin). In the case of the modern technical world produced by modern man himself, the objective representation of the logical form of consciousness is inevitably characterized by the condition of alienation, as above all Karl Marx has demonstrated.

This shows that in modernity "positivity" has come home to itself. It is positivity to the power of two. By having been applied to itself, it has become explicit positivity, literalized, absolute: Positivistic. It is now *only* positive-factual. It appears to be stripped of all negativity. Of course, soul has been invested in all the items belonging to modern technological civilization, too. But this soul is swallowed by them and has vanished in them as if in a black hole, so that it no longer shines forth, thus no longer allowing man to recognize, enjoy, and celebrate immediately his own innermost truth in them and to feel truly at home with them.

I stated that the logic that had become objectified or materialized in modern technological civilization was not the same as the one that it had been in the objective constitution of consciousness. But why not? Why is what was "sent" not identical with what "arrived"? Why did the result of the process of inwardization into consciousness (the self-definition of man as subjectivity, Self, and self-consciousness, which was by no means rigid and positivistic) nevertheless lead to positivistic positivity when it became objectively represented?

The answer seems to me to lie in the fact that subjectivity means absolute inwardization of man's nature as in-itself-reflectedness, so that it no longer needs, but also can no longer have, *objects* for any upward looking, *epiphanies* of gods, or a God, something sacred, or "the Absolute" to *believe* in. It has the form of internal duality (Jung's "twice-bornness") completely within itself and therefore exists as absolute self-relation, which also means enclosedness within itself. The time when the in-itself-reflectedness could be lived as a relation *between* subject *and* the world or cosmos, i.e., the time when truth had the form of substance and *not* of subject, is over.[15]

The moment that it is the logic of *this* self-enclosed subjectivity that becomes objectively represented in materialized form, the self-enclosedness and self-nature become also the very character of the things produced in the process of this representation. The things become themselves self-enclosed selves, and this is why the paradigmatic "things" are now *auto*mats, apparatuses: *Producing* machines (and today even more than that: So-called "*intelligent*" machines). What they produce becomes self-enclosed, too: Mute—abstract positivities. They no longer speak to man, no longer reflect back to man his objective soul invested in them (Marx)—and this naturally so, for how could they when they have not been directly produced by humans in the first place, but technically by automatic machines?

"The ego": Man as (positivistic) positivity

Now it is precisely and only this positivity that at a deep level stares man in the face, rubs off on him and imperceptibly determines the definition of his innermost nature. The positivity existing "out there" in technical reality, in his own products, is reflected in how he is now logically constituted. The question arises as to what precisely his having become permeated and defined by this positivity means for man and how it in fact shows in how man is today objectively defined.

Having himself become defined as a positivity means the end of the twice-bornness that had been discovered in and through man's first awareness of the body's "becoming cold" at death. His internal duality, the doubleness of "autochthonous animal sprung from the earth" and of decidedly being "more than that", "having his roots in the deity itself", to use Jung's

---

15 This is the reason for the diagnosis that "God is dead" and for the erosion of religion in general in modernity. Religion has become impossible (except as a private world view, personal feeling, or as a public simulation, all of which do not deserve the name of religion proper on account of their truthlessness).

phrases, has collapsed. Not only the frontier is closed (Frederick Jackson Turner), but so is also the very inner "clearance" or duality that used to be the special distinction of humanness.

The collapse of the two poles of his nature and inner definition into one means something else than merely having become deprived of the one pole, having lost the "more than that", his rootedness "in the deity" itself, and ipso facto having become reduced to nothing but the "animal sprung from the earth". Of course, Darwin discovered man's descent from the animal kingdom, which according to Freud is one of the three severe blows to human self-love, in other words, something that at long last brought narcissistically inflated man down to earth. Nietzsche also said in a like spirit: "We have unlearned something. We have become more modest in every way. We no longer derive man from the 'spirit,' from the 'godhead'; we have dropped him back among the beasts".[16] The Nietzsche quote very nicely contrasts with Jung's dictum and is clear evidence for the one half of Jung's (of course historically later) definition of man being excised so that only the other, first half is left. For Nietzsche, "spirit" and "godhead" have become a kind of superstition of bygone times, just as for Marx they have become what he called the "superstructure". With this superstition or superstructure eliminated, the animal remains as the real truth and basic reality.

But the impression of a simple removal of one half of the two-poles definition and its reduction exclusively to its other half is misleading. We have to realize that both sides of the fuller definition have disappeared and nothing of it remains, *neither* the rootedness in the godhead *nor* the "autochthonous animal sprung from the earth". Instead, the modern positivization of the concept of man amounts to the simultaneous abolition of both sides. The more the one side is abolished, the more also disappears the other side, and what "is left" is by no means the remainder, but instead a totally new substitute: *Positivized man,* into whom both sides have *collapsed* to become one. In other words, the "beasts" (*Tiere,* animals) among which man has allegedly been "dropped *back*" as well as the animal kingdom from which he derived, on the one hand, and the "autochthonous animalia sprung from the earth", on the other hand, are equivocations, the same *word* being used for totally different concepts or realities. In another context Nietzsche

---

16 Friedrich Nietzsche, *The Antichrist,* transl. by H.L. Mencken (New York: Alfred A. Knopf, 1918), p. 58.

himself saw the inevitability of the loss of both poles the moment one of the two has been excised. Thus he said: "The true world – we have abolished. What world has remained? The apparent one perhaps? But no! With the true world we have also abolished the apparent one".[17] By the same token we have to say: "Spirit" and "godhead" – we have abolished. What has remained? The beast perhaps? But no! Along with "spirit" and "godhead" we have also abolished the animal-side of the definition of man.

Positivized man is dissociated at one and the same time from both nature and deity, from both "earth" and "spirit". But since he is the result of the collapse of both poles which have become fused or amalgamated in the positive fact that he now is, they are both still in him, of course in altered form, namely each as the reversal into its opposite. The nature side has become in itself intellectualized (this is the effect of the inherited formerly divine, but now positivized "spirit"), and the spirit (*Geist*) side has taken on the status of something "natural", purely biological; it has become *functionalized* as a technical "brain function", the intellect. Each side redefines the other, and in their fusion into one both elements have exchanged their natures and become indistinguishable and distanceless. The former tension of opposites is gone; man's internal "being opened up" is closed, his illuminedness extinguished. His former logical distendedness from earth to heaven and to the underworld, from animal, nature, and matter to logos, spirit, and deity, from the transience of life to the supertemporal (to "man's inner spiritual essence that lasts beyond his death"), and along with it man's fundamental upward looking have vanished in the *black hole* of his positivity, the point-like extensionlessness and blindness of "fact". It goes without saying that his new literalized *positivity* is tantamount to the irrevocable loss of the internal *absolute negativity* of human nature as such. And this in turn means the loss of man's humanity. In his essence he has become a *functionary*.[18] *L'homme machine*.

The fusion of the two poles and their mutual redefinition in terms of the respective other leads to a double paradox. Yes, indeed, man is now exclusively derived from, and fully integrated into, the animal kingdom. But "animal" no longer *means* "autochthonous" and "sprung from the earth".

---

17 Friedrich Nietzsche, section *"Wie die 'wahre Welt' endlich zur Fabel wurde"* in: *Götzendämmerung* (Leipzig: C.G. Naumann, 1888), my translation.
18 Functionary: neither animal nor spirit. Something artificial, technical, in between.

It no longer has a personality, a face, an imaginal quality. It is not sheer vitality and wildness anymore. Instead, it has, on the level of its concept, become thoroughly intellectualized. It is an "organism", that is to say, a "self-regulating *system*", which in turn is at bottom steered by the "information" or "program" stored in its genes. As such it is in the last analysis something strictly logical. Also, it does not have a fixed inherent identity anymore (the Biblical each "after their kind"), for animals are now being genetically redesigned at will, for practical human purposes (e.g., pigs with a couple more ribs). The enormous development of reproductive medicine techniques like in vitro fertilization, and the talk of "designer babies" shows that this applies at least *logically* to the human animal, too. Dying persons become spare-parts sources for all kinds of organ transplantations, which nicely confirms once more the present-day logic of man as *l'homme machine*. We are witnessing the translation of what used to be nature into technology based on highly sophisticated science.

The logical obsolescence of "animal" shows, for example, in two opposite ways. On the one hand, on the practical side, certain domestic animals like chickens and cows have been reduced to objects, mere things or machines, in huge industrialized milk, eggs, and meat production factories. On the other hand, on the emotional nostalgic side, we need such organizations as the World Wildlife Fund or zoos and game reserves to artificially protect and conserve wild animals, more and more of which have become endangered species. What an oxymoron: Protected wildlife! To the emotional side belongs also the phenomenon of radical sentimentalism concerning animals, of *sentimental* ideologies that motivate numerous extremist animal protection activists and vegetarians or vegans.

Conversely, the second paradox shows itself very nicely in the modernistic reductive explanation, discussed above, of the origin of the idea of afterlife. It takes recourse to the allegedly "natural", instinctively felt absolute unbearableness of having to die (or of experiencing the death of one's beloved) and to wish fulfillment as a likewise natural reaction. On the one hand, the idea of death as something unbearable, which serves as explanation of the motivation for wish fulfillment, is itself precisely a modern fiction, a decidedly *abstract, rationalistic* idea. We have seen that it is by no means nature-based. (Only this type of explanation can rightly be called "naturalistic".) And "wish fulfillment" is not a kind of instinctive reaction to misery, but a technique that can only emerge once the soul, at a late stage of its development, has reached the highly *intellectual* level of the cunning modern ego, an ego that likes to cheat itself by resorting to all kinds of defense mechanisms. What the defense is directed against is nothing else but truth. On the other hand, the position of fundamental *superiority* from which the modern intellect looks down upon such archaic ideas as "psychê" and afterlife, calling them superstitions, and upon those psychic maneuvers that allegedly gave rise to them is not at all the height of spirit (*Geist*), i.e., the finite form of the infinite divine intellect, but itself the position of a human, all-too-human abstract intellectualism.

Mind, consciousness, spirit, intellect are no longer super-natural dimensions in their own right, but merely *psychic* faculties of the human organism, i.e., the human animal. Their modern truth is that they are today viewed as purely technical functions of the brain, hormones, etc., and thus as nothing but epiphenomena of biology or physiology, in other words, precisely as *not* anymore rooted in "the deity" or some supernatural sphere. Even if numerous philosophers and philosophical-minded people *subjectively* reject that clearly reductive view on the basis of absolutely convincing arguments, and even if the neuro-sciences may never be able to really make this reduction of mind to brain and to the latter's chemical processes stick, such philosophical counter-arguments are *psychologically* nevertheless idle talk (as interesting and intelligent as they may be in their own right), or at least nothing that could invalidate the psychological actual *reality* of this reductive view as the present-day objectively prevailing, *existing* truth.

The same applies to present-day religious beliefs and feelings. They are idle, mere (so-called) "spiritual" entertainments of the modern ego, or forms of consolation or comforting ideologies for it, but not prevailing objective truths. Marx spoke rightly of religion in modernity as "the opium of the people". As a private opinion of individual people there may still be an idea of an afterlife, of heaven and eternal bliss, of a supreme being as creator and wise ruler of the world, and it may of course well be that *subjectively* certain individuals may derive consolation from such opinions, just as others seem nowadays to seek their consolation in completely other ways, for example as utopian rescue-the-world activists and humanitarian do-gooders or in alcohol or drugs, in overeating or as workaholics, etc. But *objectively* the truth of these religious ideas has disappeared. "Spirituality" is just the *feeling* of abstraction, abstraction from any semantic content, and as such an *abstract* feeling. Even the great Churches today are really hard put when it comes to the topics of resurrection, everlasting life, the beyond, and Heavenly Jerusalem, and can no longer be honestly serious about them. Such topics are skillfully avoided. The irretrievable loss of the whole dimension of the supernatural and timeless is also reflected in modern cosmology, concerning which Jung as early as eighty years ago said: "We are absolutely convinced that even with the aid of the latest and largest reflecting telescope . . . men will discover behind the farthest nebulae no fiery empyrean; and we know that our eyes will wander despairingly through the dead emptiness of interstellar space" (*CW* 9i § 31). "Heaven has become for us the cosmic space of the physicists . . ." (§ 5), i.e., a positivity through and through. The truth of modernity about the cosmos is that there is no point anywhere in the universe that is not subject to the same ("technical") laws of physics.

The fact that man has in his essence become a functionary means that he is uprooted and up in the air. He has lost the "grounding ground" (Heidegger). His "spiritual house has fallen into disrepair" (Jung, *CW* 9i § 31), or rather: It has completely disappeared, and he thus has nothing to stand on, nothing that in truth expresses and *objectively* holds, backs up, his humanness. Small wonder that we witness today an increase of untamed fury and violence (Islamic terrorism which becomes attractive to some even in Western countries, numerous other forms of terrorism, unbridled extremist political movements, private persons going ballistic and out of some frustration shooting and killing numerous others at random, etc.), the loss of the last remaining inhibitions (e.g., no respect anymore by combatants for hospitals, Red Cross and other humanitarian helpers in war areas, deliberate destruction of cultural monuments) and, on the other (upper) side of society, excesses of recklessness on a large scale by high finance and industrial companies. Anything goes.

Jung's hope had of course been that modern man could find a real foundation within *himself*. According to him it is "the highest and most decisive experience of all" for a person "to be alone with his own self. . . . The patient must be alone if he is to find out what it is that supports him when he can no longer support himself. Only this can give him an indestructible foundation" (*CW* 12 § 32). The solution offered is a typically modernistic *individualistic* one, but it is illusionary. It relies on the private, atomic (and as such precisely uprooted) individual[19] and thus operates without the notion of truth.

---

19 The atomic empirical individual (as ego-personality) must be distinguished from the "atomic subjectivity" that was the latest *metaphysical* constitution of man prior to

Truth is indispensably *communal*. Without objective truth, the idea of such an indestructible foundation is just a nice nostalgic dream. Once truth, *communal* truth, as the very foundation of an indestructible foundation has been *objectively* lost, there can at best only be surrogates for it. To be alone with one's own self may, no doubt, subjectively be a most valuable experience. But it cannot restore the "spiritual house", the lost truly binding order of the world,[20] the *soul* foundation on which the humanity of man depends.

James Hillman offered another solution. He tried to restore the internal clearance or duality of phenomena by demanding that we "see through" the literal aspect of phenomena, that is, "see through to the Gods" (or to "the metaphorical" or "the imaginal") in them. Undoubtedly, with the difference between the literal and the imaginal an internal difference is opened up within the phenomena. The problem with this solution is, however, that, as the name "seeing through" suggests, it is neither a real, direct *seeing* of the God *in* the respective phenomenon (as the flaring-up of a divine light from within it), but a going beyond ("through") it, nor is it a sublated seeing, a seeing *mediated* by a (religious or metaphysical) *knowledge* of and *faith* in God as the ground of phenomenal reality. Instead, "seeing through" is, rather than a seeing, an *imagining*: The evocation of an image solely in the subjective mind of the archetypal psychologist and, furthermore, the evocation of an image that has its origin in the psychologist's acquired learning, his *purely academic* knowledge of the mythologies (the gods) of past ages. What is supposed to be an internal clearance in the phenomenon in question is therefore in reality a psychological technique ("psychologizing or seeing through") on the part of the psychologist of artificially glueing two separate things together, a given phenomenon (dream motif, behavior, or event in social reality, etc.) and the "imaginal" image *abstracted* from ancient myths, all this while nevertheless claiming internal unity or even an underlying identity for this juxtaposition, namely the *present reality* of the God *in* the given phenomenon. Clearly a reaction-formation against (and as such precisely an unwitting confirmation of) the positivity prevailing today, which is obviously experienced as unacceptable.

---

modernity and was characterized by the fact that it did not have to find a foundation, but had itself to *be, exist as*, this foundation, because with it the inwardization process had been completed.

20 "World" not in a global sense, but the spiritual cosmos of each specific community, nation, or culture.

Thinking back to our insight that in early times man's seeing was in-itself-illumined seeing, we might perhaps think that Buddhist thinking with its aim of "illumination" might offer a way out of the modern situation. But again, upon closer look it does not really resolve the problem. "Illumination" is here something to be striven for, a goal that is hard to achieve and generally requires a long practice of meditation. This makes it also the product of (pre-modern) "technical" endeavors, and in this sense something "artificial". Secondly, it happens only in the individual mind. It cannot become a shared, communal truth. And thirdly, "illumination" has in Buddhism become *abstracted* from real experience, real seeing. "Abstracted" in two ways: a) It has made itself independent of phenomena and become autonomous, *illumination per se*, an end in itself, and b) it has withdrawn into the human person, as a person's longed-for particular subjective experience or state of mind, rather than being the simple *objective* in-itself-reflectedness or clearance (internal luminosity) of the *phenomena* of the world (or their experienced inner truth). The Buddhist goal of this purified, absolutized, and self-serving illumination is probably also a reaction, of course a reaction to a historically much earlier rupture in cultural development, namely the one caused by the end of ancient *ritualistic* Vedic culture.

The "new chapter in the book of life"

With modernity the one ages-overarching process of the self-explication and slow further self-unfolding of the primordial sense of man's innermost nature as absolute negativity (which in the case of the prehistoric Greeks began with the discovery, for example, of the "psychê") seems to have come to a close. The first chapter in the book of the soul's logical life is finished. However, I already indicated that it would be better to speak of a first whole *volume* of this book than merely of the first chapter, a volume which itself consisted of many chapters. What I reported about the diverse aspects of modernity described earlier (the extra-terrestriality having become positivized and absolutized; the utter abstractness in which man, in the depth, has been immured; man's divorce from his former intimate oneness with his natural bodily process of life; the inescapable closedness of the universe at large in modernity discussed in the last section) clearly shows that the "volume" in the book of the soul's life that dealt with man's twice-bornness and the dimension of absolute negativity is definitively closed. Everything that began, for example in prehistoric Greece, with the flaring-up of the first intuition of *psychê* and unfolded itself over millennia has now—as hard as it is to admit—become undone.

For modern man living in brightly lit cities and thanks to electricity having assured access to total light around the clock[21] indoors and outdoors, the "moment in which light comes" at sunrise could not possibly open up an additional *divine* light *within* the literal light. This was possible only for archaic and for primitive man, who was still firmly contained in nature and precisely for that reason greeted the rising sun to express his reverent upward looking to the *logos* nature of humanness, the actual *realization* of which was for him still lying in distant future. By the same token, it is impossible that from the moment when a previously warm human body "becomes cold", in other words, from the *intra-natural negation* of life, a light could flare up for modern man in which he would acquire for himself the awareness of "man's inner spiritual essence that lasts beyond his death" and of *the absolute negativity of human nature* as such. Having fully integrated this awareness into his stance and, de facto, namely in his unreflected mode of being-in-the-world, existing as such, man does not have to, and cannot possibly, substantiate any longer the notion of man's inner spiritual essence as "the soul in afterlife". The time of soul is over. The ideas of soul and afterlife have become obsolete and useless.[22] Positivity rules, positivity in its radicalized sense.

But this is only the end of the first "volume" of the book of the soul's logical life. This implies that the time of soul is not really over. What is over is only the type of "soul" (and its story) that figured in the "first volume". "New *volume*" means: The soul is still alive and active. But it also means: It is a fundamentally new and different sense of soul. An utterly new story has begun. From now on another project or task seems to be set for history. We are already in the second volume, even if only on its very first pages.

A new volume of the book of the soul's life with a fundamentally altered notion of soul requires from us a new openness, a readiness to unlearn, to

---

21 "Around the clock": Note the technical metaphor. I could have said "day and night" instead, but the point is precisely that Night, once upon a time the mother of the gods, has in modernity been excised from the two-pole pair "day and night", which, as we already know, kills both poles at once.

22 "This," as Jung said, "is why we have a psychology today" (*CW* 9i § 32), however a psychology not, as Jung thought, based on "the unconscious" (*ibid.*), but a psychology based on the concept of soul merely as a strictly *methodological* principle.

give up cherished associations and expectations connected with "soul" and to learn about "soul" afresh solely *from* what is happening in this volume. It requires that we no longer look, as we have so far done, from the standpoint of the first volume when trying to make sense of our present situation and its possible future development. A rethinking, a real shift of our standpoint, has to take place, and this means *our* being translocated. As always in the sphere of the soul, such a translocation is not our, the ego's, doing (nor its duty). It is the soul itself that will have to bring it about. As always, *it* will teach us *the hard way*,[23] and only step by step, by exposing us to its self-unfolding and self-production. And only such a learning is *real* learning.

If, as I said, we are only on the first pages of this volume, not much can be said about its content as yet, and what can be said will be no more than tentative remarks. Only when the new volume has been finished in turn, only in retrospect, can it become possible to try to give adequate descriptions and interpretations.

In the following I will briefly list a number of facets that can already be seen.

1. What is absolutely special about the new technical reality (not only classical industry, but especially also computer, internet, telecommunication, medical technology, genetic engineering, nano technology, artificial intelligence, etc.) is that it has a life of its own. With an enormous momentum and constantly accelerating dynamics, it propels itself forward and insists on its further development to ever new, more complex levels and more radical forms of realization. There is an autonomous movement in it that seems to continuously demand the systematic overcoming each time of the latest stage reached. There seems to be a *will* inherent in technology, a will to head for its end. And this will and the ensuing further development are not completely irrational and haphazard. Rather, the development follows a certain internal logic. It is the unfolding of the logic inherent in technology.

There is a popular phrase, "the ghost in the machine", which was first coined by Gilbert Ryle and used to denounce the classical philosophy of mind with its fundamental distinction between mind and matter or mind and body. Arthur Koestler took up this phrase in the title of one of his books, but used

---

23 "*Páthei máthos*" (learning through suffering): Aeschylus, Agamemnon 175–178, cf. Herodotus 1.207.

it for completely different critical purposes. I leave completely aside what these authors had in mind with the *metaphor*, "the ghost in the machine", and apply this expression in its more *literal* sense to technology. The logic, will, dynamics, inherent, as we have seen, in technology can be interpreted as the presence and active force of a "ghost in the machine", as it were, and this "ghost" can be identified with what the alchemists called the spirit Mercurius. For us, what drives technological development forward at such an uncanny speed from within technology itself is the soul's logical life.

The terms "technological reality" and "machine" must not be restricted to their literal meaning. It is not just a question of actual machines or apparatuses and their breathtaking further development. Rather, the dynamic we have been speaking about has also the goal of the transformation of as many aspects of life as possible into mechanical processes, the translation of everything, if I may give this phrase a new meaning, into "machine language". Expressed the other way around, it is the powerful *program*[24] to systematically, step by step, strip all worth and feeling, all subjective, emotional qualities, all human values and the embeddedness in personal relations that have grown over time (such as feelings of loyalty) off social processes and eliminate human judgment and personal decision from them, in order to *reduce* them to absolutely meaningless countables and computables: Abstract numbers, amounts of money, bits and bytes.[25] We call this unstoppable dynamic "rationalization", "operationalization", "automation", and "abstraction", which are positive terms for what negatively would be called the radical exclusion of the specifically human factor, the abolition of spirit (*Geist*) in man, which means that ultimately man's[26] being turned into a

---

24 Despite my appreciation of many of his individual observations and interpretations I cannot approve of Günther Anders's main thesis of *Die Antiquiertheit des Menschen* ("The Outdatedness [or Obsolescence] of Mankind", 1956 and 1980), because it misses the very point of the development of technological civilization, namely that it is a deliberate *program* and the *telos* of the process to *abolish* the humanness of man and not a mishap due to man's anthropologically not being up to the superiority of the advanced technology that he produced himself.

25 This program is the exact opposite of the alchemical processes of evaporatio, distillatio, sublimatio.

26 To be more exact: The *concepts* of man, his *definitions*, being turned into that of a *mindless* operator. It is a psychological, not a psychic change. Empirically, man stays the way he had been all along, except that *secondarily* the psychological change may also slowly affect him to some extent in his empirical, psychic constitution.

mindless operator is the supreme goal. This shows in numerous smaller and larger phenomena of ordinary life. Examples are: Multiple-choice tests. DSM-5. Opinion polls. "Bibliometrics" and "impact factor" in the sciences. The requirement for researchers to acquire third-party funding. The rule in Europe that public tender has to be EU-wide and that the bidder with the lowest prices has to be chosen. Higher education and science management. Quota systems. TV viewing figures. Corporate governance rules. Quality management.

2. If we see the soul or spirit at work in the development of technology, we must be clear about the fact that it is precisely not the human soul. An autonomous movement is going on in it, and accordingly we must conceive the soul that we are concerned with here as a decidedly objective soul. It is clearly "non-ego". It is not *people* who propel technology forward. People—the scientists, engineers, inventors, and investors—have to do the apparatus's and the whole technical development's bidding. With all their intelligence and scientific or inventor's passion, they are being used for *its* purposes, for the realization of this self-propelling movement. *It* takes the lead, it dictates, while man trails behind, has to follow and serve it. The persons who seem to be the makers and inventors of new technical products are, usually unwittingly, in the grip of it, driven by it.

It is also obvious that technology does not derive from nor serve our human wishes, needs, and plans. It recklessly revolutionizes life at many fronts, and not merely on the higher level of our ideas, theories, and attitudes, but very practically, on the level of daily life. It completely ignores our human feelings and our traditional values, habits, and attitudes, forcing everybody to give up cherished habits, beliefs, and expectations, and instead to adapt to its, technology's, rules of the game. It confronts us with totally new ethical problems (e.g., genetic engineering and human dignity, the right of privacy and the needs of security through state surveillance); it creates, and challenges us, with utterly new dangers (computer viruses, internet criminality, global warming through human activities, ocean pollution through plastic waste, etc.).

3. Having used the phrase "ghost in the machine" I must hasten to emphasize that the spirit Mercurius or the soul is precisely *not* in *each* machine, apparatus, technical device, the way in mythological times dryads were in individual trees, river gods in real individual rivers, gods in their physical statues or sanctuaries. The time of the significance of "the individual" (both

individual object and individual person) is over. The soul is only in technology *at large*, as a whole, in the *concept* or *logic* of it. It escapes both the sensible and the imaginal intuition (*Anschauung*), let alone perception. It can only be thought.

When speaking of the significance of "the individual" I have of course only the *psychological* or *soul* significance (not the ego or private personal one) in mind. In their private lives, as egos, modern individuals may still find themselves being of great, if not the greatest, significance for themselves. But this is not relevant for psychology. *Psychologically*, even if not empirically, the individual is obsolete. What Jung called the "individuation process" has no legitimate place in psychology at a time when it is the logic or truth of "individual" that it has dissolved and gone under, as objectively demonstrated by the facts that globally individuals have actively integrated themselves into networks; that they reveal all kinds of details about their private lives in social networks like Facebook (violating what Jung called the "persona"), that they are day and night connected with others through mobile phones and Twitter; that they simultaneously assume virtual identities in "chat rooms" or periodically change their identity as well as their partners at different phases of their life; that people want to drown as conscious, thinking, autonomous individuals in loud, hammering smartphone or disco relayed music, at mass events, in all kinds of drug-induced states . . . The soul has lost interest in "center", "self", "concentration" and is heading instead for "différance", "dispersion", "dissemination", "multiculturalism", "diversity" in ideological regards as well as for diversion and distraction through entertainment in practical life. "Content" and "substance" as well as "subject" and "author" are also scorned. The soul's dominating goal is now absolute relationality, interconnectivity, "the web", the "field" (speech field or field of meanings), systems theory, mediality, and, in the practical sphere, team work and interdisciplinarity.

4. The unceasing drivenness towards innovation that characterizes technology, its being compelled to always overcome the latest stage of its own development, means that all technical products and scientific insights in modernity are *produced as* logically a priori *outdated* and *waste*. It is of course true, living creatures, too, carry within themselves the inevitability of their *heading for their death* from the outset. But technical products and scientific results *come* already *as* logically obsolete, which is why the

technical world is so often experienced as being composed of merely "dead things".

5. That technology is neither accessible to sensible nor to imaginal intuition, and the fact that what is accessible to sight and touch, the technical products themselves, is a priori logically obsolete, indicates that, against our expectations, technology[27] is in itself absolutely negative. What it produces is mutatis mutandis like the corpse in prehistoric times from which the first awareness of soul arose. The decisive difference is that that soul brought with it the notions of underworld, afterlife, timelessness and the supernatural, whereas technology is decidedly this-worldly. It is, we could say, the objective representation or production *of* absolute negativity *in empirical reality* and *as decidedly spatio-temporal positivities*. This becomes perhaps most accessible in the modern phenomenon of electronic, digitalized money and the likewise digitalized money market: Absolute negativity (totally invisible, unimaginable, absolutely abstract, really *nothing*), but in the form of positivity and thus of highest reality, the greatest power that moves all.

6. From here we can get an idea about the psychological function of modern (positivistic) positivity. It seems to be the objectification, materialization, realization of the objective soul. Of course, mythology was also the representation and celebration of the objective soul. However, it was this presentation *only in symbolic form*, that is to say, all the contents of the objective soul remained *subjective* experiences or ritual behavior. The dryad was seen, but this was a particular person's experience (and in addition a collective belief). The dryad did not materialize, become an independent reality. She was a kind of divinity and as such fundamentally supernatural, other-worldly, despite her location in an individual tree growing here on earth. The afterlife, the shades in the underworld, Christ's resurrection have the form of ideas, feelings, and of content of belief or visionary experiences. They only live *in* human subjects (individuals or communities, peoples). *For them*, the gods and spirits unquestionably represented the objective soul. But *in themselves* these gods and spirits were part of the subjective psyche (just as now the Jungian individuation process is part of the subjective psyche).

Technology, by contrast, is precisely not symbolic. It is hard fact, objective reality, (positivistic) positivity, and as such completely independent of

---

27 Not the technical things!

experiences, feelings, beliefs that have their place in human minds. It is the self-explication of the soul of the world in its and *as* its ruthless objectivity and autonomy.

We can understand that in order for the objective soul to become indeed explicitly objective, it had to be ruthlessly wrested from people's subjective psyche. God had to die, the "afterlife" become a fiction and lose all interest; all the mythological and metaphysical ideas including "soul" had to become the "superstitions" of former innocent, ignorant times. And man himself had to become a positivity, deprived of his "twice-bornness" and inner absolute negativity so that the soul would become free of the bond which tied it to the subjective mind. Without man's fundamental disappointment-disillusionment, his feeling of alienation, loss, and depletion, without the whole complex of experiences and ideas comprised in the name "nihilism", that is to say, without the human subject's being *relentlessly dispossessed of the objective soul* and of the whole dimension of the divine or sacred, the objective soul could not have been released into its own. Indeed, what was needed was not only man's *disappointment* (as a passive, painfully felt experience). There also had and has to be the continued active, indeed obsessive, work on his *self-abdication* as *responsible* and *thinking* (and as such in himself absolute-negative) subject in favor of, let's say by way of abbreviation: *Artificial* intelligence.[28]

In former times, the world, nature, and the cosmos served as the *stage* on which the human mind experienced the objective soul and celebrated it in its ritual performances. Technology, by contrast, *operates* quasi alchemically *directly* upon the matter of the world: It manipulates, alters the world through industry, genetic engineering, etc. And by intellectually penetrating to the minutest particles and elements and to the farthest points of the universe, it is really *archaeology*: Excavation, unearthing, of the innermost logic of material reality, a logic that used to be buried and hidden in how the world *appears* to us.

---

28 Again I have to stress that I am talking about the logic or psychology of human existence, the changes in the *concept* of man, not about man's empirical reality. *Psychically*, empirically, man of course remains a thinking being. If it were otherwise I could not have written this paper. By the same token, man still feels responsible. Empirically he is by no means a machine and has by no means abdicated as *human* being, but *psychologically*, in his essential definition, he has become a mere operator of machines and a functionary.

Chapter 3

Real Negation[1]

In this essay I will return to text material from Jung that I have already discussed previously in other contexts, above all to one paragraph from his "The Symbolic Life" (*CW* 18 § 632). But this time I will not focus on the specific content, the question of symbolism, myth, and Meaning. What I am interested in is much rather a formal or logical aspect: The function and role that negation has in Jung's discussion of these topics. The contents of the topics are here for us only concrete examples or the material in which the workings of the negation and the way it is dealt with show themselves.

After having, among other things, in § 631 pointed out, "That is the secret of the Catholic Church: that they still, to a certain extent, can live the meaningful life"[2], Jung goes on in § 632 with the following observation.

> What I have spoken of is, alas, to a great extent the past. We cannot turn the wheel backwards; we cannot go back to the symbolism that is gone. . . . I cannot go back to the Catholic Church, I cannot experience the miracle of the Mass; I know too much about it. I know it is the truth, but it is the truth in a form in which I cannot accept it any more. I cannot say 'This is the sacrifice of Christ,' and see him any more. I cannot. It is no more true to me; it does not express my psychological condition.

Nine times in these few lines we come across linguistic expressions of negation ("cannot", "no more", "not"), to which must be added another two indirect negations ("is, alas, . . . the past", "is gone"). Jung emphatically

---

1 Written in 2017.
2 As to what leading the meaningful life means we can perhaps point to another earlier quote from the same text: a "symbolic existence in which I am something else, in which I am fulfilling my role, my role as one of the actors in the divine drama of life" (§ 628).

DOI: 10.4324/9781003611400-4

hammers in his point that something is irretrievably lost, with no return. The negation is absolute. Jung does not leave any loophole open for himself or us. He relentlessly faces the situation of loss.

This insight into the loss is not an isolated point that Jung makes only in the 1938 seminar on "The Symbolic Life". No, it dates already back to approximately 1912, the time after completion of his first major work, *Wandlungen und Symbole der Libido*, if we can rely on Jung's report in *MDR*. At that time the following thoughts went through his head:

> I had explained the myths of peoples of the past; . . . But in what myth does man live nowadays? In the Christian myth, the answer might be, "Do *you* live in it?" I asked myself. "To be honest, the answer was no." . . . "Then do we no longer have any myth?" "No, evidently we no longer have any myth." (p. 171)

There is here no lack of unmitigated clarity about the loss. Also, in his Eranos lecture of 1934, Jung voiced a similar diagnosis about the modern situation ". . . our spiritual dwelling has fallen in disrepair. . . . Like greedy children we stretch out our hand and think that, if only we could grasp it [the wisdom of all ages and peoples], we would possess it too. But what we posses is no longer valid . . ." (*CW* 9i § 31). In the same text he speaks of the "unparalleled impoverishment of symbolism" in the modern world (§ 50). Furthermore, Jung tells in old age (1959) a story of fundamental obsolescence when writing the chapter on Kenya and Uganda contained in *MDR*, which fits also into our context. It is the story about an old medicine man who when asked about dreams said "with tears in his eyes" that "no one had dreams any more". Jung explains, ". . . the medicine man had lost his *raison d'être*. The divine voice which counseled the tribe was no longer needed because 'the English know better'. . . . Now the medicine man's authority was replaced by that of the D.C. The value of life now lies wholly in this world . . ." (p. 265, transl. modif.). Literally it is merely a story about an African *laibon* and his tribe, but in truth it is the mirror in which Jung could see and speak about his own truth and that of modernity as a whole. *Tat tvam asi.*

We also notice in the text passage that we started out from that Jung puts the human subject in the center: I cannot; we cannot. But the human subject is here not an agent, and the negation is not its work, *its* denial or refusal or rejection. It is not a *mental act* in the first place. On the contrary, it is a *real* negation: A fateful event or result of history that has stricken the human subject. The latter is at the receiving end and finds itself, obviously to its possible dismay ("alas"), in the objectively prevailing negation (situation of loss), much like people might find themselves in the situations left by destructive earthquakes, floods, tornadoes. Of course there is a difference. Earthquakes, floods, and tornadoes are physical events. The loss of the possibility to "live the meaningful life" (as Jung put it), by contrast, is a psychological event. It was brought about by the history of the soul and plays a role only in the logical constitution of human existence, not in the natural world. But whether physical or psychological, the objective-fact quality of the respective situations that humans find themselves in is in both cases the same. "Psychological" does here precisely not mean subjective, private, "inner". The event that Jung tries to describe, despite being psychological, hits the subject precisely as "external", simply given, fact. This is why I called it a *real* negation.

Essential concepts: Truth, history, subjectivity

The sundering of the notion of truth

Because this historically new situation is a soul situation, it involves the question of truth. Whereas physical negations such as the ones mentioned are merely destructive and as such simple negations, the soul's psychological negation does, for example in the present case, not do away with the truth of the Catholic Church, for Jung insists, after all, that it is the truth. More generally speaking, psychological negation, even as *real* negation, does not simply destroy the soul's truths altogether. Rather, like a cleaver the negation cuts into the soul's truth as such, into the notion or definition of truth, rather than into particular truths. The "real negation" breaks truth apart into two. All of a sudden, we get two radically different *senses* of truth. In our passage this becomes above all clear when Jung says about one and the same subject matter, the miracle of the Mass: "I know it is the truth" (= first sense of truth); "but it . . . is no more true to me; it does not express my psychological condition" (= second sense of truth).

"It is the truth, but no more true to me" is of course a contradictory and complicated statement. At first let us look at the first part of this statement in order to get a clearer idea about the first notion of truth: "I know it is the truth". This means: indubitably, it (1) IS the truth and (2) it is THE truth!

This truth is absolute in the sense that, other than that of statements or assertions, it is not dependent on our judgment or examination, on proofs that allow us to rightly assign the predicate "true" to it (instead of perhaps having to dismiss it as "false"), and it is not, like human opinions or hypotheses, up for discussions. It a priori *comes* as truth. *When* it indeed appears, it *is* a soul truth. In other words, the truth character is not an *attribute* of soul phenomena, not a *predicate* we assign to them, but inherent in them: To *be* truths is their very nature and essence. With respect to them, we with our opinions, feelings, and judgments would therefore always come too late.

In view of living things Goethe once was moved to spontaneously exclaim, "*wie wahr! wie seiend!*" (how true! how existent!). We could perhaps elucidate the phrase, "how existent!", by saying: How full of Being! How immediately convincing! Truth in this sense is something that *shines out* from such phenomena. In a similar spirit Jung brings truth and being together, declaring that psychology's "truth is a fact [*Tatbestand*] and not a judgment" and that an "idea is psychologically true inasmuch as it exists" (*CW* 11 § 4). As example for this conjunction of truth and being (which might even tempt one to adduce the Scholastic, *ens et verum convertuntur*), Jung also uses a living creature: "An elephant is true[3] because it exists" (§ 5).

Unfortunately Jung expresses himself imprecisely. It is of course not its existence that gives something its truth, for then all existing nonsense would also be true. Psychologically, the question is precisely not if an idea, provided that it is indeed a fact, *is* true or not. Rather the question is if it is a *soul* phenomenon and *as such* the self-manifestation of a truth, its self-evidencing shine. This also means that "fact" in Jung's phrase, "truth is a fact [*Tatbestand*]", has nothing whatsoever to do with what in modern science and in everyday positivistic thinking is called fact. Rather, it simply means that the truths psychology is concerned with happen as events. So what is at stake here is the concept or definition of truth. When Jung says, "When psychology speaks, for instance, of the motif of the virgin birth, it is only concerned with the fact that there is such an idea, but it is not concerned with the question whether such an idea is true or false in any other sense" (§ 4), it is clear that he does not want to derive truth from or reduce it to

---

3 I omitted the quotation marks around the word true that the translator of the *Collected Works*, as the rationalistic softener that he is, felt he had to add here.

fact. What he means is that psychology does not read images or ideas (such as that of the virgin birth) as judgments, propositions, assertions. It reads them as soul phenomena that ipso facto have their truth within themselves and therefore are simply convincing. They are on principle not in need of proof or argumentative support, nor are they subject to doubt. And Jung's elephant is not true *because it exists*, but when it exists it is, in Goethe's sense, an absolutely impressive and convincing reality. It *is* a truth (rather than "being true"). To be a truth is its nature or essence, in other words, part of its definition. And it is a truth because it *comes* as self-evident and self-contained *phainomenon*. Psychological truth cannot be defined in terms of either a correspondence or a consensus (general acceptance) theory of truth. It is, we might say, a "revelatory" sense of truth—the truth of soul phenomena is as self-proving as a shining light.

But other than elephants, soul truths are not physical, natural, ontological, but psychological, notional, ideational, which also means that their "truth" is more than the impressive realness of animals or natural facts, namely something in itself intelligible and spiritually (*geistig*) illumining. They possess meaning-structure, nay, they *are* this meaning-structure and nothing else. They are notions. And this alone is what gives the term "truth" its full sense. As events of something having meaning-structure, soul truths can be expressed not only in pictures, statues, symbols, etc., but also linguistically, in sentences (*dogmata*) and narratives (myths, hymns, etc.), and this in turn is also what can make it possible for people to misunderstand them as assertions, beliefs, or judgments *about* some reality *external* to them, when in reality they are exclusively "about" themselves, merely their own self-display, self-expression, self-unfolding: The representation of the idea, notion, or concept that they are. (They share this feature with animals, because the latter are of course also not statements *about* anything else, but the self-display and self-presentation of their own nature and being, which is why Jung could use the elephant as illustration. However, animals are real empirical creatures and not ideational notions.) Jung's term for the experience of soul truths was *Urerfahrung* (sometimes also *Urerlebnis*, *Urvision*—primordial experience or vision). *Urerfahrung* means that a soul truth has become, for a human being, an immediate presence, a living *present reality* (or actuality).

Two passages of Jung's throw additional light on this sense of truth. In the first one, Jung states, "It almost seems as if these images had just lived, and as if their living existence had simply been accepted without question and without reflection . . . The fact is that archetypal images are so packed with meaning in themselves that people never think of asking what they really do mean" (*CW* 9i § 22). The images *had just lived*, without question or reflection—and that also means precisely without "acceptance"! They did not need to be accepted or approved (just as we do not need to "accept" wild beasts when we encounter one). They lived, and this their living means that they simply, unquestionably *prevailed*. They were the soul truths *in which* as their medium people lived their lives. (The only thing they do need [just as the wild beasts] is, according to Jung, "careful observation and taking account of" [*CW* 11 § 982].)

In the second quotation alluded to we are informed by Jung that in earlier centuries, it "needed no *sacrificium intellectus* to believe in miracles, and the report of the birth, life, death, and resurrection of the Redeemer could still pass as biography" (*Letters 2*, p. 485, to Tanner, 12 Feb 1959). Why did the belief in miracles and the reports of Christ's birth from a virgin mother and his resurrection not need a *sacrificium intellectus*? Because all these ideas *lived, prevailed*, as self-evident and simply convincing truths, as self-evident as the air that we breathe or the sunlight in whose light we see the world.

After these elucidations of the first sense of truth, we can turn to the second sense contained in Jung's statement, "I know it is the truth, but it . . . is no more true to me; it does not express my psychological condition". Earlier in the same text (*CW* 18 § 622) Jung had made use of the same notion of truth: "If ritual and dogma do not fully express the psychological situation of that individual, he can't be cured". This second sense of truth, too, is not a predicate of judgments or propositions, but something existing and prevailing. However, in radical contrast to the first sense of truth it is not a self-manifestation and something that shines out from phenomena. It is not self-evident and self-contained. On the contrary, being defined as the state of being (or, as the case may be, not being) "true to me" and of "expressing my psychological condition" or not, it has the form of a relation between itself *and some other*, namely the relation of correspondence between a soul truth (an idea, image, soul phenomenon) on the one hand and "me", "my psychological condition" on the other. We encounter this same sense of truth in other contexts of Jung's writings. In the passage from *MDR* (p. 171) cited above about his reflections concerning the issue of myth in the present age he raises the question about the Christian myth: "Do *you* live in it?" and a few lines later, after having come to the conclusion that we evidently have no myth any more at all, he immediately asks, "But then what is your myth—the myth in which you do live?" This is the question of "my-ness".[4] It is also at work in another quotation cited earlier: We "think that, if only we could grasp it [the wisdom of all ages and peoples], we would possess it too. But what we posses is no longer valid. . . ." (*CW* 9i § 31). We can also recall in this context the passage in the Prologue to *MDR* where he says, "I can only make direct statements, only 'tell stories.' Whether the stories are 'true' is not the problem. The only question is whether what I tell is *my* fable, *my* truth".[5]

The correspondence theory of truth compares something mental, a statement, opinion, or belief, with the given reality that is the topic of the statement, and thus something subjective (*intellectus*) with something objective (*res*), which is why truth is here defined as the *adaequatio rei et intellectus*. On both sides we are concerned with empirical facts (the mental idea expressed in an articulated statement is just as much an empirical fact, even if only the fact of a statement or claim, as is the given empirical reality as the yardstick of the statement's truth). The second definition of truth that is at work in Jung's dictum involves a fundamentally different correspondence, namely one between two logically negative, not empirically given factors, inasmuch as both are soul. It is the correspondence between *ideal* soul and *real* soul: a given archetypal or soul idea, e.g., a myth (a soul truth in the first sense of truth, not a human statement or narrative in which it may be articulated, but the soul idea itself!), on the one side, and the actual constitution of my psychological condition (how I *psychologically* really am,

4 James Hillman's psychology has no place for this sense of "my-ness" and thus for the second sense of psychological truth (just as *truth* in general is not a topic for the standpoint committed to the imaginal and metaphorical). The place of "my-ness" in Hillman's thinking is, we could perhaps say, taken by his "Acorn Theory" of character and calling. Although it represents a fundamentally different alternative to our modern theories that explain character from genes and/or upbringing, it shares with them the general personalistic bias. It is a theory about empirical *people* and thus an aspect of *psychic* life, not a *psychological* theory (his book about this is entitled *The Soul's Code*, but as far as my terminology is concerned it would better be called "The Psyche's Code"). Jung's question about the "my-ness", by contrast, is precisely not about empirical individuals and their personal nature, the nature of the empirical me. It is a question of truth, a question about the myth *in which* I or we, modern man in general, objectively live(s).
5 In the two sentences, "Whether the stories are 'true' is not the problem. The only question is whether what I tell is *my* fable, *my* truth", the first "true" refers neither to the first nor the second sense of *psychological* truth. It is the commonsensical sense of truth ("correspondence theory of truth") and actually means nothing but "correct". "*My* truth", on the other hand, insists clearly on the second sense of psychological truth.

i.e., the soul's real condition at the age during which I live, not merely my individual *psychic* condition!), on the other side. While staying completely on the side of and within soul and its negativity, this correspondence, if it indeed exists in a given case, nevertheless crosses over from the (supertemporal) ideal sphere (the archetypes, myths) to the decidedly temporal real (my psychological condition).

There is no a priori here as in the case of the first sense of psychological truth. It always needs to be found out whether this correspondence prevails in a given case or not. And it can only be empirically determined. In other words, the second sense of truth has the character of being a posteriori. When Jung states, "I cannot experience the miracle of the Mass . . . I know it is the truth, but it is the truth in a form in which I cannot accept it any more. I cannot say 'This is the sacrifice of Christ,' and see him any more. I cannot", we sense the deeply painful existential experience that there is an unbridgeable conflict between wish and objective reality. Jung would like to accept that truth, but his factual psychological constitution makes it absolutely impossible for him, just as it is made impossible for him as an animal without wings to fly. This shows that it is actually not at all a question of accepting or not accepting, because the I has no say in the matter. It is a question of fact, of necessity or impossibility, that is, of whether a real correspondence exists or not. As such it is *subjectively* a question of honesty.

I mentioned how frequently in Jung's passage the human subject is mentioned. "*I* cannot . . ." (repeatedly), ". . . not true to *me*", "*my* psychological condition". Now it would be a severe mistake to interpret this "I" and "me" or "my" personalistically. The impossibility Jung experienced is not due to any preventing personal trait of his, to anything that is special to him as particular individual, as C.G. Jung. It is not his personal misfortune. The "I" in these sentences stands much rather for the subjectivity of the human subject in general and thus for the logical status in or as which modern man as such, and therefore we all, exist. This I is anybody's I, also my and your I. Jung's passage speaks about the psychological condition of all of us, that is to say, about an *objective* condition (and ipso facto an objective impossibility). It is the condition of the culture as a whole in which each individual I lives.

However, only if and as long as we are speaking of the *impossibility* of a correspondence, the I as the human subject in general is restricted to that of modern man. By contrast, the question of the relation of correspondence between soul truths or symbolism and the actual psychological condition of humans applies to the human subject of all (pre-modern) times. (Only the impossibility of a correspondence is restricted to the form of *subjectivity* or "*I*" that is the distinction of modern man.) Thus Jung once expressed himself in the following way: "Whenever there exists externally a conceptual or ritual form in which all the yearnings and hopes of the soul are absorbed and expressed, that is, for example, a living religion, then . . ." (*CW* 10 § 159, transl. modif.) and, in the next paragraph, ". . . as soon as this religion can no longer embrace his life in all its fullness . . .". We see clearly that Jung's thinking here is informed by the second sense of psychological truth. It refers to a relation between an *externally* existing religion or similar soul truth ("a conceptual or ritual form"), on the one side, and the reality of the *inner* constitution of man, on the other, but the relation is in former times, other than in Jung's own case, one of a prevailing correspondence in such a way that the inner finds itself perfectly expressed, embraced, and thus given satisfaction to, so that there is precisely not any "cannot".

The psychological indispensability of the second sense of psychological truth

The question of psychological truth in the second sense is crucial. It is not enough that images or religious ideas and rituals are "the truth" in the first sense. We could also say: For the givenness of psychological truth in the comprehensive sense or for our being able to "live the meaningful life" it is not enough that images or ideas we are concerned with are truly *archetypal* (which is Jung's usual word for something that is "psychologically true" [in the first sense]), nor is it enough that we *have* archetypal experiences, such as in dreams or visions. In the modern situation, the real test for psychological truth in the full sense comes much rather when those experienced archetypal images have to show whether they are also "true to us and really express our psychological condition" or, conversely, whether they are merely *abstractly* true in the first sense of psychological truth.

But this decisive question is frequently omitted. It is obviously very easy for people today to ignore the issue of psychological truth in the second sense, indeed, to be completely oblivious of it. In fact, this is the normal situation. It takes a veritable *psychologist*, and a psychologist of the format of Jung, to become keenly aware of the issue of psychological truth and feel it with all its consequences. The general public today, by contrast, is convinced that religion is a matter of subjective choice, private belief, of personal preference, conventional habit, and inner conviction, and that such a subjective preference or conviction is all that is needed, or, now turning to the practice of Jungian psychology, that one's mere *having* archetypal experiences is already the real thing.

The topic of psychological "correspondence" is in the case of this conviction not totally absent, but it is personalistically reduced to that of a correspondence between each individual's personal—i.e., egoic—feelings, needs, likings, or understanding, on the one hand, and the diverse religious, ideological, or psychological doctrines offered today on the market of Meaning, on the other hand. Individuals can nowadays *accept* all sorts of beliefs *in their abstractness*, the one individual this, the other that, and a third one none at all, i.e., the *belief* of agnosticism or total indifference.[6] But psychological truth (in the second sense) is, as I pointed out, precisely not a matter of whether we are willing to accept something or not. Personal acceptance rests content with the *abstract* belief contents as objects for the private (intellectual or emotional) entertainment, consolation, and gratification of the ego. It does not overcome these abstractions and thus also not reach the dimension of psychological truth. The whole idea of acceptance or non-acceptance, of what *we as people* feel or think, is *psychologically* irrelevant. The real question in this area is instead the question of *what* our objective necessity or impossibility is, the necessity or impossibility based on who we, as instantiations of modern man as such, objectively are, i.e., how man in modernity is (psycho-)logically in fact constituted and what the indispensable "external" counterpart (a conceptual, ritual, or yet unknown form) would have to be, one that could give real satisfaction to his psychological condition (to "all the yearnings and hopes of the soul")—because it is the veritable *expression* (unintentional, unreflected self-representation) of his real psychological condition.

The real psychological condition that is meant here is given to us by the time we live in. The problem of the "my-ness" of myth or archetypal ideas ("in which I do live", "Do *you* live in it?", does it express *my* psychological constitution?) involves thus fundamentally also the topic of *time*, the concrete character of the particular time in which we live.

6 The fact that the belief of agnosticism or total indifference stays clear of any particular religious creed or experience does not mean that it corresponds to the "psychological condition" of modern man. It, too, is merely an ego attitude that passes over the issue of the soul's truth.

Generally things can go wrong in two directions as far as *this* required correspondence is concerned. The one direction comes out when the question is raised: Are we really up to the soul truth in question? Are we entitled to claim it as *our* truth, or would we merely adorn ourselves with borrowed plumes? In a somewhat different context Jung once pointed to the problem of "the right means in the hand of the wrong man" (*CW* 13 § 55, cf. § 4), but mutatis mutandis it applies to our topic, too. The other opposite direction can be expressed with the questions: Is the truth (of an archetypal idea, of a religion, etc.) up to the real level or status of our objective psychological constitution, to the logical differentiation in fact reached in modernity? Or is it one that we (not we as private individuals and civilian man, but as the objective [psycho-]logical definition of modern man) have already outgrown?

Psychological truth is a two-horned issue. Two requirements need to be fulfilled, two realities must come together in a perfect fit. The two require each other in order for each to truly come into being. Each one is the other's midwife. Only when both are fulfilled do so-called archetypal images or ideas lose their status as being mere abstract intellectual or imaginal (and possibly emotionally felt and thus also merely abstract) contents and become truly archetypal in the first place, and only when these images or ideas truly express the human subject's *psychological* constitution (rather than merely its *psychic*—that is, the ego's—personal *needs* or *likings*) is a condition reached that could rightly give rise to the exclamation: "How true! how existent!"

Negation as the gift of history

"All ages before us have still believed in gods in some form or other", Jung rightly noted (*CW* 9i § 50, transl. modif.). Why were for pre-modern man the particular soul truths (in sense one) that he experienced simply "living existences", immediately convincing and unquestionably prevailing and fulfilling? Why were the respective myths, religious beliefs, and ritual practices of a people for the members of their society absolutely unthreatened and untouched by doubt? Why did people of former ages by no means experience any "I cannot" in this regard? Why did medieval man, for instance, have no difficulty experiencing the miracle of the Mass? All these questions come together in the following one: Why had in earlier times the definition of truth not been sundered and why was what we, after the sundering of truth, call the first sense of truth ("it is the truth") in those ages perfectly sufficient and all that man was aware of (in these regards) and needed to be aware of?

These questions are already the answer. Pre-modern and especially archaic man had been "unborn" man, as I termed it, that is, he was contained in the soul, had not been born out of the soul. He was completely at one with the soul. He lived in the status of (*psychological*, not psychic or empirical-practical!) innocence. Therefore the soul truths (in the form of the respective local tradition) were simply self-evident for him, *immediately* convincing (without reflection), as self-evident as the air that we breathe (of which we remain normally totally oblivious as long as there is no problem with or shortage of it). He was a priori captivated, prepossessed, by them, felt completely at home in and embraced by them as the prevailing truth.

As Jung said about former ages, man in those times lived "*in der Herde*" ("in the fold", the *Collected Works* translate: Man lived "as herd-animal" [*CW* 10 § 160]), where "Herde" probably has the Christianity-inspired figurative meaning of "the fold of the Church (or of whatever established religious practice)" as well as the fold of the village or tribal community or, later, of the nation (in contrast to *extra ecclesiam* in a wider sense). But it may of course also, as the *CW* translation seems to suggest, refer to a literal flock of sheep or other animal herd. This *psychologically* living in the fold and the primordial containment in the soul are two forms of the same psychological reality, the status of innocence and unbornness. In this psychological situation there could not possibly have been an "I cannot. It is no more true to me; it does not express my psychological condition". Because this feeling presupposes that a rupture has taken place and a wedge has been driven between the soul and man, that he has been expelled from the fold of the soul, so that now he has a psychological condition separate from and independent of the objective soul, as his own property. The primordial oneness and immediate containment is destroyed. This is the situation of born man, modern man.

It is by no means so that pre-modern man did not also have "his psychological condition" and that therefore the second sense of psychological truth did not apply to him too. Also in his case there of course had to be such a correspondence between the soul truths and his objective psychological make-up. The only difference is that in those ages this correspondence did not become an issue, simply because it prevailed as a matter of course from the outset, because it had always already prevailed, and absolutely unquestionably so. On the soul level, both sides, the "soul truths" side and "man's psychological constitution" side, or the external and the inner, were in perfect consonance. The psychological make-up of earlier (above all archaic) man was a priori informed by and thus attuned to, indeed identical with, the soul truths. This is what "not having been born out of soul", "being contained in soul", means. And because of this perfect fit (and that means the absence of any difference between the two sides), the fact remained unnoticed *that* there are two sides, *that* there is, in addition to the soul truths (the myths, rituals, religious ideas or dogmas), also a human subject with a psychological condition. The question of the necessity of a correspondence did not, could not, become explicit in its own right and could not make itself felt.

The awareness of the correspondence could only emerge when this correspondence had become problematic, or rather, when it was missing. "It required the *psychological predicament* of our time to prompt us to discover psychology", a "compelling necessity", Jung rightly pointed out (*GW* 10 § 159, my transl.). Only the loss of the correspondence makes the issue of a correspondence conscious. "So long as all goes well and all our psychic energies find an outlet in adequate and well-regulated ways", "[n]o uncertainty or doubt besets us". Only when there is a division between the soul truths and ourselves, only in "this situation of distress" (*CW* 10 § 160), "[o]nly [through] an unparalleled impoverishment of symbolism" (*CW* 9i § 50), does the sundering of psychological truth in two happen and the issue of the "correspondence" become acute and crucial.

History in the *psychological* sense consists of one single event: The birth of man, the expulsion from his embeddedness in the soul, that is, in our context, the dissolution of the fundamental prepossessedness of man by the soul and his ensuing a priori attunement to its truths. What from the ego perspective appears as a terrible loss, from the point of view of soul is the gift of history: The gift of what Jung termed the "discovery of psychology",[7] that is, the revolutionary move to the awareness of the subjective factor or of man *as* subject in his own right and in contradistinction to the soul truths, the religious ideas and rituals. "In earlier times the psychological facts were of course also existent, but they did not impose themselves

---

7 The translator of the *CW*, following his need to fraternize with commonsensical thinking, again used quotation marks: " 'discovery' of psychology" (*CW* 10 § 159), thereby taking the wind out of Jung's sails.

on consciousness" (*GW* 10 § 159, my transl.); now, however, they have become explicit and are keenly felt. The correspondence is replaced by *Zweifel* ("doubt"), "doubt" not as a particular psychic act or conscious state, but as the generally prevailing underlying logic of man's relation to soul. For, *Zweifel* contains etymologically the word *zwei*, "two". It is a logic of division, difference, non-correspondence: Of an irrevocable alienness between the two sides.

The human subject now exists *as* subjectivity, which is a radically new situation. In former ages, man was of course also a subject, but only implicitly so.

This birth of subjectivity as the inevitable psychological definition of man is the one aspect of the gift of history. The other aspect is the awareness of the problem of "form". We remember: The miracle of the Mass "is the truth in a form in which I cannot accept it any more", an assessment to which Jung added a few lines later: "I need a new form". What counts in this new situation when the issue of correspondence has become problematic is no longer merely the semantic content of soul truths, their substance and subject-matter, but also their logical form or logical status. The alienness or non-correspondence I have spoken of lies in their syntactical form, not their content. Having been born out of soul, having acquired the logical status of subjectivity, is tantamount to having advanced, above the semantic level of content, to the level of form.

It is obvious that Jung had keenly become aware of the rupture as well as the gift of history, the sundering of the notion of truth and the problem of form. In this connection it is interesting to take a look at James Hillman's psychology. When he started to come into his own and developed what, after careful consideration of all the existing names for Jungian psychology, he called "archetypal psychology", he clearly showed that he was committed to the heart of Jung's psychological concerns and redeemed it from the shallowness and mindlessness to which analytical psychology was and still is reduced in the hands of the Jungians, for whom Jung's psychology had become an intellectually scaled-down conglomerate of positive-factual ready-made doctrinal conceptions to be routinely taught and applied in the spirit ("spirit"?) of a personalistic either clinical-technical or myth-and-symbol-mongering mindset. Hillman did not only put Jung's central concern, the archetypal depth of the soul, back into the center. He also returned the character as a *living* theoretical enterprise to Jung's psychology, restoring its intellectual radicalness and challenging nature to it.

However, in the light of Hillman's later moves to the emphatically "imaginal" or "imagistic psychology", to the immediacy of "image-sense", "beauty" and "*aisthesis*", we can in retrospect perhaps already detect in the name "archetypal psychology" that penchant that became fully explicit only in his later work. "Archetypal" refers to the soul truths per se (first sense of psychological truth). In Jung's work it had, to be sure, never been without its essential counterpart, for Jung had from early on insisted on primordial experience (*Urerfahrung*), which involves both, the archetypal substance and the receiving human subject. In Hillman's set-up, there is not any essential counterpart to the archetypes or archetypal images. At least with his commitment to "the imaginal" and to "*aisthesis*" as the "conjunction of concrete sensation, psychic image and spiritual meaning" it becomes evident that he is focusing on the image in isolation, on the semantic contents alone.

Of course, "seeing-through" as well as "mining silver from lead", etc. clearly show that as far as the behavioral or practical level is concerned the human subject as psychologist and adept is required for "the work", and in this sense gets due attention in Hillman's thought. But this is of course something completely different from the *psychological* relation of subject and soul truth, as implied by Jung's primordial experience or his "no more true to me". In fact, the whole question of truth is dismissed from Hillman's theorizing. Both the truth of the images and the logical *relation* of correspondence between *two* (the soul truths there and the psychological subjectivity here in temporal reality) are not only of no interest to him, but even systematically excluded. This is the very point of Hillman's emphasis on "image as instinct", on "animal faith in the images" and on "aesthetics [a]s the *via regia*": Absolute immediacy (distancelessness and pointlike unity) of image-sense. By definition, the image *cannot* be "no more true to me". I can only have the wrong approach to image and lack "animal faith". The "no more true" would be a statement (or experience) on the psychological level, the level of the objective soul. "Wrong approach" is a statement on the empirical-practical level, the level of the ego, whereas the standpoint of "the imaginal" itself is floating in the higher ideal sphere.

It seems that for Hillman's psychology there must ultimately not be any negation—therefore also no rupture of history, indeed no history in the essential sense at all. Of course he was very much aware of history in a non-psychological sense, history as sequence of events. Thus he spoke of "ancestors" of archetypal psychology (Heraclitus, Plotinus, Proklos,

Ficino) and discussed historical topics such as the debates of the Church Fathers, the work of Melanchthon and Mersenne, the collapse of alchemy, to mention only these few. But he passionately denied, for example, that there could be an obsolescence of the Greek gods. Zeus qua image in his sense is still alive.

Through "instinct", "animal faith" and "aisthesis", Hillman's psychology implicitly aims for a psychological (not a literal) *return to paradise* and to psychological timelessness. Of course we, as empirical beings, live for him, too, in time and are confronted with the eachness of the diverse fantasy images. But the *aesthetic moment* of image itself is atemporal. Our notion of soul remains in its pristine freshness, untouched and untouchable by time. The exclusion of time from the very notion of soul is, it seems to me, the very point of his concept "the imaginal".

What, along with the exclusion from his psychology of the correspondence question and of negation and historical rupture, is therefore also excluded are the awareness of subjectivity in the psychological sense (i.e., as a status of soul) and the awareness of the problem of the logical form of the soul truths. Hillman paid amazingly careful, ingenious, and sophisticated attention to the specific aesthetic and sensual form of images. But he was blind to what Jung saw, namely, that regardless of the possible sameness of their aesthetic form, images can either possess, or have lost, the *logical form* in which they "express our psychological condition". According to Jung's notion, the soul is *fundamentally* sundered, and in itself touched by the event of history. This also comes out quite clearly in Jung's frequent citation of (Pseudo-)Democritus' axiom on nature (i.e., soul): "Nature rejoices in nature, nature subdues nature, nature rules over nature" (e.g., *CW* 9i § 234). Soul is in itself a self-*relation*, not merely something unitary: Image. And this self-relation includes the historical process of its self-negation, self-overcoming.

Having said this, I can correct a false impression that may have arisen on account of such phrases as *"man's* having been born out of the soul" as well as of the frequent emphasis on (pre-modern or modern) *man* in general. The situation of non-correspondence between the old soul-truths and "my psychological condition" is of course not really one between soul and man. Soul and man—what a mismatch! No, psychologically speaking, the non-correspondence is of course a soul-internal division. Strictly speaking we would have to speak of *"the soul's*, not man's, having (IN modern man) been born out of the *soul*". The modern non-correspondence is that between the *ideal* soul (the soul truths, the archetypal images, the gods, etc.) and the *real* soul (the soul in man as "*his* psychological condition", i.e., his *psychological* condition in contrast to his empirical psychic make-up as empirical personality or civilian man. The "my-ness" referred to earlier is, as long as it is indeed the my-ness of the *psychological* condition, the mark of the soul's having become *real*, its having taken root in a person as a being belonging to the *real* world).

Explicit subjectivity

Jung's insight into the dual, relational character of the soul and the indispensability of subjectivity reaches its pinnacle in his report about his experience in the Athi Plains, a great game reserve, of Kenya.[8]

> To the very brink of the horizon we saw gigantic herds of animals:. . . . Grazing, heads nodding, the herds moved forward like slow rivers. There was scarcely any sound save the melancholy cry of a bird of prey. This was the stillness of the eternal beginning, the world as it had always been, in the state of non-being; for until then no one had been present to know that it was "this world"[9]. I walked away from my companions until I had put them out of sight, and savored the feeling of being entirely alone. There I was now the man who recognized that this was the world and who through his knowing had in this moment first really created it.[10] There the cosmic meaning of consciousness became overwhelmingly clear to me. . . . Human consciousness first created objective being and meaning . . .[11] (*MDR* p. 255)

This passage, although literally about "consciousness", sings the praises of subjectivity. At first glance and according to Jung's explicit description,

---

8 I have already discussed this theme earlier at some length with different emphases in my papers, "Das Bewußtsein, der zweite Schöpfer der Welt", in: *Eranos 55-1986*, Frankfurt (Insel) 1988, pp. 183–239, and "Jung's *Thought* of the Self in the Light of Its Underlying Experience", in: *The Neurosis of Psychology. Primary Papers towards a Critical Psychologie* = W.G., Collected English Papers, vol. 1 (New Orleans, LA: Spring Journal Books, 2006), now: London and New York: Routledge, 2020, pp. 171–189.
9 I added the quotation marks from the German original.
10 This last sentence is my translation from the German original. The *MDR* translation is wrong.
11 In this sentence I added the word "first" and replaced "objective existence" by "objective being" on the basis of the original and its philosophical overtones.

however, it seems to be a cosmological and thus also ontological thesis. But *malgré lui*, we have to read this seemingly cosmological thesis metaphorically, *psychologically*, namely as the unfolding of the *inside* picture of the nature of soul. This is underlined by the fact that Jung is not merely and simply objectively describing an actual experience, but that he also actively stage-managed his experience by sequestering himself completely from his companions in order to be all alone. The German text does not say anything about "savoring" the feeling of being entirely alone. Jung did not try to gratify a personal desire. By purposely establishing himself as solitary individual, as "I", he unwittingly followed promptings of the soul. The point of this necessary maneuver was to transform what initially had started out from an empirical observation on the part of ordinary safari tourists by lifting it out of its realistic context and raising it to a paradigm for the inner mystery of the soul. Through his imaginary stage-management it turned for him (and for him alone) into a kind of ritual, a *mise-en-scène*, in which Jung *gave to himself (and played) the role* of Adam, the first man, while assigning to the huge animal herds the role of unconscious existence "*in der Herde*". Together these two "actors" enacted a soul drama. Jung's deliberate isolation from his fellow human beings in particular had the purpose of his leaving behind his ordinary existence as empirical or civilian man (and thus of his himself being a member of the herd) and to establish himself ritually as *modern explicit* subjectivity per se, subjectivity in the singular as the *logical form* or *status* of modern man.[12]

The "I" who was now the first man (*Mensch*) is of course not personalistically the private individual C.G. Jung. It is the *transcendental I* ritually and symbolically *represented* by Jung as one of its instantiations. And this transcendental I as modern explicit subjectivity is the form that the real soul had given itself in modernity. On the other side, the animal herds, "unheard, unseen, silently eating, giving birth, dying, heads nodding through hundreds of millions of years", symbolically represent in this enacted drama

---

12 "Only the man who is modern in our meaning of the term really lives in the present; he alone has a present-day consciousness, and he alone finds that the mental worlds of those earlier levels of consciousness have paled, their values and aspirations no longer interesting him save from the historical standpoint. . . . Indeed, he is completely modern only when he has come to the very edge of the world, leaving behind him all that has been discarded and outgrown, and acknowledging that he stands before the Nothing out of which All may grow" (*CW* 10§ 150, transl. modif.).

the simply ongoing life of the soul. This means this story is not really concerned only with literal animals. The merely factually lived life without consciousness refers also to the situation of pre-modern man who, as we heard, psychologically (of course not literally) still lived "as herd-animal" or "in the fold", and even to modern man insofar as he is (and finds his full satisfaction in being) ordinary empirical I (as was the case with Jung's companions).

Jung speaks here of the fundamental role of consciousness. But it is not really consciousness in general. For hundred thousands of years man had been conscious, he was the animal (just like those in the animal-herds) PLUS consciousness (that the animals in those herds on the Athi Plains did not possess). Because he had consciousness as a *psychic* property, he did not merely live in the world (as literal animals do), but also had a relation *to* the world, which above all comes out in his linguistic nature and his having gods, symbols, and rituals (Jung said that human consciousness first created objective being *and meaning*). He was "subject" to the extent that he not only saw and observed, but in having myths and rituals also had a reflected relation to the world and the things and animals in it. In addition to being reflecting observer, he also feelingly experienced the world.

But this subject vis-à-vis the object, this conventional and literal sense of consciousness, is not the concept of consciousness that dawned on Jung while seeing the herds in the Athi Plains. What there dawned on ("became overwhelmingly clear to") him was a, by comparison, heightened concept of consciousness, namely the consciousness *of consciousness*. This radicalized and now truly *psychological* (no longer merely psychic) sense of consciousness is one that became only possible after the rupture of history, the birth of man, the dissolution of the primordial and ordinarily prevailing *unio naturalis*. And for becoming explicit, it required in Jung's case his actively having stepped out of the "fold" of the group of his companions. In this way Jung had explicitly represented, and played the role of, the logical form of, explicit subjectivity as the true *psychological* condition of modern man or as the form that the soul had given itself in man in modernity. The deliberate and in this sense "artificial" separation from his companions gives symbolic expression to the rupture that puts an end to the *immediacy* of the "natural" (ordinary) experience of and relation to the world (in which his companions remained) and replaces it with an a priori *reflected* world-relation.

For the Jung in the Athi Plains, subject and object are no longer only an *internal* and *implicit* distinction within the *natural* human experience of the world. The insight that dawned on Jung here has its place on a fundamentally higher, purely logical level. On it, subject and object have been radically torn apart in total opposition and otherness, which produces a sharpness in the conception of consciousness. Whereas the "natural" or psychic experience of the world has its logical origin in *what* there is to be experienced and amounts to consciousness's (passively) being "impressed" by it, the *reflected* experience conversely *starts out from* the subject, a subject that has become explicitly aware of itself in its separateness and of its ipso facto standing vis-à-vis the world as the object of its experience. The reflected experience is characterized by the fact that it is an act, a doing ("creation"!), on the part of the knowing subject. Consciousness's own *active* participation in its experience of the world has objectively come home to consciousness. This is what Jung symbolically expressed by his own deliberate act of separating himself from his group.

For Jung, the radical opposition is that of the object, the world, or mere "being", *precisely as "the profoundest night of non-being"* (*MDR* p. 256), on the one hand, and *"die Bewußtheit, oder besser die Ge-wußtheit, des Universums"* (*GW* 17 § 165, "the awareness or better being-known-ness of the universe"[13]), on the other, through which alone man, I, "in an invisible act of creation gave the world its completion: objective being".[14] The position of the I, the subject, as "second creator" is nearly as sovereign and independent as God's position vis-à-vis the world. Jung also clearly emphasizes the subject's "act" and the creative nature of this act. The designation of this act of creation as "invisible" refers to the fact that it is not an empirical (psychic), but a transcendental (psychological) act.

But why is "being-known-ness" better, as Jung says, than "awareness"? *Bewußtheit* and awareness are qualities of an existing subject (humans *have* consciousness or *are* conscious) and allow one to think of the commonplace conscious experience of the world, which, we must understand, as psychic is *also* nothing but the consciousness *within the night of non-being* (although of course not the *profoundest* night of non-being that is

---

13 The *CW* translation is not usable.
14 *Erinnerungen* p. 259, my transl. *MDR* has: "put[s] the stamp of perfection on the world by giving it objective existence [being]" (p. 255f.).

represented by the literal animal herds, let alone inanimate nature)! By moving in his diction from *Bewußtheit* to *Ge-wußtheit*, Jung rises to the level of the objective soul, to the *universe's* self-sufficient *"being known"-ness* on the level of soul, through which alone the world becomes "this world" in its full objectivity. This objective being-known-ness, if and when it occurs, takes of course place in man, but it does not serve *his* self-development, the heightening of *his* awareness. It has to complete the creation of the *world*. With the term "consciousness" Jung is not referring to people, human subjects, who consciously see and experience the world (what would be special about that?), not to *our* being conscious or aware. Rather, he is referring to the *objective reflectedness* of the world itself as *its* quality through which *it* receives its finishing touches.

The *Ge-wußtheit* and thus also the objective existence of the world existed also in Jung's companions, just as in humanity as a whole from its earliest days onwards, however only as implicit (*ansichseiend*, we could also say: Not-conscious) *Ge-wußtheit* and as implicit objective being. Only when this implicit *Ge-wußtheit* becomes conscious of itself and of the fundamental role that consciousness plays in completing the creation of the world has this *Ge-wußtheit* come home to itself and become explicit. And only thereby is the creation of the world *in fact* completed. The transition from implicit to explicit is symbolically expressed in Jung's active separation from his companions in order to demonstratively become solitary I.

After having stressed the significance of Jung's Athi Plains experience and insight I now have to add two critical commentaries. The way Jung reports his experience in his *Memories* one gets the impression as if what it produced for him was an absolutely revolutionary and radically new insight. He himself, so he emphasizes, was "the first man", which is probably not only a reference to Adam, but also seems to imply that he felt like the first person who really became conscious of the cosmic role of consciousness ("for until then no one had been present to know that it was 'this world'. . . . There I was now the man who recognized that this was the world"). But in reality, the basic core of his insight is nothing new. It is part of the awareness of the role of subjectivity that had already objectively been acquired and elaborately worked out during the period of early-modern (*neuzeitliche*) philosophy from, let's say, Descartes to Kant and Fichte, of course on a much higher intellectual level and with different intent. What Jung had learned *intellectually* about Kant's "Copernican Revolution" (that objectivity is precisely not simply given to the mind, but is produced by subjectivity itself) seems only here in the Athi Plains, through his staging this vivid scene, to have fully dawned on him and truly become his own property through a *psychic experience* (an empirical sight). If so, this is another example for the curious fact that Jung needed to "translate" his own *implicit thoughts* into the alienated, externalized form of felt experiences (like dreams, visions, fantasies [*Red Book!*], ideas, observed events) that seemingly happened spontaneously to him, before he could articulate them as his explicit thoughts and claim validity for them on the ground of their now being based on these "empirical" experiences, these "facts". It is, figuratively speaking, as if Jung thought that one should not do mental arithmetic, but should much rather like little children do sums by means of the fingers of one's hand or other visual aids.

In the case of the particular Athi Plains insight this is especially counterproductive since the *creative* role of consciousness and explicit subjectivity, that are celebrated here, are of course undermined if the insight into them is dependent on empirical scenes out there: The form of the insight (the contingent happening of a real event as external object or semantic content of consciousness) contradicts the very point of the insight (that it is subjectivity that first *creates* objective being). Jung relied too much on the psychic and trusted too little in the psychological: In living thought.

My second critical comment has to do with what Jung made of his insight. The late Jung seems to have incorporated this topic into his theosophy and taken it literally, ontologically. Despite his awareness and frequent citation of (Pseudo-)Democritus's dictum, he seems to have taken the metaphor of the two-fold creation of the world as the cooperation between two separate literal beings, God as the first Creator of the world and man as the second creator of the world, just as he propounded the idea that man was literally necessary for God, for His being redeemed of his unconsciousness concerning His own shadow. One might even suspect that by actually *believing* in "the cosmic meaning of consciousness" and man's being "indispensable for the completion of creation" (*MDR* p. 256), Jung's consciousness had been inflated by this experience as a numinous one.

Psychology knows nothing about "God" and "man" and the "Creation of the world", therefore also nothing about a "*cosmic*" role of consciousness. Of course, psychology does know of the *idea* of "God as Creator of the world", but this is then only a soul-immanent motif, an archetypal idea in the history of the soul, no different from other mythological ideas or "soul truths" such as "virgin birth" or "the night-sea-journey of the hero". For us as psychologists this "second creation of the world", this "giving it objective existence", has therefore nothing to do with the literal Creation of the world in a theological or metaphysical sense, nothing with God, with the factual universe. For psychology, the change from the world's "state of non-being" to its having obtained "objective being" is a soul-internal process, and the explicit subjectivity attained to by Jung's having stepped out of the "fold" of his companions is the soul's self-distinction, self-distancing. It is the soul's need—within itself—to heighten and give more edge to its relation to (*its own idea* of) the world and to thereby catapult itself out of and above its containment within its own fold onto a new level of itself, that of explicit subjectivity. We can say that by operating with the literal ideas of God and the Creation, Jung's thinking has left the precincts of psychology. He even posits and entertains the idea of the *ultimate object* (God)! He thereby detracts from the very subjectivity whose enormous significance he, after all, wanted to highlight.

When we now compare this view of Jung's with Hillman's basic interest, it becomes immediately clear that in the *psychologically* understood conception of the Athi Plains insight there is no room either for "animal faith" or for "instinct" and "*aisthesis*". Jung's opposition of consciousness versus the animal herds that merely blindly act out their existence has a radical negation in itself, whereas "animal faith" is the denial of any negation, in fact the dream of our return to the *unio naturalis*. If we want to find what has the same systematic place in Hillman's psychology as the one that is held by *Ge-wußtheit* in Jung's thinking we have to say that it is "*anima mundi*". Although qua *anima* mundi it is not simply "the world" in its empirical factualness, the predicate Jung uses for simple being, namely, "the profoundest night of non-being", would from the Athi Plains point of view nonetheless have to be applied to Hillman's *anima mundi* as well as to his "cosmos" in contrast to "universe",[15] too, inasmuch as they are fundamentally conceived as having ultimate (even ontological?) dignity in and by themselves, without that consciousness in Jung's high-level and explicit sense as the required counterpart that alone, as "the second creator of the world", gives "to the world its objective being".

15 James Hillman, "Cosmology for the Soul. From Universe to Cosmos", in: *Sphinx* 2, London 1989, pp. 17–33.

Of course, neither of the two polarities described is identical with the relation discussed above as the second sense of truth, the correspondence between soul truths as such and the real psychological constitution of man. The "being-known-ness" of being as such, of the world, precedes the question of psychological truth. But it establishes the absolute importance that explicit subjectivity has in Jung's thinking, that subjectivity that is the precondition for any awareness of the significance of "my psychological condition" *in contradistinction to* the mere givenness of soul truths that prevailed in pre-modern times, that is to say, the precondition for *psychology* in contradistinction to the *psychic* living the meaningful life.

Hillman's passionate objection

It is not only through an external comparison that we can discern certain obvious discrepancies that exist between Jung's Athi Plains insight and the standpoint of archetypal (or imaginal) psychology; Hillman also took once directly issue with the conception elucidated in Jung's report about his experience, flatly and vehemently denying Jung's view and simply asserting the very opposite: "We can dispel subjectivity . . .. No subject needed, neither conscious nor unconscious".[16] One should not push Hillman's rejection aside lightly. His view is backed up by the whole weight of the grand theory presented in his two-part essay on "Silver and the White Earth". We will have to take a closer look at his arguments in order to determine their merit.

Hillman protests: "The objective world requires a human subject! *Horribile dictu*: 'I' crown the creation, those herds, by my consciousness!" "The plains are, and their grazing gazelle, and these images move in the soul of the world unwitting of 'Man, I' or any personal observation. Psychological faith affirms those gazelles, those images, whose appearance does not require my consent." "They do not need us."[17]

What strikes us immediately is that Hillman here has only eyes for the commonplace, *the literal*, namely the plains, the gazelles, just as for the

16 James Hillman, "Silver and the White Earth (Part Two)", in: *Spring 1981*, Dallas, TX (Spring Publications), pp. 21–66, here p. 50. I am indebted to Greg Mogenson for having reminded me of this passage.
17 James Hillman, "Silver and the White Earth (Part Two)", in: *Spring 1981*, Dallas, TX (Spring Publications), p. 50.

literally, *ego-psychologically* interpreted "Man, I" of Jung's statements. But this is not at all what Jung is speaking about. He is not talking about the gazelles, the gnus, zebras, nor about the ego, about empirical or civilian man, the empirical I—from which, after all, he had deliberately and ostentatiously dissociated himself, in order to take on the imaginal or ritual role of explicit subjectivity as such. What Jung literally saw in the Athi Plains served merely as the trigger for his real insight. Jung did not wish to claim that *the plains* and their grazing *gazelles* "need us". Of course "they are", for him just as much as for Hillman. Of course the plains and those herds are not crowned by "my consciousness" (although it can now certainly be doubted that the animals—not only the gazelles, but also, e.g., elephants and rhinos, indeed nature at large—"do not need" us and our care in a very literal sense for their continued existence!). All this is not the bone of contention.

Jung's discovery is, much rather, the much more sophisticated, higher-level, indeed revolutionizing one that this their so-understood *being* needs precisely to be *seen through* as "the darkest night of non-being"! This is the challenge of Jung's insight. And this is what Hillman completely misses, deliberately ignores, which ipso facto means that his attack does not respond to Jung's view at all, let alone amount to a refutation. His argument remains fundamentally beneath the level of Jung's idea. We can say that Hillman is, with systematic intent, concerned only "with what the eyes can see" (regardless of whether it is the physical eyes of sense perception or the mental eyes of the imagination), only with the commonplace level of visible, tangible things, with entities and personified figures, in the (unadmitted and unconscious) spirit of an ontology of substance, while—at least in this particular area—shutting his eyes to "what opens the eyes". Or we could also express the same thing by saying that he is interested only in "the semantic" and blinds himself to the breakthrough that happened to Jung, namely the breakthrough through "the semantic" to "the syntactical or logical": to the level of the syzygy of "darkest night of non-being AND objective being", or of "mere being AND *Ge-wußtheit*", i.e., to the question of the logical status of things. Hillman's vehement defense of "the event", just like that, seems to serve the purpose of the regressive restoration of the direct-access stance to the world, the stance of *naive naturalism*[18] appropriate

---

18 Of course not really naive. A *simulated* naive naturalism.

for ancient mythological consciousness, whereas his insistence on the image character of events (in his high, refined sense of "image") has the function of camouflaging the regressiveness of this stance of immediacy by presenting it as something that has been culpably neglected in our tradition and above all in modern times.

My critique of Hillman's wholesale rejection of Jung's insight into the fundamental role of subjectivity should not be understood as *my wholesale rejection* of Hillman's point. To the extent that the latter is an attack on conventional ego-psychology, on ego-psychological positions such as the view that "mental events [are] validated by virtue of my 'having' a dream, 'thinking' an idea or 'feeling' an experience" (p. 49f.), I am completely with him. But when he interprets Jung's Athi Plains insight along ego-psychological lines (e.g., his " 'I' crown the creation, those herds, by my consciousness!", "personal observation", "my consent"), when he implicitly imputes to Jung a kind of egomaniac presumption, his having inflated the everyday I with semi-divine importance, Hillman shows that in this case his own consciousness is syntactically informed by the very ego-psychological structure that he semantically fights against. Hillman states, as we heard: "Psychological faith affirms those gazelles, those images, whose appearance does not require my consent". "Consent" comes from the language of ego willing. But Jung is not concerned with consent at all. His topic is "knowing", nay, the "knownness" (passive voice!), of the world, which is a completely different matter from the ego's will, namely, one of logos. I might as well point to another problem of Hillman's sentence. "Psychological faith" is ultimately *my* or *your* psychological faith. It is not a free-floating substance, but also dependent on some subject. And is there really a great difference between "my faith's *affirming*" and "my *consenting*"? Hillman's "affirmation" has not left the sphere of the will, quite in contrast to Jung's *Ge-wußtheit*.

After the very sentence about the creation, the herds, and "my consciousness" that I just quoted Hillman says, "But what if both, all, are images?" I hail this question. Yes, indeed, *what if* they are all images?! But why then does *he* not read Jung's description of the animal herds, of "Man, I", and of "darkest night of non-being and objective being" as an image, just like a dream, and the individual elements of Jung's thought, above all also the "I", as internal to this image or "dream"? Why does he take them literally, as positivities in their everyday sense? If "psychological faith affirms those gazelles", why does it not also affirm Jung's overwhelming Athi Plains experience and his insight into the role of explicit subjectivity? Why is "psychological faith" selective, preferring certain events as good and soulful and rejecting others as being psychologically *"horribile dictu"*? About other events Hillman writes, "The event is there, shining. Have we thought it, or has it appeared, ephiphanic [sic!] . . .?" Why does he not credit Jung's "mental event"[19] as having appeared as an *epiphanic* and *shining* event, which it so obviously was? If, as he quotes Euripides as saying, "All things are full of Gods", why is not subjectivity also a manifestation of "God" or of the soul's truth? Is it not a most prominent and powerful *phainomenon* in the (last 500 years of the) history of the soul, one form of its self-manifestation? The answer to the question why Hillman did not apply his own standards when he came to Jung's subjectivity-insight can only be: Because he is committed to a certain not negotiable dogmatic position[20] of nostalgic, anti-modern[21] character.

A second serious problem is that Hillman's view is monistic. No syzygy or interrelation, no counterpart to the phenomena, such as, e.g., the relation that for Plotinus existed between sun and eye. Just the object, the event plain and simple, in isolation: "The event is there—though not in a mirror . . . Or better: the event is the mirror self-sustaining its own reflection" (Hillman, p. 50). The reflection is not completely cancelled, but it is swallowed by, has become identical with, the event. The events are so to speak *canned*. Enclosed within themselves. The world is no longer "the vale of soul-making". Soul-*making* is no longer needed. The world comes a priori as soul ready-made. The phenomena or, as Hillman says (p. 49), "events as images" come as in themselves reflected and therefore do not need our absolute-negatively reflecting, inwardizing, them into themselves.

Ultimately, this amounts to a move away from psychology in the direction of some sort of "ontology".[22] Consciousness becomes oblivious of

19 Hillman uses this phrase in his paper on p. 49, though not with particular reference to Jung's experience.
20 Cf. Jung's charging Freud with having made a dogma of the sexual theory.
21 "Modern" in "anti-modern" includes here what in German is called *"neuzeitlich"*, the period of the (15th,) 16th, 17th, and 18th centuries, whereas I usually reserve the term "modern" for the time beginning with the Industrial Revolution.
22 Cf. Jung's contrasting psychology and things or events: "If psychology did not exist, but only concrete objects . . ." (*MDR* p. 152). Cf. also Jung's idea that "There are peoples and epochs where it [the soul] is outside, peoples and epochs that are unpsychological, as, for example, all ancient cultures, and among them especially Egypt with

its participation, one might even venture to say its hidden complicity, in the coming about of images and is in its turn ultimately reduced to nothing more but a *touristic* one ("Take joy in witness", Hillman proclaims). But in reality the grazing gazelles only *become* image and mirror reflection *in human consciousness*, in a consciousness's dream, thought, vision, experience. "Mental events as images" (p. 49) do need us to *be* mental, to *be* image (and for becoming truly psychological they need in addition the particular work of our absolute-negative interiorization of them). Even epiphanies need us, and not only as a receptive mirror or "witness", but also for their coming into existence in the first place. One cannot factor out the "Man, I" from the *anima mundi*. If you subtract human subjectivity, human apperception, human naming, what is left? Is *it*, the *anima mundi*, really what is left?

Concretistic negation: Negation as loss and lack

No present: Truth on vacation

That Jung faced and unrelentingly respected what I called the *real* negation—the loss of myth, symbolism, and thus of the capability to "live the meaningful life"—has been shown. In addition we have seen that ipso facto he also received the benefits of this gift of history: The awareness of the question of *form* and the awareness of the fundamental significance of consciousness in the sense of *explicit subjectivity*. What we now need to explore is how Jung dealt with these insights he had gained and what his response was to the—after all, depressing, if not devastating—loss of the soul truths.

In "The Symbolic Life" Jung's answer to his "It is no more true to me" is "I must have a situation in which that thing becomes true once more". By the same token, his "it is the truth in a form in which I cannot accept it any more" is countered with his statement, "I need a new form".

---

its magnificent objectivity . . ." (*CW* 10 § 158, translation modified). One could think that what Hillman wants is a *psychology* that is in itself precisely "unpsychological" and "objective" in the sense of this Jung quote. "Image" seems for Hillman to be the compromise-formation between his modern consciousness that is already subjectivity and aware of itself (in contrast to the "magnificent objectivity" that Jung ascribed to the ancient Egyptians) and that very objectivity that he desired. The result is the idea of the self-sustained reflectedness of the *anima mundi* or "the imaginal".

There are two decisive problems with Jung's response to his correct diagnosis. One concerns the question what it means for life in the present. The other is whether this response does really do justice to his own insight into the *real* negation: Into the obsolescence of the inherited soul truths and into the problem of form.

Jung establishes, high above our present situation, a wide arc today, crossing over from the one extreme to the other: From the "no more" to the "once more" or from past to future. The past-ness is strongly articulated in his text and explicitly mentioned ("... is, alas, to a great extent the past"), whereas the future is only indirectly hinted at by a few phrases ("I need", "I must have", will become "true once more"). In a late letter Jung speaks more clearly of "the coming guest" (*Letters 2*, p. 591, to Read, 2 September 1960). One is reminded of Heidegger ("Only a god can save us") and Samuel Beckett (*Waiting for Godot*). It is a situation of expectation (*exspectare*: To look out for, long for) and of anticipation.

Jung settles in the empty hole between the "no more true" and the not yet of the longed-for "true once more". Past and future? Yes. But the present is missing, or it is precisely a "present" of the *absence* of truth and thus not a present in the full sense at all. Rather, Jung lives in an intermission, a no-man's land,[23] in an empty time during which soul and truth are on vacation, off duty. The intermission may be a long one: For Jung it began as early as with the emergence of Protestantism (*CW* 9i § 22ff.), i.e., 500 years ago, and for all we know it might just as well continue indefinitely. The soul has no *present reality* in this Jungian conception. In the psychological hollowness of the present Jung merely *dreams* of the future coming of "a new form" and takes this dream for the real thing. It is his longing, indeed, his *need*, which only indicates his, in reality, being needy, poor, empty-handed. In his cited Eranos lecture of 1934 Jung speaks directly of "our spiritual poverty, our symbol-lessness", of the "void" and the "vacuum", of our status of "beggary" (*CW* 9i § 29).

But it is not sufficient to speak of "our" or "Jung's" poverty and symbol-lessness or truth-lessness. For this expresses only the ego standpoint. Much more serious is the poverty that in Jung's theory befell time itself and with it the objective soul, the logic of the soul's life: The fundamental

---

23 Cf. the already quoted statement: "Indeed, he is completely modern only when he has come to the very edge of the world, leaving behind him all that has been discarded and outgrown, and acknowledging that he stands before the Nothing out of which All may grow" (*CW* § 150, transl. modif.).

present-lessness in Jung's psychological thinking, its sense of fulfilled time being reduced, much like in the philosophy of Schelling, only to past and future. The factual present is a mock-present, in which, psychologically, we can at best live a pseudo-life by merely going through the motions of living, but cannot live in the true sense of the word ("live the meaningful life"). It is nothing but "banality", i.e., utter soul-lessness, as we learn from Jung's confession: "My whole being was seeking for something still unknown which might confer meaning upon the banality of life" (*MDR* p. 165).

With this sundering of time into the two poles of past and present without real present, Jung exemplifies Niklas Luhmann's analysis about the present in our time, an analysis coming from a very different starting-point. Luhmann writes about the new situation concerning the nature of time:

> . . . the difference of past and future (which of course had also already been known before) enters into the position of a guiding difference [*Leit-differenz*] for the understanding of time and here replaces the distinction between ever-present eternity and time. The consequence of this is that the present is defined by the difference of past and future, that is, that it turns into a now-point of time (that it previously had only been on the level of the temporality of *events*), a now-point of time that "between" past and future makes possible the constant switching from the one time horizon to the other, but *itself* is *not time*. [. . .] With this, the present turns itself into the paradoxy of time: into the unity of the difference of past and future, into the third excluded by it, but included within it, into the time in which *one does not have time*.[24]

The time in which one does not have time and the emptiness of a present that is itself not time (and this means for us soul-less) is what in Jung appears under the keyword "banality of life". Jung beautifully demonstrated (and caricatured) this time in which one does not have time by telling us in "The Symbolic Life" (§ 630) about a woman he met

> in Central Africa who had come up alone in a car from Cape Town and wanted to go to Cairo. 'What for?' I asked. 'What are you trying to do that for?' And I was amazed when I looked into her eyes—the eyes of

---

24 Niklas Luhmann, *Die Wissenschaft der Gesellschaft*, Frankfurt a. M. 1992 (1st ed. 1990), p. 613 (my italics, my translation).

a hunted, a cornered animal—seeking, seeking, always in the hope of something. . . . Hers is a life utterly, grotesquely banal, utterly poor, meaningless, with no point in it at all."[25]

A life without any fulfilled present.

It is illumining to see that Jung, to be sure, in his psychological *theorizing*, i.e., on the intellectual ego-level, emphatically upholds the vertical distinction of and relation between the archetypes, the transcendent, "an extramundane authority which acts as counterpoise to the 'world and its reason'"[26] (i.e., what Luhmann called "the ever-present eternity"), on the one hand, and the temporal, the "world and its reason", the empirical or human-all-too-human sphere, on the other hand, but that in truth—in his *actual existential life experience*, in his real "psychological condition"—he has precisely lost this verticality, and along with it the fulfilled present (a present fulfilled by the ever-present eternity), and has succumbed to the modern strictly horizontal difference of past and future, the bygone and the longed-for, the "no more" and "not yet". His psychological doctrine contradicts his own inner *truth* (remember: "My whole being was seeking for something still unknown which might confer meaning upon the banality of life")—and possibly (or probably?) has the function of counteracting this truth (which is of course not his idiosyncratic truth, but the "psychological condition" or situation of modern man as such).

The topic of the missing present calls to mind for us a part of a dream of Jung's discussed in *MDR*, a dream[27] which began with Jung's meeting his father, who in the dream was a highly learned scholar and the custodian guarding the sarcophagi of great personages, famous people and princes in a crypt. Later on the dream text reads:

> . . . In the dream I suddenly saw that from the center a steep flight of stairs ascended to a spot high up on the wall. . . . At the top of the stairs

---

25 In view of Jung's own seeking for something unknown which might confer meaning upon the banality of life we might again be induced to say to Jung (and ourselves to the extent that we seek "meaning"): *Tat tvam asi*. What he says about that woman applies to himself.

26 *CW* 10 § 258, transl. modified.

27 I discussed this dream in my "Jung's Millimeter: Feigned Submission—Clandestine Defiance. Jung's Religious Psychology", in my *Dreaming the Myth Onwards. C.G. Jung on Christianity and on Hegel* (New Orleans, LA: Spring Journal Books, 2013), now: London and New York: Routledge, 2020, pp. 3–46.

was a small door, and my father said, "Now I will lead you into the highest presence". Then he knelt down and touched his forehead to the floor. I imitated him, likewise kneeling, with great emotion. For some reason I could not bring my forehead quite down to the floor—there was perhaps a millimeter to spare. But at least I had made the gesture with him. Suddenly I knew—perhaps my father had told me—that that upper door led to a solitary chamber where lived Uriah, King David's general, whom David had shamefully betrayed for the sake of his wife Bathsheba, by commanding his soldiers to abandon Uriah in the face of the enemy. (*MDR* 218f.)

In order for us to better see why I quote this dream part we need to turn to the actual German text because the English translation obscures an essential point. According to the German text, what his father said is more complex: "'Now I will lead you into the highest present [*Gegenwart*]!' I felt as if he said: 'highest presence'". The latter phrase, which in the German text appears in English, is obviously the dream-I's subjective interpretation of what his father literally said. It must be of importance that the dream introduces the ambiguity of *Gegenwart* ("the present", also, in Grammar, "the present tense") and "presence". The dream could easily have made the father say directly "highest presence", if that was the only meaning intended. I don't want to put down the dream-I's interpretation as mistaken or as an ego defense against "*Gegenwart*". The reverence paid by the father by kneeling down and touching his forehead to the floor supports certainly also the sense of "highest presence". Nevertheless, we must not overlook the dream's intended ambiguity. I think that what is meant is that Jung's father wants to lead Jung indeed into the *present* (*Gegenwart*), but the present *as* the highest *presence* and in this sense as the vertically fulfilled present (i.e., as a time in which one can "live the meaningful life"). But the dream-I rejects this offer of a fulfilled present that would once and for all end all seeking and longing for something that could confer meaning upon the banality of life; it rejects this present by defiantly, even if secretly, refusing to bring his forehead all the way down to the floor.

The question is of course *why* this refusal of something that, after all, was desperately sought for? The dream does not explain. My suggestion is that it is not so much and not only the dream-I's ego pride (that comes out in Jung's explanation of not wanting "to be a dumb fish" and his ridiculously farfetched attempt to justify his arrogance by blathering about the necessity of "some mental reservation": "Otherwise, where would be his [man's] freedom? And what would be the use of that freedom if it could not threaten Him who threatens it?" *MDR* p. 220.). It is also more. It is above all the dream-I's refusal of allowing himself to be led into a present (*Gegenwart*), if that present is such a one whose "highest presence" shows *only* in man's total, honestly reverent submission *without* any spectacular, glorious manifestation of the divine or archetypal soul truth, but if it is nothing more than the relentless submission *to* Uriah, the image of man in his utter misery as guiltless victim (and a Uriah who, to top it all, does *not* appear, but is merely hinted at). This was the verticality offered to the dream-I by Jung's father, a verticality that could have led the dream-I (and probably also the real Jung as the dreamer of this dream) into the fulfilled present. It is the vertical axis of: Absolute humility and veneration below and the idea of *God-forsaken*[28] man above, i.e., Uriah as prefiguration of the Crucified (but precisely not the Crucified himself, not Christ. Only Uriah! And, more than that, even Uriah only as absent, *not*-appearing!). It is *this* soul-truth, *this* ever-present eternity, *this* verticality, that the dream-I (and probably Jung himself, too) abhorred. But *it* is precisely the "highest present (*Gegenwart*)" AND "highest presence" that the dream, and in this dream his father, wanted to offer to the dream-I.

The highest present/presence into which Jung's dream-father wanted to lead—and *initiate*—the dream-I is *absolute negativity*. And what the dream-Jung (just as the Jung who interpreted this dream) refused was thus ultimately the *negativity* that characterized *this* highest presence of the present. But we learned from Jung himself that, as the gift of history, psychology comes into existence only through the "real negation", through the loss of symbolism as such, that is, through the negation of the entire semantic form of truth: Psychology depends on absolute negativity. Jung's insistence in real life, "I must have a situation in which that thing becomes true once more", and his "seeking for something still unknown which might confer meaning upon the banality of life" amount, by contrast, to two things: First, (in contrast to negativity) to a clinging to the positive, semantic form of truth (that of symbols, archetypal images, the imaginal) and secondly (in contrast to true psychology) to the demand for the *psychic* or *egoic* form of fulfillment: Through his own *having*, *possessing*, symbols as felt experience

---

28 Jung quotes, "My God, my God, why hast thou forsaken me?" (*MDR* p. 219).

("I must have", "I need"). The second feature, the fact that truth or meaning has withdrawn into the inner and can only be imagined as personal psychic *experience* and must gratify the I, is proof of Jung's irrevocable modernity, and at the same time it is proof of the fact that what was desired was— in truth but unwittingly—not *truth* at all any longer. Conceived as bound to the ego's felt experience, the very concept of psychological truth had already been decomposed. Pre-modern man's "living the meaningful life" had not been experiential. It had essentially been a ritual enactment and a metaphysical knowledge: not psychic, not personal feeling, but psycho*logical*, the sober active affirmation of the objective soul's objectively *prevailing* truth. The dream-Jung's refusal to touch the ground with his forehead, as the deliberate (even if unconscious) act that it is, is ultimately *the refusal of a wholehearted move from the psychic to psychology*.

Fake present, or: Alternative truth

Only four years before the "Symbolic Life" seminar Jung had, in his Eranos lecture of 1934 "On the Archetypes of the Collective Unconscious", advanced another thesis about the change brought about by what I called the *real* negation. It is the thesis that "the stars have fallen from heaven" (*CW* 9i § 50), that "the spirit . . ., as Heraclitus says, has descended from its fiery heights" and turned to water; that we are "children of an age in which the spirit is no longer up above but down below, no longer fire but water" (§ 32, transl. modif.). The stars, the gods, once up there in everybody's Heaven and as such cosmic truths have—in this theory—become introjected into people's unconscious and been psychologized. Now "a secret life holds sway in the unconscious"; our unconscious "holds living water, spirit that has become nature", and we have been able "to rediscover the gods as psychic factors, that is, as archetypes of the unconscious" (§ 50). All that now needs to be done is to salvage "the treasure" that "lies in the depths of the water" (§ 51). All this points to the topics of the quest, the individuation process, the possibility of *Urerfahrung* (primordial experience), topics that are central to a main line of thinking in Jung's psychology and dominates the thinking and endeavors of the Jungians and Jung fans alike.

Despite the different view in this area expressed in the 1938 seminar, Jung never revoked the basic position about the secret life of the archetypes in the unconscious and the necessity of our retrieving this treasure from its depths, just as he never, it seems to me, critically distanced himself explicitly from earlier theses on the basis of his not quite compatible insights gained later (in his old age one can, despite certain shifts in emphasis and orientation that had meanwhile happened in his thinking, see him still upholding earlier concepts at times). The particular views just described remained bread-and-butter stances up to the end of his life, and they probably also antedate the more detailed discussion given in his cited Eranos lecture.

What is the difference between them and the other 1938 idea of the need of a new form, of "a situation in which that thing becomes true once more"? Whereas there, truth was pushed off into an unforeseeable future, here the soul truths ("the stars", the gods, the spirit) are sunken into "our unconscious". This does not only mean that the horizontality of the past-future opposition is replaced by an (even if reversed, upside-down) verticality and that verticality is thus retained. It also means that truth is not on vacation; there is a sense of the present (*Gegenwart*) as fulfilled one. And it means that in this view the soul truths have the status of a *present reality*. The beyond, Heaven, the stars are already in *this* world here on earth and thus immediately true. This uplifting sense of a "fulfilled present" and of the soul truths' present reality comes out especially in the enthusiasm with which Jung speaks about the secret life that holds sway in the unconscious and in the exuberance with which he claims, "But 'the heart glows'" (CW 9/I § 50)!

"The archetype is ageless and ever-present"[29] (*Letters 2*, p. 394, to Trinick, 15 October 1957). "Our consciousness only imagines that it has lost its gods; in reality they are still there . . ." (*Letters 2*, p. 594, to Serrano,14 September 1960). Primordial experience is possible here and now ("It is one of the self-delusions of our time to think that the spirits do not ride again [. . .]. We are only removed from the place of such happenings, carried away by our madness [*Wir sind nur von dem Ort solchen Geschehens entrückt oder verrückt*]. He who is still there, or has found his way back again, will be smitten by the same experience, now as before"[30]). Jung's vision thus entails the promise that to "live the meaningful life" is still possible here and now, after all.

---

29 As soul truths in the first sense of psychological truth the archetype is indeed ageless, supertemporal. But this does not mean that it is for all times a present reality (second sense of truth).

30 *Letters 2*, p. 612, to Olga von Koenig-Fachsenfeld, 30 November 1960. Transl. modif.

With the idea of the possibility of *Urerfahrungen* (primordial experiences), Jung insists on a fundamentally fulfilled present and on those experiences as present realities. But in the last analysis, the primordial experiences are fake. True, the kind of experiences that Jung has in mind can occur. But they are precisely not *what*, according to his theory, they are supposed to be: Neither primordial nor present realities. They are not primordial, not *immediate* presences (let alone "the highest presence"), because they are fundamentally mediated by Jung's psychology, his theoretical concepts. And for their being taken seriously and being fully appreciated as primordial experiences they depend, conceptually, on his psychological doctrine and, practically, on the work of the whole profession of Jungian analysts to prop them up. Where they are considered to be primordial experiences with all the significance attributed to them by Jung, they are (unwittingly and unadmittedly) *results* of a decidedly modern psychology-industry and despite their emergence from "the unconscious", they are brain children; where, by contrast, outside of Jungian thinking they may happen spontaneously, they tend to go by without much notice and to have the status of no more than curiosities.

As to "present reality" and to the question of "living the meaningful life", we have to say that they remain fundamentally "compartmentalized": They belong to the sequestered compartment of *merely* private, subjective experience and feeling, without relevance to real, objective life as a whole in the modern situation and conversely also without the power to express the modern world's inner logic and truth, thus also without the capability of illumining and ensouling it from within. But if they cannot do that, they can also not bestow meaning on modern life. (Or else one has reduced the notion of "meaning" to that of a particular consumer good or an ideology, a belief-system.)

No matter how we evaluate this "alternative truth" about the ever-present archetype and primordial experiences, one thing is certain, namely, that this whole view amounts to the undoing of the underlying irrevocable experience of Jung's, the experience of the *real* negation. The gift of history is rejected. This view does not directly mean, but in effect amounts to, the fact, that the experienced negation (the "unparalleled impoverishment of symbolism", the "No, evidently we no longer have any myth", the "God is dead" of 1912) is seen as merely an illusion. There is therefore not *really* a change according to this view, a change in substance. The change is no more than a *translocation* of the *same*. We have already seen that what used to be up above as *cosmic* truths has become introjected into people as merely contents of their unconscious. The gods are now "psychic factors", as Jung explicitly stated in *CW* 9i § 50. Irrespective of Jung's notion of the *collective* unconscious, the standpoint that views the gods as "psychic factors" is inevitably personalistic.[31]

This theory, instead of doing justice to the negation experienced by Jung, has the purpose of pasting something over the gap torn open by it and of regressively restoring the status quo ante, while, as an unavoidable tribute to modernity, paying for this benefit the high price of exchanging the gold standard for paper money, or real gods and real truths for something psychic. Instead of "pasting something over the gap" it might be better to say: It tries to fill in the hole between the "no more true" and the not yet of a "true once more" with the regressively restored soul truths now "rediscovered as" "archetypes of the unconscious", claiming them to be untouched by the negation and truly ever-present, truly present realities, so that they are supposed to be in fact able to confer meaning upon real life in modernity—even if only a "meaning" on paper or by credit card and not in gold.

The soul truths have been translocated. But what happens to the negation itself? Having been pushed away from the constitution of life and the order of the world itself as *their* new character of negativity, the negation is unloaded onto people's ego or ego-consciousness as its, consciousness's, blindness, its lack of understanding, its being *entrückt oder verrückt. It* has to shoulder the blame. The negation itself is disposed of as waste or mistake.

Why was it possible for Jung to brush aside the "*real* negation" with his "the 'heart glows'" and the "secret life" that "holds sway in the unconscious", despite the fact that the negation was *his own* deepest experience and starting point, the insight that initiated him, after his separation from Freud, into his truly own thinking? How could the trick of reducing the

---

31 Jung tried of course to escape this trap by simply stating: "But I am not at all convinced that the unconscious mind is merely *my* mind, because the term 'unconscious' means that I am not even conscious of it" (*CW* § 64). But I am not conscious of many or most of the organs and processes in my body either, and yet they are undoubtedly *my* body organs and internal processes. These organs and processes could also be called "collective" in the sense that they are structurally of the same type in all humans. And yet they are exclusively each person's own organs. Jung has never demonstrated that "the unconscious" is truly "collective" or, as we should rather say, "communal" and not each individual's own unconscious (this is true even if it is certainly not identical with what Jung rightly distinguished from it as the "personal unconscious").

negation to a mere translocation from above to "in here" or "down here in us", in the unconscious, successfully eliminate for him the impact of his own devastating experience? The answer must be that all this was only possible because the whole issue of whether the soul truths, the archetypal experiences from out of the unconscious, are "true to me or not" and "express my psychological condition or not" has *in this context* been completely ignored. Jung dug his heels in exclusively in the first sense of truth, so that he is "only concerned with the fact that there is [in one's inner experience, e.g., one's dreams] such an idea, but . . . is not concerned with the question whether such an idea is true or false in any other sense", *including in the sense of true or false to my psychological constitution, my "I cannot" or "I can"*. The mere positive fact of the appearance of archetypal images and the fact of "numinous high-feelings" that may have occurred is taken *abstractly* as proof of their truth. This means that Jung, to the extent that he fosters this described theory, has exclusively eyes for the object or content of consciousness in its isolation, for the "that" and "what" of archetypal experience, while seeming to be oblivious of the subject (the subject of course not in the sense of the empirical I, but as transcendental I, as explicit subjectivity).

Thus, with this exclusive insistence on the fact "that there is such an idea", Jung established himself, so we might say figuratively, among the "gigantic herds of animals" in the Athi Plains, or at least among the group of companions with whom he had first watched them and who—despite their consciously *watching* the herds—nevertheless themselves represented man living "as herd-animal" (*CW* 10 § 160) or "dumb fish". For the herd-animals only go by immediate facts (including inner impulses). *That* Jung who believed in primordial experiences defended in himself the primordial *unio naturalis* and "the profoundest night of non-being" that inevitably prevails in the state of *unio naturalis*. Jung's enormous learnedness, his being an intellectual, and all his psychological reflection belong to the psychic or behavioral level and thus do not contradict the *Urerfahrung*-Jung's *psychological status* of being on the level of "herd-animal" (although we must of course immediately add that this status is only simulated or regressively restored long after the soul's *real* expulsion from it into modernity). This Jung betrayed that other Jung who in view of the animal-herds deliberately had isolated himself from his fellows in order to ritually establish himself with conscious awareness as *modern explicit* subjectivity. That subjectivity has entered the level of *Ge-wußtheit*. As such it is ipso facto only irrevocably distant observer of, be it animal-herds or archetypal dream images, and is logically separated from them by an abyss. It knows that "I cannot" go back because they are "no more true to me". And for it the heart therefore does *not* glow. The enthusiastically celebrated dream of immediacy and present reality is over.

Deferred present, or: Postponement of truth

The passage from which we started out, taken from § 632 of *CW* 18, "The Symbolic Life", is undoubtedly not haunted by that undoing of the experienced negation that we saw at work in the claim of the present-day possibility of "primordial experiences". By explicitly emphasizing that what he had spoken of in the preceding paragraphs (relating to the symbolic life in general and "the secret of the Catholic Church" in particular) "is, alas, to a great extent the past" and by settling in the empty intermission between "no more" and "not yet", the negation is obviously acknowledged and allowed to rule over the present. Nevertheless, we will have to examine if this his respecting the negation does give the negation its full due.

The first thing that strikes us is that with "truth on vacation" and existence in the no-man's land between past and future the negation is taken literally and simply acted out. It is understood as absolute absence of meaning, as nothing, "no truth", "no symbolic life". The negation imparts itself exclusively to the object, the soul truths. *They* are the past. *They* have become obsolete or have been lost. The negation is kept "out there" as the real situation *in which* (or exposed to which) the human subject finds itself. The subject on its part, by contrast, remains *psychologically* unscathed, for although it of course suffers from the effects of this new situation—from the experience of loss, from its all of a sudden being spiritually empty-handed—this suffering affects the subject only emotionally (i.e., psychically), not logically, not in its very nature: Its psychological constitution or definition. The pain felt by the loss and emptiness with which the subject is smitten proves precisely that it, the subject, has remained intact. More than that, precisely in its misery, the ego is even edified; in its suffering it feels *itself* as subject much more strongly than under unproblematic conditions and thus becomes quite intensively aware of itself as ego. If the subject itself were negated, it could not uphold itself so keenly as itself in opposition to the new situation as when the latter causes pain.

The spiritual emptiness of the present in the hole between the "no more" and the "not yet" is only the one aspect of this theory. The other equally important element is the hoped-for "new form" or the "coming guest". To the extent that the present is fully acknowledged as being empty, the negation is indeed given its due, and yet, as we have seen, only in an external sense and only partially so. This assessment of the merely partial acknowledgment is supported and even intensified when we look at the "new form" aspect. For one thing, the longing for a new form alleviates the experience of the emptiness of the present because this one's "now", *in the present*, toying with the idea of "a situation in which that thing becomes true once more" reduces the time of loss to a mere intermission, to whose concept it belongs that it will not last. At the same time, the hope for the new form, as an anticipation and promise of the redeeming future, takes away our total empty-handedness. With this anticipation, there is already now something to hold on to, to rely on, something that carries us through the period of drought and privation. Already now it provides a foretaste of what is to come. The negation is not definitive, does not deprive consciousness completely of its previous possessions.[32] The present may be the time of painful emptiness, but it is overarched by a bridge that leads directly from the no longer to the not yet, from the past form to the new future form, which relativizes this emptiness. Also, by being in possession of the idea of such a bridge, consciousness *has mentally already crossed over* to the other side, leaving behind the present of deprivation, even if not literally and practically, then at least psychologically. *Psychologically* the future is already present, even if only *on credit*.

Very telling is also the wording in the phrase "in which that thing becomes true once more". *That thing*! New form or no, it, that thing, i.e. *the same* as before, will survive, will come again. The soul truths that now are "the past" are nevertheless not really, not once and for all, negated. Despite the explicit admission of the negation, the essential core, "that thing", is precisely being retained *over its having been lost*.[33] We are not, for better

---

32 This formulation is not quite accurate. Strictly speaking it should read: "of what from the modern ego point of view is imagined as consciousness's previous possessions". Premodern man did not *have* or *possess* gods, symbols, Meaning. He lived *in* the objective soul whose property they were. He had to religiously, ritually *serve* the gods.

33 Jung's cited 1912 self-questioning, "'No, evidently we no longer have any myth.' 'But then what is your myth—the myth in which you do live?'" follows the same pattern of

or worse, committed to and stuck in our real present without any knowledge about what the future might bring. We already really know now that it will be "that thing" that becomes true once more, and becomes true really "once more". The negation is fundamentally half-hearted.

By clinging to the idea of "that thing", consciousness does not only *not* allow the negation to destroy the idea of the return of the same, it also paradoxically *preserves that old logical form* that has decidedly been declared to be obsolete and to be in absolute need of being replaced by a new form. The old *form* is ultimately what we could call the general thinking in terms of an "ontology of substance", that form that thinks (imagines) in terms of "things", "persons", "objects", "entities".[34] In other words, the positivity in the *form* of natural thought is rescued. With the idea of "that thing" becoming true "once more" this traditional form of thinking is retained and even, as it were, set in stone forever.

We see this unwitting retention of the old form also quite clearly in how Jung in his old age imagined what the psychological task of the future might be. Jung anticipated the psychological future not only in a general way, in abstracto. He also had more or less concrete ideas, at least in outline, of what could happen and what we could and should do to advance the psychological process in the direction of the future. I am referring here to his idea of "the further development of the myth", that is, the Christian myth. "Our myth has become mute, and gives no answers. The fault lies not in it as it is set down in the Scriptures, but solely in us, who have not developed it further, who, rather, have suppressed any such attempts" (*MDR* p. 332). Essential for this further-development is in Jung's view the correction of the traditional Christian concept of God as exclusively good (as even being the *summum bonum*) and as Light through a splitting of His wholeness into a light and a dark realm, that is, the inclusion into the very idea of God of evil, of Satan (as God's unconscious and repressed shadow and as Christ's

---

retaining the very thing that has just been declared to be lost. "No longer any myth" is countered by "But then what is your myth".

34 When Hillman declared "Personifying" to be one of the major forms of soul-making, he also de facto tried to resurrect, retain, and eternalize this outdated mode of thinking as *the* psychologically valid mode. Of course, in the consulting room personifying, as a form of *psychotherapeutic method* for practical purposes, may be quite helpful and is certainly legitimate. But as such it is a fundamentally sublated, merely psychic, not a psychological way of thinking.

dark brother). This correction adds the Fourth to the Trinity, thus changing it into Quaternity.

It is obvious that this is not really a *new form* at all, neither the new *form of thinking*, a new logical status of consciousness (which would be what is actually required), nor at least a new form *of the inherited Christian myth* in the strict sense. What Jung offers is much rather an entirely different, to some extent even diametrically opposite myth to the traditional Christian myth. Jung *adds* a fundamentally new element to the Christian God-image and thus revolutionizes it. He also radically changes the whole point (aim, goal) of the Christian message, by claiming that God is the one who needs to be redeemed in and through man, redeemed from His unconsciousness. Not Christ is the redeemer of man. No, it is conversely God who is dependent on man (". . . the darkness of the Creator, who needs man to illuminate His creation", *Letters 2*, p. 597, to Serrano, 14 September 1960). In other words, we get a "new *myth*", not a new *form*. What is new is the content, the substance.

The contents that in Jung's vision are to be added to the Trinitarian God-image to change it into a Quaternity are Evil and the Feminine. Both appear as personifications: Satan and the Virgin Mary (cf. Jung's exorbitant praise of the 1950 Roman-Catholic dogma *Assumptio Mariae*). Both the abstract concepts of "evil" and "the feminine" (as *elements* or *components* of wholeness) and their personifications betray the "old form", what I above called the conventional thinking in terms of entities or of the ontology of substance. It obviously prevails here, too.

Furthermore, the addition of new "information" to consciousness, regardless of whether it is the discovery of bacteria and viruses to scientific knowledge or "Evil" to the God-image, may no doubt have great practical consequences, but does not in itself amount to a *form* change of consciousness. The layout of journals may stay the same even if revolutionarily new ideas are published in them. In order to be able to hold on to the old idea of God as something he possessed and to protect it against the already experienced real negation (that is, against its obsolescence), Jung had to regressively construe "new form" as merely meaning added content, thus only seemingly complying with his need for a new form.

We can see this same old style of thinking confirmed once more when we take another aspect into consideration. The change envisioned by Jung is to happen in and to the nature of God. The problem with this particular change is not so much the resulting ambivalence and split[35] of the God-image. No, what is psychologically the real problem is that the idea or image of "God" and thus of "substance", of an "entity" or "person" as the *bearer* of qualities or attributes (e.g., good and evil, masculine and the feminine), is held on to, in other words, it is the style of representational or pictorial thinking, of *Vorstellung*, which, in the way it imagines, inevitably merely *acts out* the envisioned change *out there* on the *level of object* or *content of conscious- ness*, rather than to *erinnern* (inwardize) it. The object, here God, has to change. This thinking remains external. Consciousness itself, by contrast, that is, its logical form, is not affected.

Jung's great discovery in the Athi Plains of the *psychological* duality of being and knownness (*Ge-wußtheit*), of merely lived (acted-out) life and explicit subjectivity, is thus disregarded, if not lost. The subject (explicit subjectivity) drops out of this theory. With the essential change being shoved off onto the object or content, on the one hand, and pushed off into the distance of the future ("the coming guest", the promise of the "new form", the expected "true once more"), on the other hand, the I is simply left out of consideration and can thus *remain the same* (untouched in its form of constitution). The only change is that it has lost the *present reality* of meaning, of the soul-truths.

Or we could express the same the other way around and say that for being able to escape the necessity of having to undergo a revolutionizing change of the logical form in his *thinking*, in the very heart of subjectivity itself, Jung paid the price of condemning the present to being nothing but a truth-less, soul-less intermission ("concretistic negation")—which in the last analysis amounts to no less than *psychological* suicide—and of having the desperately needed "new form" only on credit, as a postponed future, if not a phantom. By deliberately renouncing the soul's fulfillment and com- mitting itself to that empty, soul-less present, the I keeps itself free to retain *itself* in the form of its old mythologizing, personifying, ontologizing, pictorially-thinking—in that very form that has already been emphatically recognized as *not* being able to express "my psychological condition". The negation, which is exclusively directed against the psychological truth and the fulfillment of the present, can therefore not hit the I, penetrate it, and

---

35 On the splitting of God's wholeness, on the "metaphysical split" in Christianity, and "the split God" see *MDR* p. 333f. and, of course, "Answer to Job".

revolutionize *its* form. The subject functions only as the one who theorizes *about* the change in the nature of God in the future (the object of thinking) and thus remains uninvolved and, as far as its form and logical constitution is concerned, unchanged. But what does "new form" mean, if not that everything, the form of the world, of existence, of subject and object, that is to say, the logical status of consciousness, is "trans-formed"?

But is my analysis not an unfair description of Jung's late thinking? After all, old man Jung precisely stressed that the fault lies not in the Christian myth, but solely in us, who have not developed it further. So he assigns precisely to us the task of developing it further and, fundamentally more than that, of ourselves becoming the place of God's "continuing incarnation" (*CW* 11 § 746). "[T]the uniting of his [God's] antinomy must take place in man" (§ 747). Only in him, in man's becoming conscious of the great problem of Evil and the Shadow, is He redeemed of His unconsciousness. In other words, the subject is essentially involved in Jung's vision of the psychological future.

But of course, what we see here—in addition to the fact that consciousness would only become conscious of those *contents* and not itself acquire a new form—is precisely only that vision's *view of* the role that the subject has to play, that is to say, the subject functions here only as the object that Jung thinks *about*. It is precisely not man *as subject* in the strict sense, as explicit *subjectivity* and transcendental I, who is supposed to be the place of this momentous transformation process of God, but man as empirical *individuals*, that is, as *people*. In other words, the very thought of the incarnation of God in man (as a thought of an *interiorization*) remains itself fundamentally external. It is a theological or theosophic theory because it is a theory about the relation between God and man, both understood literally. But psychology knows nothing about "God" and "man", as I pointed out above. Its topic is exclusively the soul's logical life.

What as *psychological* truth would have to take place on the strictly logical level is reductively brought down to the level of a temporal and as such contingent, haphazard event. It is imagined empirically, naturalistically, and, above all, practically: A person's becoming aware of Evil and the Feminine as absolutely essential in "metaphysical" regards is *structurally* not unlike one's becoming aware of the importance of healthy food for one's physical well-being. Just as health freaks preach as ego's and to the ego, so Jung with his theosophic theory speaks as ego, propounds an ego program and appeals to the ego in us. No doubt, his 1938 statement, "I cannot. It is no more true to me; it does not express my psychological condition", was a psychological insight. His earlier realization about the role of consciousness and explicit subjectivity was also a psychological insight. His theosophy is not. It is a human *project*: (1) There is an ego will behind it. (2) It operates with a moral blame ("The fault lies . . . solely in us who have not developed it further") and a moral exhortation, a "should" ("The further development of the myth should probably begin with . . ."[36]). (3) Psychological changes are the soul's doing, not our work. And they cannot be anticipated, ideologically spelled out beforehand, but only *noted* after the fact, as changes that happened behind our backs. The tense of psychology is the perfect, not the future. We are not doers, technicians, social engineers, world saviors, but concerned with what *is* because it has already happened.

Real negation: Truth as ever-present

No evasion or compensation

When Jung had to state that the traditional soul truths he had referred to are "the past" and "we cannot turn the wheel backwards", I called this an insight into a *"real* negation", "real" negation (in contradistinction to merely mental negations, our subjective denials of statements or ideas) because it is one which is objectively brought by the history of the soul and to which the subject is merely exposed. In the previous chapters we were concerned with the question how this experienced real negation was honored by Jung and to what extent it entered into his theorizing. We had to realize that despite his outspoken acknowledgment Jung's actual dealing with his own experience of this negation did not *really* give it its due. He did not abide by it, allow it to come home to itself (and home to his own consciousness) and thus to fulfill itself. Jung partly counterfactually rescued the old soul-truths from their own negation as the gods now *rediscovered* "as psychic factors, that is, as archetypes of the unconscious", and partly he held the effects of the negation at bay through literalizing it, concretistically acting it out, or pushing it off onto an object, or through consoling himself with the hope of a return of the lost in new form in an indefinite future. This means that what in one sense is indeed the "real negation" was not permitted to *be* a *real* negation in the altered sense of "full-fledged" or *"psychological* negation".

---

36 *Erinnerungen* p. 335. My transl., cf. *MDR* p. 333.

Much the same applies to Jung's declared absolute need of a "new form" that was concomitant with the experience of the loss of symbols. He did not really advance to what "new *form*" means and requires. So we now have to ask what "the *real* negation" in the altered sense would be and how it would be reflected in psychological theory if this theory relentlessly abided by its own experience of and acquired insight into it.

For the real negation to *be*, all attempts at evasion and circumvention are of course out of the question. We cannot come up with the idea of an alternative truth through the trick of translocating the old soul truths from the public sphere of generality, where they would immediately come under fire from the negation, and of safely encapsulating them as "psychic factors" in the private "inner". We can also not resort to an imaginal escape from the scorched earth of the present into a hope for a new fulfilling future. Rather, we have to stay put and let the negation relentlessly do its thing. No exit, no escape, no toying with hope nor with surrogates. This is the sine qua non of the negation's being able to come home to itself and home to us. *No coming guest.* Why? Because the experienced negation of the traditional symbolism *is itself* the arrival of the guest or the guest *that has already arrived.* It is not a wrong condition to be corrected, a wound to be healed, a problem to be overcome.

Negation not of contents, but of the structure of consciousness

This needs a few words of explanation. The first observation is that the negation we are here concerned with is not a specific one that merely negates this or that particular soul truth, such as "the miracle of the Mass", or a number of soul truths that can be replaced by others. No, the "no more true to me" applies to the entirety of the traditional soul truths, the symbolism embodied in myth, religions, rituals, and metaphysics. It is the soul's wholesale negation of its own truths as they used to be known in all their variety. That is to say, the negation is not one of semantic *contents*, but a structural one, the negation of a whole logical status of consciousness. (Jung intuited this when he interpreted it as the Fall of the stars and a transition to "an age in which the spirit is no longer up above but down below", namely in the unconscious, in the human psyche. But this interpretation, as radical as it attempts to be, also reveals that Jung was not radical enough. He still remained on the semantic level, within the *cosmic* space of the imagination, and merely conceived of the psychological revolution as a removal within the same old cosmic space from one place to another, from up above to down below or in here, when what was actually required by the correctly observed radical change was the insight that the sphere of the mythic imagination and the thinking in terms of space and entities or figures in space had *psychologically* altogether been left behind.)

The necessity of the interpretation of the change as a structural one is highlighted when we secondly consider what it means that Jung can say: "I know it is the truth", but it "is no more true to me". When Christianity emerged and was confronted with the preceding pagan religions it negated the old gods by declaring them to be false gods, idols of human making. By the same token, the Enlightenment declared the belief in witches and numerous other religious ideas as superstitions. In both cases, the negation attacks the semantic contents and throws them into the wastebin of history. But this is precisely what Jung is not doing. The semantic content, the phenomenon of the Mass (and by extension all traditional soul truths) remains intact and is unreservedly honored as "the truth", still now! Nothing is wrong with it. It is not illusionary, superstitious, merely a figment of the mind of former ignorant people. But despite being perfectly alright, "it is no more true to me". This discrepancy clearly shows that the negation negates the symbolic, imaginal, mythological, ritual, archetypal *form as such* and not the phenomena themselves as semantic contents, not the individual symbols or archetypal images or ritual practices. The entire *level* of symbolism and semantic contents is recognized as psychologically outdated, which implies that the soul has reached and now irrevocably lives on a fundamentally new level, which makes the whole change a structural or logical one. This is why Jung also introduced here the notion of form: "I need a new form", even if de facto, in his further theorizing, he regressively tried to deal with the form-problem, in a few different ways, as if it were a semantic one and could simply be taken care of on the semantic or content level.

A third point to be made is that in keeping with what I just said the negation is not a judgment or insight by the human mind. It is not intellectual, not about whether something is true or false, reasonable or not. The negation does not attack the old soul truths, is not directed against *them*. It is not even interested in or concerned with the contents. On the contrary, it is only concerned with the "I cannot", with "my psychological condition". Or, to put it the other way around, this real condition *is* the negation, and the negation on its part is simply the expression of the truth of this psychological condition. Jung finds himself really and irrevocably in a new psychological condition. Without his own doing and even, it seems, against his own preferences, he has, for better or worse, been catapulted into a new logical constitution that is absolutely incompatible with the old symbols. This new logical constitution expresses itself as "It is no more true to me", that is to say, as the objective rejection of, and pushing off from, the symbolic mode as such and thus as *its* self-discrimination from *them* in order to come into its own. That is to say, the negation is the very character *of the new "psychological condition"*. It is not the *act* of negating, but the logical *form* of negativity. Negativity is what the new psychological condition itself is about. It is the self-manifestation of the latter's own essence.

Autonomous negation

The negation is *the message*! As such it is precious. It IS *the guest* and as guest brings *itself*—itself as negation or better negativity. The negation IS itself the very "new form" that Jung felt he desperately needed and looked out for to come in the future, and it is the new form as the new *present reality* of the soul's truth. But Jung experiences and misconstrues the "I cannot" merely as the negation *of the old soul truths*, as *their* loss, because he has only eyes for the semantic contents, the symbolism, the archetypal images and *not* for his "psychological condition" as his new truth.

As long as the soul was experienced in myth, symbolism, ritual, and imaginal form in general, it was still exiled, appearing only in external form, in various semantic guises. The Greek god Zeus was known to appear literally in numerous guises, as bull, swan, eagle, rain of gold, Amphitryon, etc. To Semele, and upon her own insistence, however, he appeared not in one of his guises, but in his true form, his absolute, pure form as lightning. In a somewhat analogous way we could say that in "the guest" the soul comes to Jung and shows itself in its pure form, in its truth: As absolute negativity. The new present reality does not have the form of guises: contents, images, substances. It has the form of form.

What from the experiencing ego's point of view that clings to the symbols or the imaginal is experienced as man's having been born (and thus expelled) out of the soul, which is tantamount to his having lost the entire traditional mythic symbolism and the meaning it used to provide for human life, from the soul's point of view looks very different. For the soul, it is she herself who has been born (expelled) out of herself, but this her birth and expulsion is precisely the soul's coming home to herself from her exile for the first time, home into her true form.

The point that the negation is the message is essential, which is why I want to circumambulate it a little more. If the negation is the message, this confirms my point that negation is here not a judgment. Negation does here not mean a logical operation or mental act performed on something else, some content or whatever. It is not a logical instrument (Symbolic Logic speaks of "functors") for denying something. Its purpose is not to undo the old soul truths. It has no stake in them. It has simply left them behind.

It would likewise be a crucial mistake to see in the experienced "*real negation*" a destructive fate that befell the soul truths as a mishap, comparable perhaps to tsunamis that wash away whole villages, or to volcanos that bury them under lava and ashes. Instead of such *external* negations inflicted on the traditional symbolism, the negation we are concerned with is *autonomous, self-referential and complete in itself*. It has come fully home to itself as something in its own right; it is inwardized into itself. This is what makes it the *real* negation (in the altered sense). The new psychological condition in which Jung finds himself has the character of being in itself negative, having left behind the positivity of semantic content. It is the logical status *of* logical form, *of* syntax.

Much the same can be said about "form". The soul has objectively moved Jung, as I indicated, to the form *of form*, that is, not the form *of* something, of some content, but to form as such, form that is its own "content", as it were. Jung's phrase, "the truth in a form in which I cannot accept it any more" does not only (or rather not at all) amount to the fact that the symbols and contents are being lost (while possibly nevertheless at a later point returning once more in altered form). It much rather means that such a thing as symbol or myth, indeed the *very form* of symbol or myth, has become impossible (if by "symbol" or "myth" or "imaginal content" we mean something that immediately enables us to "live the meaningful life" or that at least contributes to it).

However, when Jung subjectively felt that he needed "*a* new form", this "*a*" shows that for his subjective consciousness there is a variety of forms, that "form" is still external to what it is the form of (i.e., "form" as the form *of* something), and that he stayed on the semantic level wanting to rescue it after its already experienced definitive obsolescence. His thinking was not really up to and did precisely not do justice to the new psychological condition that was already his own and that he himself had discovered as the reason for the old soul truths' no longer being true to him. The new form he hoped for was no more than the form in which, as he put it, "*that thing*" would have become true once more. But what, instead of "*a new form*", was really required by his new psychological condition was that "form" comes home to itself and as such is form in the singular. Only the form that is fully inwardized into itself, fully autonomous, and ipso facto has become in itself negative (because of not being the form *of* some positive content) would be that form that Jung really needed.

We now have to see what the consequences of the new status reached are. The guest is already here: *As* Jung's "psychological condition", *as* his "I cannot". As such he is Janus-faced. As the "I cannot" he assigns, on the one hand, the status of "historical presence in Mnemosyne" to the miracle of the Mass (as well as to "the imaginal" as a whole), while on the other hand as "the new form" he is the new "present reality". First I will turn to the consequences that the status of reflectedness and the form of form has for the inherited symbolism, such as the Mass, and only thereafter look at the effects on the form of the development of present-day reality.

The historical presence of the past

Jung said, "I cannot experience the miracle of the Mass; I know too much about it". It is of course not knowledge that prevents him from experiencing the miracle of the Mass (knowledge in the sense of all the pieces of information and insights which Jung had acquired about the Mass). There have been enough learned Catholics with extensive knowledge about the Mass in the long history of the Catholic Church for whom this knowledge was not an obstacle in the least. Rather, what "I know too much" refers to is that Jung finds himself thrown onto the level of *reflection*, of knownness (*Ge-wußtheit*) and explicit subjectivity. (Just as in the case of "form" and "negation", "reflection" is here a singular; it does not refer to all the various empirical acts of reflection performed by humans).

The *immediacy* of experience that existed "in the fold" or in the status of the *unio naturalis* is over, which also means that the for any real rituals indispensable "suggestive power of primordial images" (*CW* 7 § 269) has been lost, or rather, with the loss of immediacy the human subject cannot be reached by this suggestive power. From this advanced standpoint of reflection Jung can no more than look back upon the Mass as "the past" and think *about* it, *understand* it,[37] imagine it, perhaps empathize it, but he cannot psychologically get truly *into* it as his present reality, the way people on previous levels of consciousness—with or without knowledge—were able to, without the least problem. The Mass cannot become his present reality. Jung is irrevocably cut off. This is why he stresses: "We cannot turn the wheel backwards" and, repeatedly and emphatically, "I cannot". Understanding and emotional feeling are the mediated, reflected relation to ritual and symbol. They are already on the other shore, the ego's standpoint. The Mass, just as any other ritual, could only provide fulfilling Meaning for people as long as it was performed and participated in *without* understanding or emotion, when it worked exclusively *ex opere operato*, that is, as long as the standpoint was immediately the sober one of the *objective soul*.

Jung also said about the miracle of the Mass (and by implication about the traditional symbolism and the psychologically relevant semantic contents in general): "I know it is the truth". Despite being "the past", "no more true to me", and thus obsolete because of no longer expressing his psychological condition, it IS nevertheless still THE truth! For Jung it is precisely not the mere belief or illusion or superstition of former ages. This means that what is rendered obsolete is not its truth, or the truth of the symbols, the archetypal images, and semantic contents in general. And conversely, the "IS" indicates that this truth *is* a *present* one. But if that is so, what then is that which is negated by Jung's psychological condition? What precisely is no more true to him? The answer must be: What the symbolism has lost is its immediacy, its immediate validity for Jung as truly modern man and not its truth; what it has lost is merely its status as a "present *reality*", its

---

37 It was Jung's view that our *understanding* of dream images, symbols, myths, etc. is indispensable. For this purpose he introduced the method of amplification. Cf. his comment about his not finishing the *Red Book*: "Therefore I gave up this estheticizing tendency in good time, in favor of a rigorous process of *understanding*" (*MDR* p. 188). And at the end of the following paragraph (*Erinnerungen* p. 192, omitted in *MDR*) he adds: "In order to free oneself from the tyranny of unconscious presuppositions both are needed: fulfillment of the intellectual as well as the ethical obligation" (my transl.). The lack of understanding is for him even the cause of the death of the gods and symbols: "The gods of Greece and Rome perished from the same disease as did our Christian symbols: people discovered then, as today, that they had no thoughts on the subject [*daß sie sich nichts darunter gedacht hatten*, i.e., that they did not know what they, the gods, were about or what they mean]". I think that this is not the cause of the death of gods, but the fact that Jung thought so shows the importance of "understanding" in his psychology.

immediate relevance for his "living the meaningful life" and its being the expression of the unquestionable cosmic truth (the stars, trees, rivers and most natural phenomena used to be gods, and all cultic life was concerned with this divine truth of the real world).

Only now that the symbols and archetypal images exist *as* "the past" (as Jung had said), and only if their pastness remains *abstractly* the past, has it become possible to eternalize them as "*the* imaginal" in Hillman's sense: As on principle cleansed of all temporality and as to be approached strictly aesthetically, under imaginal psychology's category of "beauty", or in Jung's sense as "archetypes" that are "ageless and ever-present". As atemporal and "ever-present", the archetypes and "the imaginal" are fundamentally abstract concepts.

But the symbols' pastness ("no-more-true-to-me-ness") does not have to be taken abstractly. Then their pastness turns their still remaining presence into a "*historical* presence". As a historical presence it is a presence only in Mnemosyne.[38] It is the presence that has its own negation integrated into itself; it has obsolescence, renouncement, its own having been lost, *within* itself, so that it is not threatened by them. But conversely, as "historical presence", all the precious symbols and images of the past do not need to be disposed of. They remain precious, however precious no longer directly for the *soul*, but only for *psychology*, the already in itself *reflected* soul, the soul as consciously thinking one. While not providing Meaning (in the singular), i.e., the possibility of living "the meaningful life", they are a treasury of deep meanings in the plural which are *present* today. They can be cherished as our psychological heritage. They enlighten us about who we are by showing us how we psychologically became what and where we are. There is much to ponder in them.

Since in Mnemosyne the images are in the status of "*historical* presence", the mind can—in contrast to "*the* [abstract, atemporal] imaginal"—be very conscious of the concrete historical-cultural setting to which the diverse images belong and of their historical evolvement. However, even despite such a decided attention to the specific historical locus of the various images and ideas—what is "in Mnemosyne" is, as "historical *presence*", ipso facto *objectively* simultaneous. It is this simultaneity that can seduce

---

38 Apropos Mnemosyne we remember Jung's dream, cited above, in which his father is the custodian of sarcophagi in a crypt.

psychological consciousness, as above all in Hillman's case, to exclude the aspect of their historicity in favor of a purely aesthetic conception.

The "I cannot" is the self-display of "the guest". But if the guest shows himself as the "I cannot", if the guest is the negation or negativity, he is nothing imaginal: Not a being, figure, or person, just as "the message" is not a literal message in the sense of some semantic idea, exhortation, or advice. Both are strictly logical, abstract, the form of the constitution or logical status of the "psychological condition", namely, the status of absolute negativity.

After having seen what the new "psychological condition" means for or does to the inherited symbolism, I now turn to the second aspect, the effects it has on present-day reality.

The new present reality

If the guest is already here, if "the new form" (not "*a* new form") is already real in Jung's psychological condition, it follows that truth is not on vacation. *Malgré lui*, Jung does in truth *not* live in the empty hole between "no more" and "not yet". He is wrong to speak of our time as of "our benighted present" (*Letters 2*, p. 396, to Trinick, 15 Oct. 1957), at least if this verdict meant as a *psychological* one. The idea of the idle, truth-less intermission can now be seen as the result of the defensive refusal to receive the *real* guest, a refusal caused by the egoic and nostalgic (or regressive) insistence that truth must have the same old semantic form to which we have been accustomed ("I must have a situation in which that thing becomes true once more"). Jung's focus stayed fixated on archetypal or imaginal contents, he looked out for *their* coming in such a "new" form that would be acceptable to his psychological condition, *instead of examining this psychological condition itself* that was already there, with a view to seeing in detail what *it* in fact expressed, and instead of allowing himself to be taught by *it* about his already prevailing truth. The very point of his "I cannot" (as the negation coming from his psychological condition) is obviously the destruction of any "once more". There *is* nothing to be looked out and hoped for: Because the new present reality and highest presence is already present.

On the other hand we on our part must not reject and denounce the idea of "truth is on vacation" as totally false. No, it is itself true. "On vacation" is simply the expression for the *not acknowledged*, but correctly apperceived new form of truth: For truth in the present-day form of absolute negativity.

Certainly, the "I cannot", the experienced negation, amounts to a loss. It has deprived Jung of something. But the negation did not leave an empty hole because it also *brought* something: It brought *itself*. The negation or better negativity as the very "new form" that Jung felt he desperately needed (but postponed into the future) is the new *present reality* of the soul's truth. Therefore no present-lessness. The present is fulfilled as always. Even if what it is fulfilled by is this negativity and status of reflection as the new truth. Truth and soul are always with us. Continuously. Truth is what uninterruptedly accompanies the process of life, but what, as we have seen, may undergo fundamental, at times radical form changes ("metamorphoses"[39]), such as, with the transition to modernity, from the semantic to syntax or the form of form. There is no gap between past and future. The nihilistic interpretation of the present is psychologically illusionary (and, as I pointed out, a defense).

If the guest is already here, namely, precisely *as* Jung's own "psychological condition", *as* his "I cannot", sort of as his own nature as truly modern man, then the question arises why he is nevertheless "guest" and in this sense a stranger to Jung? One would expect that one's own psychological constitution is intimately one's own, that it is even identical with oneself. That his own psychological constitution is nevertheless "guest" can only mean that his own psychological condition is psychologically not really, not fully his own condition, or more exactly: It is only implicitly his own. The guest who is already in his house also needs to be officially received and honored. Psychologically it is never enough that the truth factually exists and factually rules over consciousness, so to speak from behind. It must also be actively made explicit. As the new truth his "psychological condition" wants to be integrated into consciousness and interiorized into itself. It wants to come fully home to Jung and be consciously appropriated *as his own*, by becoming his actual style of thinking, feeling, and experiencing the world. It wants to overcome his *thinking* in terms of the "ontology of substance", his clinging to the style of representational (pictorial) thinking, and his exclusive devotion to the semantics of the imaginal, and instead

---

39 Jung spoke repeatedly of the "metamorphosis of the gods". See my "Jung's Idea of a Metamorphosis of the Gods and the History of the Soul", in: W.G., *The Soul Always Thinks* = W.G., Collected English Papers, vol. 4 (New Orleans, LA: Spring Journal Books, 2010), now: London and New York (Routledge) 2020, pp. 531–562.

initiate consciousness into the *form of form*, into *reflectedness, absolute relationality*, syntax, logos and "concept".

That the new form is really the new present reality can perhaps best be seen from the fact that we are now witnessing the technical fabrication and objective representation of autonomous "reflectedness". I am thinking here of Google Earth and Google Maps, of the billions of photos and moving pictures that exist of all types of phenomena in the world, from outer space scenes to ocean ground sights and to microscopic details, and of the obsessive, almost indiscriminate picture-taking by tourists of whatever site they are confronted with; of the compulsion to shoot selfies and post them as well as all sorts of personal details "out there" on Facebook; of the widespread routine observation of public places by surveillance cameras, the use of automatized face recognition, of body scanners, earth observation from satellites, spy software, key logging software; of the digital storage of "all" human knowledge and incredible masses of information outside the actively knowing mind (Wikipedia as only one example); of the recordedness of all email traffic, all internet use, individuals' shopping preferences, telephone calls, airplane passenger data, financial transactions via banks or credit card, and so on. All this is, apart from the diverse subjective and conscious intentions that people, firms, and institutions may have with these recordings, from a soul point of view objectively in the service of the establishment of objective *Ge-wußtheit*. This is (part of) the soul's new present reality.

That "reflectedness" is the soul's new logical status may also be confirmed *ex negativo* by the extremely powerful tendency in today's society to dope oneself. I am not only referring to alcohol and literal drugs, but also to the enormous role that entertainment, television, computer games, noise (constant accompaniment by often deafening music), the craving for sensations and heightened emotionality, the cult of the trivial through one's staying in ceaseless mobile phone contact with others on "what one just now happens to be doing", the love of "chats" in "chatrooms" and of the need to undo serious topics by exposing them to the shallowness of talk-show discussions, the popularity of "spirituality" in all its variety, furthermore the attractiveness nowadays of suicide bombings and shooting massacres.[40]

---

40 How very symptomatic and thus revealing that a punk rock band could give itself in our age the name "Random Killing"!

All this can psychologically be seen as the completely unconsciously attempted flight out of the actually prevailing reflectedness, a flight partly into the simulation of pre-reflected containment and immediacy (back into the "fold"), partly into the absolutely perverse form of a *momentary* "living the meaningful life" (through the existential act of breaking the absolute taboo by random killing and through unreservedly sacrificing one's life in suicide attacks). The simulation-character in the one case and the perversity in the other expose these tendencies (underneath their possible particular subjective conscious or ideological motivations) as absurd regressive reaction-formations to reflectedness as the already real objective status of consciousness.

In closing, I have to point to and dispel a likely misunderstanding produced by my diction and apologize for the latter. When using Jung's metaphor of "the guest" and speaking of the necessity of honoring this guest by integrating the negation into consciousness, even more so when charging Jung with a defensive or regressive reaction to his experience of the negation, all this suggests a subjective, egoic, personalistic point of view: As if the guest were coming *to Jung*, *to us*, and as if it were *Jung's* or *our* task to integrate the negation into consciousness or his or our failing in this task. But psychology has no stake in "the relations between the ego and the unconscious", in the relations between human being (empirical man, "ego-personality") and soul, which would be a totally wrong pairing. For psychology it is the *soul* that is coming as the guest to *itself*, and not we but it, the soul, needs to integrate its own new form of negativity into *itself*, into *its* form of constitution so as to *really, explicitly* attain that new logical status that factually is already its own. We must not attach so much importance to ourselves and not see ourselves as the focus. As pointed out earlier, psychology is not concerned with "man" and "people" in the first place; they are not possible psychological concepts. We and our consciousness are merely the stage where alone this process of the objective soul can take place. Or we are the material in or through which alone it can become real and explicit—become real and explicit *to the extent that* this *empirical* and thus (in different persons always to different degrees and in different ways) *inept* material allows. "Real" and "explicit" means in our particular context: Real as the *real* negation (in the altered sense).

Chapter 4

Soul and world[1]

If psychology wants to establish itself as a discipline of interiority it must show that it is capable of accounting for external reality, for the "world", *in terms of its own standpoint of interiority*. For if it simply turns its back on the outer, then the inner lies just as much *outside* the outer as the outer outside the inner, which has the unpleasant consequence that ultimately the logic of externality rules over both, even over our so-called interiority. Hillman taught us to look at the world as the vale of soul-making. But as the vale—and thus vessel—of our soul-making and interiorizing, the world is confirmed to be external to soul. The externality of the world as a given out there around us seems to be inescapable.[2]

1 This paper was written in January 2012 and presented as Keynote Address at the 1st Conference of The International Society for Psychology as the Discipline of Interiority, in Berlin, 23–25 July 2012.
2 Some years later Hillman himself found his earlier idea of the world as the vale of soul-making inadequate, saying it "still focuses on one's personal destiny. . . . The exterior world's value is simply utilitarian, for the sake of soul-making. It provides obstacles, pitfalls, monsters to be met in order to make one's interior soul". "It actually neglects the world, even while finding a soul use for it" (James Hillman and Michael Ventura, *We've Had a Hundred Years of Psychotherapy—And the World is Getting Worse*, San Francisco [Harper] 1992, p. 51). Perhaps Hillman is here a bit unfair to this own earlier idea. For what this earlier idea, coming from the Romantics, probably implies is an intimate connection between world and soul. The world must be soulful to begin with if it can serve as the vale of soul-making, and "vale" does not really suggest a hostile exterior reality full of obstacles, nor a world that provides merely the raw material for our utilitarian exploitative soul-making. "Vale" could much rather imply a hugging reception. Hillman's later interpretation of his own concept is probably a somewhat soulless one so that he misses a potential that this idea may have had without its already having been able to realize it explicitly in itself. Nevertheless, as I pointed out, the notion of a receptacle does uphold the externality of the world. And interestingly enough, Hillman's move beyond "the world as vale of soul-making" to the fully developed idea of the *anima mundi* and to the soul in things certainly translocates the soul from "in us" to the real world outside, but ipso facto it also unwittingly maintains the very "split between inner and outer" that he

DOI: 10.4324/9781003611400-5

Contourless wall of Otherness?

According to the myth theory developed by an influential German philoso-phy professor of the last century, Hans Blumenberg, this externality pre-vailed, even in an extreme sense, already in the primordial condition of mankind.[3] For Blumenberg the initial condition was what he calls an "abso-lutism of reality", a state of reality's overwhelming superiority and total alienness. Therefore at this stage the world could not be called a "world" in the proper sense at all, because, being totally uncanny and radically unfa-miliar, it was in truth the opposite of "world", namely "chaos". The reality that Man (according to this theory) was confronted with was Chaos because it was, without exception, hostile and appeared as a shapeless, contour-less wall of Otherness. Reality as such caused horror and fright. And here, according to Blumenberg's theory, myth came in. Myth was fundamentally a strategy to enable Man to gain a distance from a primordial horror, to depotentiate the terrifying power of reality and thus to assert himself vis-à-vis it by *naming* the unknown and uncanny and by telling stories about it. Story-telling made Man forget what was terrifying, and by giving a name to the powers feared, it became possible to invoke and exorcize them. In this way the function and achievement of myth was to make the utterly unfa-miliar familiar for Man and to satisfy Man's elemental need for a feeling of trust and confidence in the world.[4]

---

criticized on the very same page. Hillman's whole later emphasis on *aisthesis* and the face of things obviously operates within the despised subject-object relation. His attempted *direct* access to the things of the world does not remedy the problem that he wanted to leave behind (concerning his wish to leave this split cf. the following statement: "This insight from Keats . . . also separated me from my classical colleagues who, I believe never really left the Cartesian split between inner and outer . . .", *ibid.*).

3 Hans Blumenberg, *Arbeit am Mythos*, Frankfurt/Main 1979.

4 Considering this description of the role of myth we could be put in mind of the early C.G. Jung's much-cited dictum, "The psyche creates reality every day. The only expression I can use for this activity is *fantasy*" (*CW* 6 § 78), despite the fact that in this statement Jung does not speak of the earliest prehistoric times, but of a "continu-ally creative act" going on "every day". But what his idea and Blumenberg's view have in common is that what we call "world" is the result of a human psychic production vis-à-vis, and projected upon, a given utterly external reality. Blumenberg's shapeless, contourless wall of Otherness finds its less outspoken equivalent in the late Jung's con-viction that "The psyche cannot leap beyond itself. We cannot see beyond the psyche. / Science is tacitly convinced that a non-psychic, transcendent object exists" (*MDR* p. 350f.) and, furthermore, "We are in truth so wrapped about by psychic images that we cannot penetrate at all to the essence of things external to ourselves" (*CW* 8 § 680). For Jung, too, the "things external to ourselves" are, strictly speaking, not yet distinct

I question this thesis of the absolute otherness of reality.[5] Let us begin by looking at the situation of plants and animals. *Logically* (although of course not necessarily in empirical reality[6]) plants and animals are perfectly adapted to their environment, each according to its kind. *They* do not have to adapt to an antecedently given, and as such radically external, reality. No, they are from the outset born into this adaptedness. There is a priori a harmonious correspondence between the various species and their particular habitat. They are made for each other, in a similar way that the sun and the eye are made for each other, as Plotinus said. The correspondence comes first, and the different species and their respective habitats are moments within this correspondence. We cannot even think of animals or plants *in isolation from* their habitat. Such an abstract animal or plant species could

---

and formed things at all (they become this precisely only through the creative act of the psychic faculty of fantasy). What is "external to ourselves" is absolutely unknown and even on principle inaccessible to us and in this sense similar to Blumenberg's shapeless wall of Otherness.

5 One might think that Jung's dictum that "Individuation does not exclude the world, but encompasses it" (*CW* 8 § 432, transl. modif.) presented precisely an approach to the world from the standpoint of interiority. The problem with this statement is of course that it is merely an assertion. It is easy to *claim* the interiority of the external world in the individuating soul. But what would be needed is a demonstration *how* individuation can encompass the world and *that* this is in fact the case. Another idea from within our Jungian tradition that we could also come to think of as providing an answer to how external reality might be viewed in terms of the standpoint of interiority is Jung's late conception of the *unus mundus*, of an ultimate oneness of psyche and matter and thus of psychology and physics. However, as far as our question about true interiority is concerned, this idea has to be ruled out from the outset, for four reasons. First, it has the status of a mere postulate or dogmatic speculative idea and thus amounts to no more than a vague possibility. Taking its psychological function for modern Man into account, we could perhaps even say that it amounts to a salvational promise for the healing of modern Man's suffering from the feeling of alienation and uneasiness, a promise which merely appears in the guise of a theoretical claim. Secondly, much like scientific statements it is conceived from and confirms the standpoint of an outside observer high above both psyche and physical reality and is thus of no use for a discipline of interiority. Thirdly, precisely by responding to the need for a unification of the opposites, the thesis of the *unus mundus*, contrary to its intended purpose, emphasizes their really prevailing duality and opposition. And fourthly, Jung's move seems regressive (in a theoretical, not a personal clinical sense) because on a merely semantic level it goes back to an alleged deep natural level of unity that the human mind and soul have irrevocably overcome, rather than teaching us how to syntactically learn to in actuality think about reality in a not dissociating way.

6 This also implies that all my statements in the following about animals and the human animal refer only to the species or genus, not to individuals.

not exist. The smallest unit is the living species and its habitat as a pair. Life is not only what goes on within the abstract organism; life IS within itself the *relation* between itself *and* the habitat.[7]

In principle, animals and plants are always already at home in their habitat. The latter is familiar to them. Even their enemies and what they must fear are not totally alien but known from the outset. What we call "environment" is for them not something absolutely "other" but rather an integral part of their own being-alive. Their environment could perhaps even be imagined as an extension of their body, as their own "extremities". No division. No vis-à-vis. For a dung fly, dung is part of its very own life reality. An elemental confidence and trust in what *we* call the external world is biological life's inherent presupposition. It is part of being alive, part of the logic of life.

If *animals* are a priori at home in the world and if for them their habitat is fundamentally familiar because they are made for it and it for them, there is no good reason why this should on principle be different for the human animal. The first human beings were to a large extent adapted to their environment, fully familiar with it, and on principle at home in reality. They *knew* how to live, what to eat, how to protect themselves, even if this was not their *conscious* knowing in our sense. If this had not been the case they would not have survived. The first humans were not "thrown" into an utterly alien, hostile environment.

The alleged absolute otherness which according to Blumenberg existed at the very beginning does not have its true origin in the situation of prehistoric Man, but much rather in the modern *logic of difference* prevailing in 20th century consciousness. This otherness is *modern* Man's deeply felt *logical* experience of alienation and uneasiness retrojected into the past. Myth and language do not, as he asserts, have a *strategic*, i.e., *instrumental*, function as defense mechanisms against an alleged absolutism of reality

---

7 Just as wounds, pain, illness, death are the living beings' *very own* experiences, so also is the encounter with a ferocious predator not an experience of otherness in the radical sense. Precisely because life *is* in itself relation to habitat, its very own form of being requires its own staking its life in this relation. Life does not have the innocent form of being to be found in inanimate things. The harmonious correspondence, to the extent that it is immersed in empirical reality, in the world of finitude, encompasses both yes and no, victory and death, fulfillment and denial. But even if *empirically* it is denied, the relation itself, its logic, is affirmed.

and as an escape from the horror of Chaos. They are not the result of a secondary fight against a primary fright.

Blumenberg's wall of Otherness versus Jung's "wall of fog"

Here we have to remember a crucial insight of Jung's. "The loss of the great encompassing connection [*des großen Zusammenhangs*][8] is the prime evil of neurosis" (*CW* 10 § 367, transl. modif.). This prime evil is nothing other than abstraction, the *abstract* construal of things, which becomes clear from the preceding sentence in Jung's text, "From this universal foundation no human soul is cut off; only individual consciousnesses that have lost their connection with the whole of the soul remain caught in the illusion that the soul is a circumscribable area of smallest size, a fit subject for 'scientific' theorizing" (transl. modif.).

We must not lose sight of the great encompassing connection. *It* must be our basis. And so I repeat that the in-ness in life, as the great encompassing connection between the living being and its habitat, is inescapable and that this also applies to the human *animal*. But of course, our topic is soul and world, not animal and habitat. The question is, what is the difference?

Animal existence is characterized by the fact that the animals' in-ness in life is an in-ness to the power of two, namely the in-ness *in* this in-ness. Their in-ness is not such that one could speak of their being *in* the world or *in* their habitat, because they have no sense of their being in their environment nor of themselves as distinct from their habitat. I pointed out that their habitat could even be considered as a kind of extension of their bodies. They have no distance to what is around them. The encompassing relation in which they exist is therefore only an *objective* one. They factually embody and live this relation. It is enacted, i.e., acted out, by them, but *they "subjectively"* do not themselves do any of this relating, so to speak. They are totally enveloped in it and identical with it. It is not *for them*. This is what I mean by their in-ness in their in-ness in life.

---

8 In the passage in which Jung speaks of the *große Zusammenhang*, this expression refers to something different from what I have in mind here. When Jung spoke of the great connection here, he thought of the connection between humans and the gods. That is, he gave a particular semantic interpretation to the *große Zusammenhang*. I give it a much wider, namely syntactical, structural meaning. But this does not alter the validity of Jung's sentence.

The situation is different with humans. Man knows of himself as distinct from his environment and is aware of his in-ness in his habitat or environment, and this is why his environment is not merely "environment" or "habitat" but truly "world" in the full sense. In Man the great encompassing connection is no longer merely acted out as a fact, but has become explicit, explicit as a relation. Man *does relate* to the world, he himself, as a subject, to the world as object.

This is a truly revolutionary change over against the situation of animals. In order to make comprehensible what this revolution involves and how it was possible, I will make use of a brief passage from Jung's *Memories, Dreams, Reflections* about an experience Jung had in his twelfth year.

> Once there was a moment when I had the overwhelming feeling of having just stepped out of a dense fog, with the conscious awareness: now *I* am. Behind my back it was as if there was a wall of fog behind which I had not yet been. But at this moment, I *happened to myself.* Previously I had existed, too, but everything had merely taken place. Now I knew: now *I* am, now *I* exist. Previously things went on with me, but now *I* willed (*MDR* p. 32f., transl. modif.).

What Jung gives us in this passage is a description of a modern, late 19th century boy's experience of his revolutionary shift from childhood consciousness to adulthood consciousness. With our present focus on early Man, we only need to be interested in the logic of this shift as a general principle, not in the specifics of a boy's development in the modern situation.

Right away we become aware of one striking similarity of Jung's passage with Blumenberg's fantasy. This is the similarity between Jung's "wall of fog" and Blumenberg's "wall of Otherness". The *fog* character of Jung's wall of fog is equivalent to the "shapelessness, contourlessness" of Blumenberg's wall. But apart from these similarities, both fantasies are fundamentally different.

Jung's wall lies behind him, whereas Blumenberg's wall of Otherness is in front of early Man. Only because it was in front of him could it be a cause of fright. But Jung did not have to feel threatened by his wall of fog because the moment when it appeared he was precisely liberated from it. He had already come out of it. It was a thing of the past. No challenge. Jung *begins* with an experience of having *emerged*, Blumenberg with early

Man's feeling of being *oppressed* by the absolutism of reality and its over-whelming superiority.[9]

For Blumenberg, the wall of otherness was *reality* as such. In other words, it had the character of a hard literal fact, whereas for Jung the wall of fog was something subjective, his feeling "as if . . ."

Correspondingly, Blumenberg's fantasy begins with a factual condition of nature, reality's absolute superiority, whereas Jung's experience begins with the feeling of an abrupt *act* or *deed*, namely, *his* having just "stepped out"[10] of something that was now behind him. The *initium* is his own hav-ing made a move, not Man's being oppressed. In Jung's story it all starts with a spontaneous human action, not a reaction to an external condition. The act performed by Jung was of course not a literal stepping out, leaving an earlier condition, the way, for example, that astronauts who take off for the moon in fact leave the Earth. It was a *logical* stepping out. Literally, Jung stayed of course put where he had been before: With the same parents, in the same home, in the same school and with the same things around him, and also in his old body and personal identity. The stepping out is an inter-nal revolution *inside* the same in-ness.

Now we have to ask: From where did "the dense fog" out of which Jung stepped all of a sudden come? Prior to this moment, there had not been any fog at all for Jung. He had been a bright boy with open eyes and rich and deep inner experiences and reflections, most of which had been fully con-scious. There was nothing muddleheaded about him. Paradoxically enough, the fog here is the product and result of Jung's having stepped out of it. The act of stepping out first produces that very wall of fog from which this

---

9   Hillman, when he distanced himself from his earlier idea of the world as the vale of soul-making, had said about the world as it functioned in that earlier conception that "It provides obstacles, pitfalls, monsters to be met in order to make one's interior soul". In much the same way the world viewed as a wall of otherness amounted according to Blu-menberg for early mankind to a terrible obstacle or monster. This monster did not have to be met *in order to make* myth, but on the contrary, it had to be met *by means of* making myth (and human culture as a whole) as a gigantic *defense strategy*. This theory of myth and culture is causal-reductive, not final-constructive in Jung's sense of the terms.

10   Jung's experience does not invite the idea of a natural and gradual *transition* from an earlier to a later stage. It is about a decisive *act*, his active and instantaneous "having stepped out". This is why the official English translation in *MDR*, which instead of "hav-ing stepped out" has "having just emerged", is misleading, implying a more passive and gradual process.

stepping out takes place. The "wall" is the product of soul-making, not the necessitating cause and origin of myth-making.

This takes us to the next question: What is this fog? It is the image into which Jung's entire childhood was logically collapsed. In this moment, all the previous years of his life with all their colorful and impressive experiences were contracted and condensed into one single nondescript and in itself differenceless image, the absolutely abstract image of this dense fog. His whole childhood experience was negated.

I spoke of "result" and "product", which would imply that there are two events, first a stepping out and then the production of the fog. But what we have to realize is that there is only one single act or event. At one and the same time it is the involution or collapsing of the whole past "in-ness in childhood" AND the stepping-out of it into the entirely new logical space of I-ness. Or conversely: The stepping out *is* the pushing-down of the whole in-ness in childhood into the past, into obsolescence. The logical doing-in and pushing-down of his whole past existence IS the pushing himself off into a new dimension.

Jung had said, "at this moment, I *happened to myself*". So I have to revise my earlier statements that Jung had stepped out of his childhood. The boy Jung did no such thing. Rather, he suddenly *found himself* in a situation in which this stepping-out had already happened for him. It was not his doing. It had been nature's doing, part of his growing up. His natural development had performed this logical act for him. And this act *is* the contradictory unity of a closure and an opening-up. As such it is a revolution.

What Jung experienced was thus of course not merely a restructuring, the way companies are frequently reorganized nowadays, whereby positions and responsibilities are merely shuffled around. Rather, it was a restructuring that amounted to a breakthrough into an absolutely new openness. It achieved the conquest of something new that did not exist before, a new stage of consciousness. It was a vertical change, a change in the sense of a *self-transcendence*.

The principle that we found at work here can help us to describe the logic of the revolution through which the human animal's in-ness in its in-ness in biological life could be turned into Man's explicit relation to the world. It, too, required the *happening* of a logical act. Man is that animal in whose nature it lies that this act takes place or, rather, has always already taken place.

Inwardization of the end of life

The animal, I said, is totally enveloped in its in-ness in life. A freeing from this imprisonment in the in-ness in life cannot happen by escaping from it. So much we have already learned from the foregoing discussion. A coming out of it can only happen by entering it more fundamentally, more deeply, that is, through an involution of the in-ness in life. How this works will have to be analyzed. I will begin with a passage from Hegel. Discussing finitude, Hegel said:

> When we say of things that *they are finite*, we understand thereby that they not only have a determinateness . . . but that, on the contrary, nonbeing constitutes their nature and being. Finite things *are*, but their relation to themselves is that they are *negatively* self-related and in this very self-relation send themselves away beyond themselves, beyond their being. They *are*, but the truth of this being is their *end*. The finite not only alters, . . . but it *passes away*; . . . the being as such of finite things is to have the germ of their passing away as their in-themselves-ness: the hour of their birth is the hour of their death.[11]

The innermost being of finite things is their end. They carry the germ of their passing away within themselves *as their in-themselves-ness*. This applies of course also to living things, to plants and animals. But despite the fact that the innermost truth of the life of living beings is their death, animals do not have access to this truth of their life. They know not of their finitude. And despite the fact that the hour of their birth IS the hour of their death, in the actual process of life death precisely marks the *outside* border of their life and appears as the radical opposite of their birth. Time holds birth and death neatly apart as two separate events, making life appear as an extended line leading from the one end that we call the beginning to the other, the literal end.

Now, what happened in the human animal was that the border of life, its end, death, was pulled inwards. Death was interiorized into life, infolded. That is, life as a whole, the entire extension from birth to death, was collapsed into the one notion of *mortality* as an equivalent to the boy Jung's

---

11 G.W.F. Hegel, *Science of Logic*, trans. A.V. Miller (Atlantic Highlands, NJ: Humanities Press International, 1989), p. 129 (transl. modif.).

wall of fog: Humans do not merely have to die; they *are*, they define themselves as, "the mortals". Its, life's own, finitude, which on the animal stage
is only the animal's *factual* truth, in Man had thereby come home to life
itself. It had become explicit to life itself, as its, life's, own core.

It is crucial to note that I did not say that life's finitude had come home to
Man, that *he* had become conscious of it. It is an objective process, an event
that happened to life itself, not to Man.[12] For how could Man have made
himself conscious of his own mortality when to begin with he was still a
human *animal* without any consciousness?[13] (This absence of consciousness is comparable to and reminiscent of Jung's statement that "behind"
his wall of fog "I had not yet been".) To become conscious of something
presupposes an already existing consciousness. But this did precisely not
yet exist at the outset. It is only the objective event of life's involution
upon *itself* that WAS the creation or invention of consciousness in the first
place.[14]

We usually reify consciousness as a kind of organ that Man possesses, as
a part of the make-up of the personality. But consciousness is performative.
There are not two things, biological life plus—on top of it—consciousness as a separate "layer" or additional reality, a new component, such as a

12 This event can be understood in the light of the logic of ritual killings described in
    my paper on "Killings" (Chapter Five of my *Soul-Violence*, Coll. Engl. Papers vol.
    III [New Orleans, LA: Spring Journal Books, 2008], now: London and New York:
    Routledge, 2020). In the human animal's killing its own living other, be it in big-game
    hunting or in sacrificial slaughtering, *life's* innermost truth was *explicitly* brought
    home to *life*.
13 I must warn the reader of the equivocality of the term "consciousness". There is of
    course also a type of consciousness already on the merely *psychic* level of the human
    animal, a pre-linguistic consciousness (self-feeling and waking states). But my word
    "consciousness" here tacitly refers to linguistic consciousness, consciousness as Intel-
    ligence, self-consciousness, the capability of having representations and notions, which
    depends on the subject-object distinction, that is, on the psyche's relation to its own
    contents (which originate in its sensibility and irritability) *as* representing an other, a
    relation on account of which, when it exists, the psyche is no longer psyche in the termi-
    nological sense, but already *soul* or *mind*.
14 To be more precise: Not of a fully developed consciousness that was in actuality con-
    scious of a plentitude of contents, of itself and of the things in the world, but rather of
    no more than the principle of consciousness, the condition a priori of the possibility of
    a concrete consciousness, the actual faculty to become conscious of things. The human
    animal is that animal in which nature has performed the logical act of this infolding. The
    human animal is born with this potential.

special organ. No, there is only life, but if and where life turns in on itself, is reflected into itself, there we get consciousness.[15]

Hegel had said, "Finite things *are*, but their relation to themselves is that they are *negatively* self-related and in this very self-relation send themselves away beyond themselves, beyond their being". In finite creatures, this their sending themselves away beyond their being is, we could say, pointlessly squandered, wasted on their simply passing literally away. Their self-transcendence is acted out as a positive-factual temporal process and as such leads nowhere. It leads only into their literal nonbeing. In Man, the negative self-relation of finite things is interiorized into itself. And this makes all the difference. Now the self-transcendence becomes productive and affirmative. I want to show what this means in three points.

1. The finite things' "*being* negatively self-related" turns into life's actual "negatively *relating* to itself". Having become truly *human*, the human animal in fact has always already been sent away beyond itself. It transcends itself, that is, it has a distance to itself as animal. Within its animal nature it has overcome its animal nature and has attained a totally new *status* of existence, the status of *being* mind or soul, and being "I".[16] To the extent that I am I, I am, so to speak, inevitably an "*extraterrestrial*" who landed on the "earth" of my animal body.

2. The *negativity* of its "being *negatively* self-related" becomes itself something affirmative, something in its own right, namely the sphere of *absolute negativity*, the sphere of the *logos* and intelligibility, the (to stay in my image) "extraterrestrial" realm of *meanings, ideas, concepts*.

3. The *effect* of the finite things' negative self-relation is, as we heard, that they send themselves away beyond themselves, transcend themselves. Now, if life's "sending itself away *beyond* itself" is reflected or inwardized into itself (rather than merely acted out), then what

---

15 Again: "Consciousness" in the sense of Intelligence. It is not to be confused with that consciousness that exists already on the level of the "*psyche*" of the human animal, in contrast to the "*soul*".

16 Whereas for finite things their "being sent by their negative self-relation away beyond their being" means that they simply cease to be, for the human being it means that it is sent beyond its animal status into the status of being human. The human being qua human is always already out of its animal nature and beyond it, irrevocably out of its animal body. The real animals *are* bodies. Man *has* a body and inevitably perceives it from outside. He has to relate to it.

emerges instead of literal death as a temporal event in empirical-factual reality is the idea of **the beyond**, the notion of **Transcendence**
as the very *horizon* of existence as such.[17] Thereby Man has indeed
caught up with the finite things' being sent away "beyond their **being**",
having transcended the sphere of mere BEING as such, of positive-
factual existence. The moment his *mortality* had come home to Man
he ipso facto was also *beyond* it—of course logically, negatively (not
literally) beyond it. And because he *was* beyond it he possessed an
immortal soul,[18] a *life after death*, and even his descent was ultimately
an "extraterrestrial" one from above, from Heaven, from the gods. The
notion of Transcendence, conquered through this interiorization, congealed into the imaginal ideas of the immortal soul, of ancestors, the
underworld, the yonder and into the philosophical concepts infinity and
eternity. The "immortal soul" is nothing else but the *reflected, interiorized* DYNAMIC of finite life's "*sending* itself away beyond itself"
represented IN *imaginal, substantiated* FORM.

This reflection allows me to correct my earlier description in my discussion of mortality and immortal soul and to admit that I have put the cart
before the horse. For in truth, just as Jung's "I *happened to myself*" sort
of retroactively produced the notion of the "wall of fog" behind him, so
here, too, it is really the attainment to the higher status that produces the
notion of the lower one and not the other way around. That is to say, we
must derive the human animal's awareness of its mortality or the humans'
self-understanding as "the mortals" from their having been transported to
the awareness of "*the immortals*" and to their having comprehended their
own (ultimate) *infinity*, their continued existence as *souls* in *afterlife*, rather

17 Conversely we could say that only because of and in the notions of "the beyond" and
of "Transcendence" does existence have a *horizon* in the first place. Animal existence
is without a horizon. "Horizon" and "transcendence" are more or less the same thing
inasmuch as a "horizon" refers to the *horos* (boundary, border) of existence and with the
notion or experience of a "border" this border has logically already been overstepped.
And it is the fact that there is a "horizon" for Man that distinguishes the *world* of Man
from the *environment* of animals.

18 Please note the equivocation that the word "soul" involves. In point 1 above, "soul" is
more or less synonymous with "mind" and is something that Man *is*. Here in point 3,
"soul" as immortal soul is something that Man possesses (because he stays animal and
mortal).

than falling for the typically modern fallacy of interpreting the ideas of an afterlife and of the immortals as a reaction formation, an attempted compensation and consolation for Man's disappointing and shocking insight into his mortality.

What happens in the described process or act is that life encounters this its own finitude and self-transcendence. The finitude clashes with itself. It becomes aware of itself. This coming home to itself is—logically—like an electric shock, an explosive event. It breaks open the animal's in-ness in the in-ness of natural life and catapults life to the higher level of mind and notions.

In Man, life has, as it were, "stepped out" of its containment within itself in much the same way that the boy Jung had stepped out of that wall of fog into which his childhood had logically collapsed. But just as Jung's stepping out of his childhood was only a (psycho)logical as well as, consequently, an attitudinal or psychic change while physically he remained in the same body and the same environment, so also is the change that we are here concerned with only a logical change. The self-transcendence that we have in mind here only inwardized deeper into itself that very reality which is transcended, which is why the change is invisible from outside.[19] Being an internal sublimation or distillation, it did not turn the human animal literally into a higher being such as an angel or spirit. Rather, the human animal became an *animal* characterized by the fact that *within* it and *for* it, an internal breakthrough to the dimension of logical negativity had happened and that for it literal being had been transcended so that "being" or "life" had turned into *existence* within a *horizon*, and "environment" into *world*. Aristotle called this animal, i.e., the *animal* which is not an animal, the *zôion logon echon*, the living being that has access to the *logos*.[20]

19 As indicated, the higher category cannot be derived from a lower one and thus be reductively explained. The act through which the dimension of absolute negativity is first generated must in itself already be a logically negative act. It cannot be derived from anything empirical or positive. It is its own origin.

20 Because life or nature performed this infolding as a *logical* act, as *thought* and in absolute negativity, the human animal became Man. Whereas, if this act (provided this would have been possible at all) had been a *literal, positive-factual* act of infolding, life would have literally become uroboric in the human animal, a circle that returns into itself. And thus it would have been literally eternal life.

Consciousness as second creator of the world

Jung had a clear insight into the truly revolutionary significance of the emergence of consciousness over against mere life. And because his insight connected consciousness with "world", with the following Jung passage we finally return to the second term of our topic, the world. In Kenya, Jung visited a great game preserve.

> From a low hill in this broad savanna a magnificent prospect opened out to us. To the very brink of the horizon we saw gigantic herds of animals. . . . Grazing, heads nodding, the herds moved forward like a slow river. . . . This was the stillness of the eternal beginning, the world as it had always been, in the state of non-being; for until then no one had been present to know that it was "this world". . . . There I was now, the first human being that recognized that this was the world and had through this knowing first really created it in this moment. . . . / . . . Now I knew . . .: Man is indispensable for the completion of creation; in fact, he himself is the second creator of the world, who alone gives to the world its objective existence—without which, unheard, unseen, silently eating, giving birth, dying, heads nodding through hundreds of millions of years it would have gone on in the profoundest night of non-being down to its unknown end. (*MDR* p. 255f., transl. modif.)

In this experience Jung turned into Adam, the first Man. In his imagination he experientially repeated, so to speak, the first human beings' dramatic breakthrough from the unknowing mindlessness of biological existence *into* the light of mind.

I will only touch on two points of this in many ways admirable story and take issue with them, (a) the notion of "knowing" and (b) the idea of the "second creator".

(a) In this passage, Jung equates "consciousness" with "knowing". The term "knowing" shows that he has more in mind than prelinguistic consciousness. "Knowing" suggests that here consciousness means linguistic intelligence, conceptual knowing.[21] It implies a subjective clarity of mind, a personal awareness.

---

21 "I happened to myself. Previously I had existed, too, but everything had merely taken place. Now I knew: now *I* am, now *I* exist. Previously things went on with me, but now

However, if we go back to the situation of the very beginnings, I think that what existed was precisely not yet any clarity of mind. Subjective knowing is rather a much, much later acquisition. At first the mind did not exist *in* Man, subjectively, as people's personal insights ("in their heads"). Rather, such an intelligent knowing was first *objectively produced* in words and sayings as the shared, the collectively-owned property of a whole community or tribe. This knowing existed exclusively "out there" in public and objective form as the communal cultural reality of the *names* of things and what was *said* about them. Only very slowly, through the endless centuries-long repetition of the objective store of sayings did the essence of these sayings become interiorized into the mind of people, thereby creating a subjective mind.[22]

(b) Jung's idea of Man as the "second creator" of the world operates within the opposition of consciousness, i.e., the subject-object divide, and harks back to his idea of "a non-psychic, transcendent object". Another time Jung had spoken of the "*Ge-wußtheit* [knownness] of the universe" (*CW* 17 § 165, transl. modif.). But the actual character that "knowing" had in his own experience has nothing whatsoever to do with the relation of a subject to an external reality. If we stay true to what Jung *really experienced*, then the question of an external reality does not arise at all. What

---

I willed." It is the change from an implicit to an explicit, a *knowing*, I. Before, he had of course been aware of himself, too, had had a sense of his identity, had referred to himself as (and felt himself to be) I. Just like, on a different level, the grazing animals are aware of and know their environment. But now the I had come home to the I *itself*. It had thus become his center, his "headquarters". Before, the I had been a condition that he had been in. Now it, and this means: *He*, was in charge. *He* had to assume full responsibility for himself.

22 The soul was "objective", "out there", not subjective and in the mind ("in the heads of people"). In his reflections about soul history Jung had clearly gained the important insight into the priority of the deed and thus of the primordial objectivity of the psyche. "I am inclined", he said, "to think that things were generally done first and that only a long time afterwards somebody asked a question about them, and then eventually discovered why they were done". "Faust aptly says: '*Im Anfang war die Tat*' (in the beginning was the deed)" (*CW* 18 § 540 and 553). But it is interesting that the moment when it was a question of his own theorizing, of reflecting about consciousness as such, about life and the role of Man in relation to God, Jung himself thought on the horizontal and subjective level in terms of knowing and epistemology, not of veritable objectivity and not of production. It was Hillman's great merit with his term soul-making to have introduced into psychology the notion of making, production.

Jung experienced was the intuition (*Anschauung*) of the difference between
(a) the animals' undivided enactment of life, that is, what I called their in-
ness in life to the power of two, or what Jung called the "profoundest night
of non-being", and (b) a sudden emergence, a dawning, an awakening from
this immersion in the in-ness, on the other hand, a being transported into
a new status. The latter is analogous to the boy Jung's experience about
which he said, "at this moment, I *happened to myself*". The question of the
universe does not arise at all.

There was not a given reality whose creation Man could have completed by adding "knownness" to it. Knownness could not be added
"to it" because "it", the world, cosmos, or universe, had not come into
existence at all. All that could possibly happen with the arrival of Man
on the scene was that the human animal's own specific life experience
opened up for him. This opening up, this internal breaking open of the
human animal's in-ness in its in-ness, amounted to an internal clearance,
Lichtung in Heidegger's sense, which can be described in less imaginal
terms as the establishment of the radical difference (or should I say *différance?*) between the "horizon" of existence mentioned earlier and the
existence or what existed within this horizon. This opening-up is the
event in which *MAN happened to himself.* Mythology had imagined this
clearance as the separation, and constantly holding apart, of the world
parents, Heaven (= horizon) and Earth (= what appears within this horizon). This clearance, this having "stepped out" (certainly not out of the
in-ness of life, but out) of the *immersion* in the in-ness in life, is the
"knowing" Jung really had in mind. And this knowing gave birth to such
a thing as "world" or "universe", rather than being an addition to an antecedently given world. "World" is the result of the clearance and exists
only within this so-called "knowing".

There was not and never is a knownness of the *universe*. Rather, all
knownness is the explication of Man's own *life experience*. Consciousness[23] *is* the OPENED-UP human life experience. And it is that *into which*
his life experience opened up or bifurcated, namely into the internal opposition of consciousness, the vis-à-vis of subject and object, Man and world,
"me" and "my body", as well as on a reflected, second-order level: Horizon

---

23   Again I have to stress that "consciousness" has in this paper the sense of Intelligence, of
     Jung's "knowing". Consciousness as a light.

(consciousness as such) and content of consciousness, the ontic and the ontological, the semantic and syntactical form.

Language

This logical explosion happened as language. Primordially language, I claim, was not an *instrument* of communication for the practical purpose of coping with reality. Primordially it was a revelation. The *event* of a word or sentence spoken WAS a flash of lightning,[24] a flash of lightning that illumined "the [thereby *created*!] world" rather than subjectively the human mind.[25] Language IS nothing else but the "same old" specific life experience of the human animal,[26] *however* this life experience turned in on itself and dirempted: Having become *linguistic*.

Language, in what it does, in fact establishes for Man a distance to himself as animal as well as the difference between act and fact, subject and

---

24 As such, primordial speaking was the *sublimated* equivalent of primordial ritual killing that occurred in big-game hunting and blood sacrifices. In my "Killings" paper (in: *Soul-Violence*, Coll. Engl. Papers vol. III [New Orleans, LA: Spring Journal Books, 2008], now: London and New York: Routledge, 2020, p. 204) I wrote that "the blood gushing forth from the open wound [caused by the sacrificer's axe blow] ignited a light". This idea of a revelation, of a light that is ignited, of the event of a flash of lightning should be distinguished from the idea of reflection as a "replication of reality within itself" (Markus Gabriel and Slavoj Žižek, Mythology, *Madness and Laughter: Subjectivity in German Idealism*, London: Continuum International Publishing Group, 2009, p. 13, cf. p. 3 as well as p. 35 "reduplication") which amounts to a *petitio principii*. Reality, which is the result of the flash of lightning, is presented as that which is replicated or reduplicated.

25 Just as a word spoken, so WAS the "objective" and cultural *event* of the sacrificer's killing blow or the hunter's killing spear shot the lightning. The light was *in* the word, *in* the act, *in* the deed, not in the subjective mind nor *for* the mind. Therefore it was not a light to be *seen*, neither by the literal eyes, nor by "inner" eyes (in the way be it of "insight" or actual "visions"). It is time for us to take Jung's notion of the "objective psyche" seriously. *Insight* comes much later. It is due to acts of inwardization.

26 There is not *the* world, there are only the radically different and specific life experiences characteristic of each species. A mole has a different life experience from a shark, a jelly-fish, a deer, a butterfly, or an eagle. The sun, the sky, do not exist for the mole. Mountains do not play any role in the life experience of sharks. A bookworm, although it lives off books, does not become aware of what a book is. The same applies to the human animal. It has *its* specific life experience, and when it is opened up into what we call the world, this is not *the* reality "external to ourselves", but only its very own world.

object, between "in us" and "out there".[27] It performs a *separatio*, a bifurcation. The names of things exist as the performance of a division, and this is what causes the names to *be* the clearance. The word *is* in itself a logical doing or happening. The one word "tree", for example, establishes at one and the same time and within itself the difference between the name as such and the referent, between the mental *notion* "tree" and the *thing* that is meant by the word, and thus also between subject and object or soul and world. The word points simultaneously in two opposite directions. It is not something static like a mere label stuck on existing things. By dissolving the human animal's *identity* with its biological life experience and by creating within itself the difference between notion and thing referred to, language sets *us* off as selves, as subjects, over against "things external to ourselves".[28] Both we and they exist only in the OPENED-UP interiority of *our* in-ness in the in-ness in life.

Adam could not, as the Bible thinks, name already-created things, because contoured things with gestalt-character and a structured, ordered world originate only in that very naming. As Jung had correctly seen, Man is indispensable for the creation of the world, but in contrast to Jung's view Man is precisely not the *second* creator, not the completer of the creation. Neither a notion nor a thing existed before or outside the word. Only through language is there now an "external world" and a "vis-à-vis" for the first time, and only *in and through it* can we conceive of the animal's in-ness in the in-ness in biological life that we claim was opened up in Man into the clearance of consciousness.[29]

27 This *horizontal* setting-apart (a) of the opposites (subject and object, self and other, human mind and world, inside and outside) goes along with (b) the *vertical* diremption of heaven and earth (immortal gods and mortals, living humans and the dead souls, the ancestors, this world and the beyond), as well as with (c) the *internal* one of human animal and logos (or body and mind, empirical "I" and immortal, absolute-negative soul). All three aspects are modes how the *internal, self-inwardizing* self-transcendence of the finite human animal manifests and realizes itself.

28 With respect to myself as "me" or personality or soul my body is also a thing external to myself.

29 The animal's in-ness in the in-ness in biological life must not be viewed as a positive fact on which human existence as the existence of mind or soul (as the opened-up in-ness) is based and from which it is ultimately derived. It is the other way around. The higher category (mind, soul, the opened-up in-ness, absolute negativity) posits within itself the lower one as its *internal* basis from which it pushed off to itself.

Wilhelm von Humboldt had a crucial insight about how language operates. Having in mind the image of a spider or certain cocooning insects he stated the following.

> Through one and the same act by virtue of which Man spins language out of himself, he cocoons himself in it, and each language draws around the nation to which it belongs a circle, to leave which is possible only to the extent that one at the same time takes one's place within the circle of another language.[30]

I said that consciousness and language are the OPENED-UP interiority of our in-ness in the in-ness in life. But von Humboldt shows us that this opening-up is itself a closed circle, a kind of prison that cannot be left but only be exchanged for another similar prison. The opening-up is not an escape from our in-ness in the in-ness in life. It is merely a transformation of it, its alchemically distilled form, namely Man's self-cocoonment in language.[31]

Language is an activity, a producing. But production ipso facto produces products that have an existence of their own and that Man is confronted with and surrounded by. Jung had said that "We are in truth so wrapped about by psychic images that we cannot penetrate at all to the essence of things external to ourselves" (*CW* 8 § 680). From von Humboldt we learn that the images in which we are enwrapped are produced by language. By speaking, Man makes, so to say, the bed that he then must lie in. No radical otherness. It is a dialectical, uroboric relation. The tail-eater produces itself and ipso facto devours, cocoons itself in itself.

What this means for our topic, soul and world, is that soul-making is in itself world-making and self-cocoonment in the world thus made. Logically, the world is not really the vale of soul-making, an antecedently given vessel. Conversely, the world is itself the result of that soul-making that takes place in its vale. *Only empirically, only within* our in-ness in language, does

---

30 Wilhelm von Humboldt, "Ueber die Verschiedenheiten des menschlichen Sprachbaues [1827–1829]", in: *Werke in 5 Bänden*, ed. Andreas Flitner and Klaus Giel, vol. III (Darmstadt: Wissenschaftliche Buchgesellschaft, 1963), pp. 224f. [= p. 180, vol. VI, 1 of the edition of Humboldt's collected works by the Königlich Preußische Akademie der Wissenschaften] (my transl.).

31 We have to emphasize the word "self-" in "self-cocoonment" because it is the human counterpart to the animal's *natural* "cocoonment" in (absolute determination by) its instincts. Language is *"contra naturam"*, a manifestation of soul.

soul-making take place in the vale of an antecedently given world because we are never in the position of Jung's first Man, of Adam, who spoke the very first words and for whom there existed a created world already *prior* to his naming and speaking. Yes, through language there *is* a world external to us, the world in which we live. Yes, we *have* a distance from the things around us and stand vis-à-vis them. But this externality exists only in and by virtue of language and thus in the interiority of soul.[32] As Wittgenstein said, "The boundaries of my language are the boundaries of my world".[33]

In Blumenberg's myth theory and in Jung's idea of our being-so-wrapped-about by psychic images that we cannot penetrate to the "essence of things", the Great Connection has fallen apart into an unbridgeable difference.[34] In this thinking, both the human mind and reality have been removed from the great encompassing connection. Both are set up as *extra-linguistic*, that is, as positivities existing outside of and prior to language, language which is the in-ness in the sphere of absolute negativity (which is the in-ness in the "extraterrestrial" sphere "beyond ourselves, beyond our being" in Hegel's sense: In language we are in our home *because* in it we are beyond ourselves).[35]

---

32 And yes, there is fear in the world, and not only the concrete empirical fear of specific dangers. No, there is also an "ontological" fear, Heidegger's "*Angst*", about which he said, "The what-of Angst is the world as such", in other words, an abysmal fear, a fear without concrete object. However, this is precisely not the Chaos and absolute Otherness prior to naming and myth, not Blumenberg's horror and fright that could only be banished through naming and story-telling. No, it is conversely a fear that *presupposes* language, myth, and the humanization of the human animal, a fear that was *created* through and within language. And it is not an absolute horror either, but rather a noble mystery, the *mysterium tremendum*, the numinous, which, as we know, in addition to being *tremendum* is in itself also *fascinosum et augustum*. It is the *Holy* (Rudolf Otto). It is that fear of which at a much later date we read in Job 28:28, "The fear of the Lord, that is wisdom" and of which Jung said it leads to γνῶσις θεοῦ (*Letters 2*, p. 333, to Arnold Künzli, 16 March 1943). Only for a being that had already left the in-ness in the in-ness and was already in language and consciousness could there be a strangeness and the vis-à-vis of "the other" in the first place.

33 Ludwig Wittgenstein, *Tractatus logico-philosophicus*, trans. C.K. Ogden (London: Kegan Paul, Trench, Trubner & Co., 1922), 5.6.

34 With his concept of the "unprethinkable", Schelling was of course a thinker of the difference. But we must not think of him here because he never left the ground of the logic of classical metaphysics and the Great Connection, and so *his* difference was not yet an unbridgeable one.

35 Language in its turn must ipso facto have dwindled in this scheme of Jung's from the great encompassing connection to no more than a separate third thing (another positive

The problem, as I see it, is that in Blumenberg's theory of the wall of Otherness, and likewise in Jung's idea of the unreachable essence of things external to ourselves, the issue to be discussed is construed *horizontally* in *epistemological* terms, in terms of the modern logic of *intentionality*. For me the "cosmic significance of the mind" that dawned on Jung in Africa lies much rather *vertically* in the breaking open of the "profoundest night" of the human animal's in-ness in the in-ness of its undivided experience of life, in the flash of lightning which occurs in and through language. *It is the bursting-open of a bud into a flower*. It has nothing whatsoever to do with the horizontal subject-object relation. Both soul and world are *vertically* the product of the opening-up and internal "en-lightenment" of the human animal's in-ness in the in-ness of its life experience. They are not in a horizontal epistemic or intentional relation to each other. This is also why for psychology "truth" has nothing to do with epistemology, nothing to do with a penetration to the essence of the "thing in itself". Truth refers to a vertical correspondence between what is said or thought and the inner depth of the logic of actual lived life at a given historical moment.

Man and world are not fixed, existing entities, not ontological. They are equiprimordial moments contained in and posited by that great encompassing connection that we call language. They are fundamentally linguistic, soul-internal.

And because language is the opening-up of our in-ness in our life experience, this our life experience is not, like that of animal species, once and for all biologically fixed. For this breaking open of the in-ness in our in-ness in life also entails a *liberation in practical regards*, namely with respect to our determination by instincts.[36] The life experience of humans can be enormously extended, altered, and even[37] manipulated and thus become highly

---

fact) in between the two, namely, to a mere instrument of expressing and communicating the knowledge that the human subject has gained about the object, the world.

36 Man's being freed from the compulsive determination by instinct has been given a solely negative interpretation by Arnold Gehlen (on whom also Blumenberg relied concerning this topic), a negative interpretation in the sense that Man is a *Mängelwesen* (a "being of deficits or structural lack").

37 See my "The End of Meaning and the Birth of Man", Chapter Nine in *CEP* 4, *The Soul Always Thinks* (New Orleans, LA: Spring Journal Books, 2010), now: London and New York: Routledge, 2020.

artificial and abstract.[38] And this is why "Man" and "world", the two poles into which this life experience opens up, are fundamentally historical, subject to change. The form of in-ness in life that, for example, opened up into

38 Immediately preceding Jung's cited sentence about the fact that "we are in truth so wrapped about by psychic images . . ." (*CW* 8 § 680) we find the following statement: "My psyche even transforms and falsifies reality, and it does this to such a degree that I must resort to artificial means to determine what things are like apart from myself. Then I discover that a sound is a vibration of air of such and such a frequency, or that a color is a wave of light of such and such a length" (transl. modif.). For one thing, this quote of course highlights once more Jung's naive belief in the "true world". If the images that we are enwrapped in *falsify* reality, then reality must be something that can be imagined as existing as an absolute Other (an absolute X) outside and independently of our experience ("apart from myself") as the actual "true world" (the "essence of things"). The proof Jung provides for this thesis of his is that we have to "resort to artificial means to determine what things are like apart from" ourselves. Through these artificial means, Jung believes, we can correct the "falsification" caused by our cocoonment in psychic images, so that we arrive at the truth, at how things *are* (sound IS, according to him, vibration of air!). But this whole binary opposition of true and false has no place here. The sound that we hear, the colors we see are not false, and "vibration of air" or "wave of light" not any truer. Our unarmed eyes, our eyes with sunglasses, our infrared camera pictures, our magnetic resonance imaging all correctly show what they show. They present varieties of human life experience. In the same way, our psychic images do not falsify what is seen through them. (A wholly different matter are prejudices, projections, and ideologies as well as TV news, because they do not *show phenomena*. They are *opinions* and *interpretations* . . . that are taken or presented as phenomena.) But on the other hand—and with the topic of the "artificial means" alluded to by Jung I come to the second point and the real reason for why I quoted this passage in the present context—Jung does not realize that these "artificial means" are merely crutches that rather than helping us to get at the truth merely alter, technically manipulate, and in this limited sense perhaps even precisely "falsify", *our real human life experience*. Modern physics, e.g., is not really an epistemic endeavor. It, too, with all its ideas about a big bang, collapsing stars and black holes, about the relativity of time and curved space, antimatter, and with its totally abstract mathematical formulas only *makes* soul and *makes* world *in an artificial way* by means of technical devices like radio telescopes and electron microscopes, by particle accelerators, by space shuttles or X-Ray machines and, methodologically, by systematized exploration, experimentation, and (often computerized) mathematical calculation. Science does not transcend our cocoonment in language and images. It does not get us any closer to the essence of things. Rather, (in *possibly* all too extreme ways) it *expands* our language (e.g., mathematics!) and thus the very specific life experience of the human animal. It *extends* this experience beyond the human animal's natural form and dimension, even beyond the biosphere into regions absolutely hostile to life (outer space, nuclear physics, nano technology, etc.), above all beyond Intuition. The most-modern physics no longer observes and analyzes *phenomena*, but for gaining its ultimate insights experiments with second-order, if not third-order, "phenomena", namely

early shamanism and its form of Man and world was fundamentally differ-ent from those of the later agriculturalists, the citizens of the classical Greek *polis* or those of modern Man since the Industrial Revolution.[39]

The history of the soul is nothing else but the slow transformations of *the whole relation* of human mind (or soul) and *its* world, their ever-new mutual redefinition, within the great encompassing connection. The moment the one side changes, the other has already changed with it. One could try to trace the metamorphosis of the forms in which the in-ness in the human life experience is opened up at the various historical loci down to our days and then perhaps even find out why today's in-ness in life had to open-up into, and ipso facto cocoon itself in, the logic of the unbridgeable difference, the logic of externality, that logic that informed, for example, Blumenberg and, at times, also Jung and that tends to construe Man and world as extra-linguistic positivities.

Now one could think that with the insight that inherent in our speak-ing and soul-making is our inevitable self-cocoonment I have arrived at a position of solipsism, absolute idealism, and "anything goes". But since the revolutionary breaking-open of the occludedness of the in-ness in the

---

Man-made mathematical *equations* (e.g., Stephen Hawking's work). It *does* something to our life experience, something which is analogous to what animal breeders nowadays sometimes do to natural animals, such as when they breed monster pigs with additional ribs to optimize them for industrial meat production. No living being is confronted with "*the* world", which is an abstract fiction. Harking back to Heraclitus and Wittgenstein we could say that the incredible expansion by science and technology of the *human* animal's particular undivided experience of life is the attempt to travel every road to the ultimate boundaries of our language as the boundaries of *our* "world" and to exhaus-tively explore, one after the other and to the extreme, all possible avenues within those boundaries, all potentials lying in the logic of the mind of *born* Man. The fundamental difference between born Man and unborn (or traditional) Man is that with all his explo-ration, his inventiveness and craftiness, with all his artificial productions, unborn Man nevertheless stayed within the phenomenal sphere *provided* by his, the human animal's, life experience, whereas modern or born Man *directly focuses on and manipulates this his life experience itself* (in other words, his soul-making/world-making).

39 In the biological sphere, the different kinds (species) of flowers (as well as animals) display their variety side by side, synchronically. This is so because life embodies itself in positive beings. As *logical* life and as absolute-negative, the soul's life, by contrast, unfolds its variety predominantly as time—if I may say so following up on my image of the opening-up of a bud into a flower: As the historical *transformation* from one "flower" (form of culture) to another. Metamorphosis. At one moment, one historical locus, there is always only one truth. This is so because soul is absolute-negative. Soul does not positivize itself in ontological beings.

in-ness of the human animal's real life experience occurs as language and since language is a communal or national reality, if not one of the human race as such, the alleged solipsism could also only be one of the human race as a whole. And apropos the charge of idealism and "anything goes", we have to remember that the revolutionary breaking-open of the in-ness in the in-ness in the human life experience is *grounded* in that very life experience, in the unrelenting *reality* of this life experience. Soul-making is not free, not ad lib. It has no choice. It is, in a vertical sense, committed to and bound by our specific in-ness in our historical locus, in the truth of our real situation. And so soul-making is ultimately nothing else but our saying the truth. But the project of saying the truth is totally different from the partly delusional, partly technocratic idea of "horizontally" having to penetrate to the essence of things external to ourselves.

Chapter 5

Homemade dilemmas[1]

On Marco Heleno Barreto's "The 'Great Hunt': Psychology and the question of truth"[2]

The words "great hunt", often capitalized "Great Hunt", are both the very beginning of Barreto's essay (namely its title) and the very last words with which the main text of his paper ends (followed only by the merely summarizing "Conclusion"). Furthermore, the beginning of the text is a Nietzsche quote, the quote from which the phrase "great hunt" has been taken. This modern, Nietzschean origin of the idea of the "Great Hunt" needs to be noted. It, and even more so the fact that both the "Introduction" and the end section of Barreto's exposition are devoted to lengthy discussions of Nietzsche, seem to indicate that this essay is under a Nietzschean star. When Barreto states that the initial quote from Nietzsche about the "great hunt" "could well have been quoted in *The Soul's Logical Life*" (p. 211), he shows that the idea Nietzsche expressed in that quote, on the one hand, and my chapter in *The Soul's Logical Life* about Aktaion and Artemis, on the other, stand for him (1) logically on the same level, i.e., are immediately comparable, and (2) that they are both about the "Great Hunt". Both claims and their unity are made explicit in the heading of the "Introduction": "Two Versions of 'The Great Hunt'". If they are two *versions* of the same, they must stand side by side on the same logical level. And if they are two versions of *the same*, there is no difference between their ultimate concerns.

Both assumptions are erroneous.

1 This essay was written in January 2024.
2 Marco Heleno Barreto, "The 'Great Hunt': Psychology and the Question of Truth", in Jennifer M. Sandoval, Colleen EL-Beijjani and Pamela J. Power (eds.), *Essays on "The Soul's Logical Life" in the Work of Wolfgang Giegerich: Psychology as the Discipline of Interiority*, London and New York (Routledge), 2023 pp. 211–228.

DOI: 10.4324/9781003611400-6

The Great Hunt?

I begin with the second assumption, that about the "Great Hunt". A brief look at the Aktaion story shows us that this concept is out of place. The hunt that is the topic of our myth is a very ordinary hunt. Aktaion *simply goes hunting*, which during the early age in which this myth originated was a normal everyday activity performed by all or most men. There is nothing "great" about it, nothing that would single it out from the range of the other ordinary hunting expeditions during the times of the early hunters and fundamentally raise it above them.

Myth and psychology: Self-manifestation, not "hunting for"

No doubt, in *The Soul's Logical Life* I also said that Aktaion was hunting for truth. But it is really the soul that in and through Aktaion wants to "hunt for" its truth in the sense of making that which it, the soul, from the outset *implicitly* is, also *explicit*. It wants to give its implicit truth reality (presence in reality) and thus come home to itself. For this purpose Aktaion is needed. Only in *his* seeing the soul as naked Artemis can the soul become consciously cognizant of itself in its truth.

For Aktaion himself in his humanness, by contrast, such a thing as "*the truth*" was over his head; he was practical-minded. However in *myths*, such figures as Aktaion are not real persons existing also outside the myth, the way historical kings appearing in stories about their feats certainly have an existence outside those stories. The figures in myth are myth-internal imaginal figures, invented by the myth itself. Thus they have to be seen as having a dual role in accordance with the psychological difference. *Ostensibly*, on the narrative level, they represent a real human being that (in our story) miraculously encounters a real divine Other. But on the deeper level of the psychological meaning, they represent the initial, still unconscious *soul* intent upon becoming fully aware of itself through seeing, *as* the limited initial form of the soul, itself in some other as its truth. Soul is self-relation. In myths (and numerous dreams), it is ultimately the soul that speaks about itself through the diverse figures and events. In certain dreams the dream-I has its own intentions, but by pursuing them fulfills, unwittingly and unintentionally, the soul's bidding, showing that underneath the obvious appearance the dream-I (in *such* dreams) is already the soul itself in its present deficient form of realization in the empirical world. In such cases, the soul is on both sides, on the side of the dream-I and that of the "other".[3]

That the initial unconscious soul in our story took on the shape of *hunter*, of him who ventures into and exposes himself to the wilderness, indicates that in this myth the soul's interest appears, right from the beginning, itself in its aspect (one of many aspects) of untamed, uncivilized primordial wildness and ruthlessness, and in this sense implicitly corresponds already with its later discovery of Artemis, the goddess of the wild (indeed, the very personification of its logic).

The inflated phrase (and idea) of "the Great Hunt" is probably due to a misunderstanding not only of *this* myth, but of what the nature of myth as such is. To view the Aktaion tale as a tale of "the Great Hunt" is only possible if this myth is read as if it were like a modern story telling us about a succession in time of empirical-factual events (to be more exact: Poetically invented events presented as empirical-factual ones). But myth is *tautegorical*:[4] With all seemingly new "events", it is always merely "saying the same" once more shown in a different light or on a different logical level. What narratively appears as successive is in truth simultaneous. The narrative form acts like a prism that disperses the *one* beam of white light into its internal constituents, which also means that in truth the movement in time implied by "the Great Hunt" or the normal hunt does not exist in this myth, or only narratively so.

There certainly is in the narrative of the Aktaion myth a spectacular "happening": The discovery of the goddess Artemis bathing. The idea of a *Great* Hunt comes about when the myth is viewed as the story of a finite human being's directly and literally reaching for something absolutely out of the ordinary: Something *superhuman*, the goddess Artemis as the naked truth. But on the narrative level, Aktaion was, I have to say it again, simply going on a hunt, which means that what he as human hunter wanted was no more than to kill some game and thus to get food for himself and his family or clansmen. Very much down to earth. No higher aspirations.

Rather than having been hunted for, the discovery of the goddess in her sacred grove was an unexpected and completely serendipitous lucky *find*. It

---

3 Jung's early idea of "The Relations Between the Ego and the Unconscious", by contrast, started out from the idea of real otherness.
4 "Tautegorical": See W.G., *The Soul's Logical Life*, 5th edition (Berlin: Peter Lang, 2020) (1st edition 1998), pp. 119ff.

was an epiphany, an apparition. Against appearances, Aktaion did not come *to* her, but she, together with her pond, suddenly *appeared* before him. She cannot be sought; one cannot go "hunting for" her. Apparitions come of their own accord.

What the myth, understood as *myth* (in contrast to the impression created by its narrative form), presents with the appearance of Artemis is in this sense not a new and separate event in the story. It is simply the portrayal of the successful hunt, the actual happening of the killing of a stag, but this event *as seen from within*, perceived with the eyes of the soul and not from the "empirical-fact" perspective, not with the eyes of civilian man, the ego-personality. Artemis in this myth *is* nothing else but the inner image or truth of *the moment of the kill*, its opening out, the way a bud blossoms out into a flower. It is nothing else than this (*empirically real*) moment of "the kill" *once more*, but now inwardized into itself. What the myth simply tries to do is to present the inside view or essence of the *normal-life* reality of the hunt (without first having given us the factual view). It wants to give us the Notion of what the epitome of "hunt" (the kill) in essence is and means: A moment of truth.

Myths of this type are, so to speak, the archaic equivalent of modern definitions, with the only, but crucial difference, that a myth gives the soul's, not the ego's, definition. It teaches us, to say it with Jung's words, what there is "behind the impressions of the daily life—behind the scenes"; namely "*another* picture" that "looms up, covered by a thin veil of actual facts"[5] (where Jung's word "behind" must not be taken literally, in a spatial sense, but as meaning "inside", in its own inner depth). Just as for the mythological mind in general this real tree here IS *in truth* a dryad, this ordinary empirical river a river god, the physical flash of lightning the self-manifestation of Zeus, so the ordinary hunt culminating in the kill has as *its inner truth* the image of naked Artemis.

The point to be emphasized here is: As the *internal* logic, *Inbild*, or truth of the normal *empirical* event of any hunter's kill, the image of naked Artemis is not a new spectacular event in addition to the kill (neither spectacular, nor event) and nothing *meta*-physical. Factually speaking, there

---

5 C.G. Jung, *The Visions Seminars*, From the Complete Notes of Mary Foote, Book One (Zürich: Spring Publications, 1976), Part One (Lectures October 30 – November 5, 1930), p. 7f.

is only the kill. It has its truth *in itself*, regardless of whether this truth is actually *seen* or not. Artemis is the reality of the empirical, ordinary hunt's *opening itself out* from within itself *to the mythological or psychological eye*. Very sober, completely down to earth. And specific: Only this one phenomenon's truth, its soul or essential being, not *the* Truth at large, truth in a philosophical or metaphysical sense. If one wants to use "metaphysical", then it is the real phenomenon's *internal* metaphysic, its *internal* self-transcendence.

The form of perception of the world and the events of life that prevailed on the mythological level of consciousness decidedly predates religion and metaphysics, for which the gods or the God have already, although to differing degrees, become transcendent and independent of both the physical or empirical reality and of the eachness of the concrete moments of their realization. For mythological consciousness the psychological difference was directly the "ontological" character of the things in the world as well as man himself.

Turning from the myth to psychology in the rigorous sense, as "psychology *with* soul", I can say that psychology's project is likewise not that of the "Great Hunt". In fact, no "hunting-for" at all, no searching. On the contrary, psychology always starts out from what is *found*, what is already *given*: It begins with the stone *in via ejectus*, with dreams already dreamed, with symptoms troubling a patient, with ancient myths, rituals, religious ideas, and so on. And what it does is no more than to methodically, patiently *work with* the respective given psychological phenomena, and to work with them in the spirit of soul-making, that is, with a view of inwardizing each psychological phenomenon into itself and at the same time interiorizing *oneself* into the (thus emerging inner truth of the) psychological phenomenon. It is a kind of alchemical work of sublimation, distillation, vaporization, we could also say with an entirely different metaphor: Of hatching out the given phenomenon. In cases where this work happens to be successful, "the truth" of the phenomenon in question reveals itself of its own accord.

So much on the grandiloquent thesis that Aktaion and psychology as the discipline of interiority are committed to, or can be defined in terms of, the "Great Hunt". Now I come to Barreto's second assumption, the idea that, e.g., Nietzsche's conception, on the one hand, and the conception of *The Soul's Logical Life*, on the other, are two different versions on *the same logical level*.

Only the one plane of ego reasoning and the epistemological question: A "psychology" without soul

What we observe is that throughout his entire paper Barreto argues only on one and the same level, formally, the level of ordinary rational reasoning and, content-wise, on the level of *epistemology*. The epistemological question is basically, as Kant put it, "What can I know?" Constitutive for epistemology is that it begins with the logically isolated human subject or mind vis-à-vis the world and the things in the world as object. How and to what extent can the isolated and not-knowing subject gain true knowledge about the object, despite the fundamental gap between the two that is a priori set up by the epistemological scheme itself? Or can it perhaps not gain any true knowledge at all? It is easy to see that the question of knowledge that needs to be gained by the isolated subject about "the object" lends itself to being metaphorically expressed as a "hunting-for" (a desire, striving, searching for) knowledge, for truth. It is also understandable that when the philosophical mind realizes the enormous difficulties that stand in the way of achieving true knowledge and that require heroic efforts to overcome, this "hunt" can easily appear to this mind as "the *Great* Hunt". Just as different philosophers like Kant and Nietzsche, among numerous others, have tried to answer these questions each in their own different ways, so Barreto takes it for granted that what I state in the last chapter of *The Soul's Logical Life* is another, *my* answer to the same *epistemological* question.

This is astounding. One would have expected that Barreto, being not only a philosopher but also a practicing psychologist and active member of the ISPDI, would have seen the fundamental discrepancy between the logic of philosophical epistemology with its basis in the subject-object relation, on the one hand, and the logic prevailing both in the Aktaion myth and in psychology as the discipline of interiority, on the other. The decisive question "Who is the 'subject' that knows according to the discipline of interiority?" is not raised. Why does Barreto dwell on Kant and Nietzsche, when it is a question of a psychology *with* soul? Neither Kant nor Nietzsche had any idea of "soul" (in psychology's sense of it); it remained completely outside their purview. The psychological statements based on the myth's motif of the epiphany of Artemis, on the one hand, and Kant's idea of the radical difference between appearance and thing-in-itself or Nietzsche's perspectivism, on the other, are worlds apart, which also means that the notions of "true knowing" are fundamentally different, indeed incompatible.

Never is in Barreto's essay the plane of the ego-personality's rationalistic argumentation, the plane of external reflection, left in favor of the dimension of soul, of interiority. There is "no alchemical retort" that would demand concentration on the one prime matter with a view of interiorizing it into itself. Barreto's movement is instead that of going from one (given) passage or idea to the other, from one book or author to the next, comparing and contrasting them from an external observer or arbiter standpoint. Throughout, his thinking style is remarkably devoid of speculative strength.

There is no trace in Barreto's essay that the psychological difference is at work in his writing. But psychology as the discipline of interiority is constituted by the "psychological difference", the difference not only between man and soul, the psychic and the psychological, but above all more specifically, for example,

(1)   between the standpoint of everyday or commonplace reality *and* the soul standpoint, between "the impressions of the daily life" and "the other picture" that looms up, as well as

(2)   between "the I, i.e., the empirical man", "the civilian man" *and* the autonomous objective soul. (This distinction is especially relevant with respect to the two different notions of true knowing.)

But concerning this last-mentioned form of the psychological difference we must note that, in devoting himself in his essay to the last chapter of my book, Barreto totally ignores what was written in the first chapter of this book about psychology's entrance requirements: That in order to begin to do psychology you, so to speak, have to have died to the ego-world. Psychology has to have pushed off from the level of empirical man or the standpoint of the ego to that of the soul. The true-knowledge claim of the "discipline of *interiority*", like all its themes, cannot even be conceived if you stay *outside*.

In epistemological discourses, "true knowledge" (*provided that* according to the respective epistemological theory it can be achieved at all) would always refer to (the knowledge status of) *our* ideas, theories, propositions, to what *we* think or believe *about* this or that feature of reality. "True knowing" in psychology, however, would be *the soul's* knowing, and, furthermore, its knowing *of itself* (always in the, at each respective *now*, relevant one of its innumerable moments or guises). The place of epistemology's logic of radical otherness (subject vs. object) is in psychology taken by the *uroboric* logic of soul (or, also, by the logic of the "transference"). Of course, since the soul is not an existing entity, *its* possibly arriving at its knowing *itself* would need *us* in order for *it* to become a reality: It would need to happen in and through us, through our soul-making, without, however, thereby ceasing to be *the soul's* knowing and instead becoming *our* knowing of the truth. And when this happens, then *we* merely stand *in* this event of truth, in its *effulgence*, its radiating *shine*. This means, it is not our subjective knowing, not our (not psychology's) truth, but truly *objective* truth, absolute truth.

And the way the soul's knowing of the truth (its own truth) comes about is through the soul's freely *showing* itself, its appearing to itself of its own accord. Truth must *happen*, *give* itself. In the modern epistemological scheme, by contrast, the acquisition of knowledge requires the ego's "attack" on nature, one's summoning nature before the court of reason:

> Reason must approach nature with the view, indeed, of receiving information from it, not, however, in the character of a pupil, who *listens* to all that his master *chooses* to tell him, but in that of a judge, who *compels* the witnesses to reply to those questions which he himself thinks fit to propose.[6]

The soul's knowing its truth allows us to claim that this is what Kant would call a true knowing of the thing-in-itself. However, "the thing-in-itself", of course, *not* as the counterpart of the Kantian "appearance", because here, in psychology, the thing-in-itself is itself appearance pure, *phainomenon*, epiphany: The soul's self-manifestation, its own speaking about itself.

Psychology's anti-Kantian paradigm: The appearance as the thing-in-itself

Interestingly enough, this is and has been also the Jungian position from the outset.[7] By way of illustration of this assertion and at the same time

---

6 Immanuel Kant, "Preface to the Second Edition, 1787", *Critique of Pure Reason*, B XIII, trans. J.M.D. Meiklejohn (New York: P.F. Collier & Son, 1902), p. 24, my italics. The figure of Kant's "judge" is not far away from Barreto's implied figure of the "Great hunter". By the way, the compelling of the judge in Kant's statement is a reference to times when witnesses were put to the torture.
7 With the one exception, namely, when it came to phenomena like "the Self" or the "god-image", which deplorably made Jung desert his own phainomenal theory and escape into the Kantian scheme of the radical difference between appearance (only image in the

of the *psychological* sense of true knowing, I now go down into the low-lands of psychology, the daily work of psychotherapy, and turn to something very ordinary, inconspicuous, namely the phenomenon of dreams[8] (using it merely as one well-known example representative of what is valid for psychological phenomena in general). Jung insisted that the dream is not a façade ("Kant's appearance") behind which is hidden the true meaning of the dream ("Kant's thing-in-itself"). The alleged façade is *itself* the real thing.[9] The image has everything it needs within itself (*CW* 14 § 749). The dream is even its own interpretation (*CW* 11 § 41 and elsewhere)! The dream as the soul's speaking *is* the internal relation of itself in its immediacy (in which it gives to *us* only "the impressions of the daily life") and its own *true cognition of itself*. Within itself it comes home to itself, has always already come home to itself. It is (ultimately!) completely perspicuous to itself. In other words, it *is*[5] already *within itself* the logical movement from implicit to explicit. It is complete in itself.

No "hunting-for" on our part is necessary because the aim is already present from the outset; the psychological phenomenon *comes* with its aim always already reached. It does not need *our* speculations *about* its meaning. And because *we* do not need to interpret the dream, we would, if we came to it, for example, with Nietzsche's scheme of perspectivism in mind, only bypass, or even violate, the very nature of this soul phenomenon.

The crucial point is that in this Jung's view of the dream, the *dream* (as a soul product, and thus as a real instantiation of soul itself) *is* its own interpretation, its own knowing itself. The psychological notion of knowing is not ego-knowing. It is *objective* knowing. Another important insight to be gained is that with the dream conceived as in principle completely perspicuous to itself, Jung follows the logic prevailing in classical metaphysics.

---

soul) and thing-in-itself (real God), because, I claim, it was his personal ego need to (at least in this utterly curious and inconsistent way) keep the logical *slot in his mental system* of "the transcendent, supra-worldly God" of theology and metaphysics alive.

8 What here will be discussed does not apply to *all* dreams. There are also many superficial dreams that are not really soul phenomena, but rather psychic phenomena.

9 The "is" in this sentence and in similar statements is not to be misconstrued as an *ontological* one. It means: if you are in psychology or if you want to do psychology, then what the sentence says has to be, and in fact *is*, so for you. The "is" is a methodological presupposition that is in turn the condition of the possibility of psychology.

This one example may give the reader a hint why I could state elsewhere that the psychology of interiority "gives asylum to the ancient metaphysical logic of identity, of the copula . . ." within an utterly post-metaphysical world.

To us, as dreamers as well as analysts, however, the dream appears only in its first immediacy, evoking in us merely "the impressions of the daily life". This is so because we always, with each new soul phenomenon, see with our fundamentally deficient ordinary everyday mentality. *By devoting ourselves to* the soul phenomenon, we have to work our consciousness slowly deeper into psychology, to bring the constitution of consciousness more and more into conformity with the truly psychological, with *soul* thinking. It is not *we* who make sense of the dream, *we* who understand it. It is the other way around. It is precisely the *ununderstoodness* of the dream (or other phenomenon) that serves as our teacher. We dwell with the not understood dream and all of its words and images, immersing ourselves into them, sort of humbly turning each of them round and round in our hands, patiently hatching *it* out. In this way we interiorize ourselves into it and simultaneously inwardize it into itself.

If and when this work happens to be crowned by success, which would be one's good fortune and cannot be counted on, then the dream may open up and from within itself disclose the "interpretation" that it in truth, but only implicitly, has been from the outset. This would be the moment of truth, of true knowing. However, as I must again impress on the reader, not our knowing. As far as we are concerned, it is our being bathed in the shine of this objective event of truth.

But the event of truth, as an event or happening, is essentially momentary and therefore lasts only as long as it lasts and as consciousness is able to hold itself on this level; this means as long as consciousness is able to really remain in its having, as *our* consciousness (i.e., as ego-consciousness), truly "gone under" into the objective soul's (i.e., this particular *dream's*) knowing its truth. The dream truth *is* only for the consciousness that has indeed gone under (and thus been sublated) into the moment of the dream truth's self-manifestation. This truth cannot be had outside (nor be preserved beyond) its own time, its own actual happening.

Looking back from here to the Aktaion myth, we can say that what I described corresponds exactly to the logic portrayed in the myth.

Insistence on and denial of true knowing: A blatant contradiction?

From here we can take a look at some of the fatal contradictions that Barreto believes to have detected in the psychology as the discipline of interiority. For one thing, he believes "we are thrown into a difficult theoretical dilemma" or "blatant contradiction" (p. 218) by finding in *The Soul's Logical Life* an explicit claim for true knowing, whereas in *What is Soul?* we find a just as explicit denial of this claim. No doubt, the two relevant statements in the two books he refers to, if taken literally and in isolation, say the exact opposite of each other.

The internal contradiction of psychology itself and the two subjects of true knowing

Let me here, before discussing the issue of the alleged contradiction, first mention that psychology as the *discipline* of interiority itself exists as a contradiction. It is empirically a human undertaking engaged in human theorizing, requiring psychologists who are, and remain, first of all ordinary, civilian people, ego-personalities. But at the same time, it is, as discipline of *interiority*, *within itself* constituted by the *soul standpoint*, the non-ego standpoint, which it can only be if and when (!) the thinking of these psychologists has left ("died to") the level of the ego-personalities that they are and has, as far as their own outlook and method of approach is concerned, become "initiated" into the soul perspective so that they are able to do the work of soul-making.

Now, when we read in Barreto's text that ". . . if we advance to the 'non-positive, negative notion of truth', . . ., then **we** reach *soul* as *truly knowable*, and **psychology as the discipline** of interiority becomes a form of *true knowing*" (p. 219, my bold), we see that the ego level and the epistemological scheme have not been left behind.[10] My point was (1) that it is not *we*

---

10 A little before this quote, but in the same paragraph, Barreto states, "But absolute negativity is a *metaphysical* notion . . ." (p. 219), which is not correct. It is a *logical* notion, the result of ordinary logical operations, namely, of the negation of the negation. When he goes on to claim that absolute negativity "is indissociable from the claim for true knowing" (p. 219) and offers Jung's notion of the archetype-in-itself as an example of absolute negativity, he shows that he has not comprehended this concept. In reality, absolute negativity is neither connected with a claim nor has it anything to do with any knowing. Instead it is the general name for a particular logical status which is the result

who need to reach (in a Great Hunt!) the soul as truly knowable because the soul is already from the outset present in any psychological phenomenon we study, and (2) that psychology as a discipline is not, cannot have to be, a form of true knowing. Psychology is, as far as truth is concerned, for me simply a "psychology *with* truth" (i.e., with the *claim* [ultimately our claim] that truth and true knowing can happen), no more. Truth itself is thus not arrived at *by* psychology, not *in* psychology *as a human-all-too-human discipline*, but it is arrived at in events of truth (true knowing) that are beyond our control and whose producing subject is not we. It is only *the soul itself* that achieves true knowing. It is crucial to keep the two subjects, the human subject with its empirical knowing and the soul as the subject of true knowing, clearly apart.

With respect to the present conflict of the true knowledge claim and its denial, we need to pay attention to the respective contexts and aims of the two statements.

The Janus-faced-ness of psychology

Using the political metaphor of "Foreign Ministry" and "Home Office" (a crucial and necessary distinction, which under different names was also very much alive in Jung's psychological thinking[11]), we can say that denial of the knowledge claim in *What is Soul?* belongs to the department of the

---

of a logical further determination or inwardization. And Jung's archetype-in-itself is nothing negative, let alone absolute-negative. It is a *hypothesis*, the hypothesis about something that is imagined as a *positively* existing "factor" (Jung's own word).

11 Cf., for example, "One must have a good exoteric 'dans ce meilleur des mondes possibles'. For, to have none does not get you anywhere", *Briefe I*, p. 221, to Hermann Hesse, 18.IX.1934, my translation (for the context see *Letters I*, p. 170 f.). The distinction between the *exoteric* (or Foreign Ministry) and the *esoteric* (or Home Office) presentation of the same topic is at least formally related to such other psychological distinctions as extraversion/introversion, persona/individuality, ego/self, and may even be considered as one aspect of the psychological difference. That Barreto has no place for the Janus-face distinction in his "metaphysical psychology", but insists on the immediate validity of the, to use Jung's terms, "esoteric" (psychological truth) for the "exoteric" is probably already indirectly reflected in the fact that he needed to view the Garden of Eden in the Biblical story as "the mythological expression of the idea of absolute infinity" and thus to resorb this garden, that clearly belongs to the finite created world, into metaphysical spheres. See Barreto and Giegerich, *Human Dignity and the Garden of Eden Story*, ed. Greg Mogonson (London; Ontario: Disk Owl Books, 2024), p. 73 (for his view) and pp. 99ff. (for my critique).

Foreign Minister. This comes already out in the fact that the whole para-graph from which the quoted *What is Soul?* passage is taken, has the task of demarcating psychology from Hegel's philosophy. It describes the "foreign relations" of the discipline of interiority to, in this case, "Hegel" (and, by extension, to the societal environment in which psychology finds itself). And the purpose of the denial of any true knowledge is to serve as an exhor-tation to humility directed *at us psychologists* and to ward off a possible overestimation of psychology. The need for such an admonition is directly motivated by the bad examples of psychology's grandiosity-ideas in our tradition, examples set, e.g., by Jung who sometimes felt that the function of psychology in the world is nothing less than "the rescue of the world" and believed that "the salvation of the world consists in the salvation of the individual soul"; furthermore, by Hillman hoping that Archetypal Psy-chology could bring soul and a sense of the aesthetic to the world or that it could bring about a change back from "universe" to "cosmos"; or, one last example, by many Jungians nowadays who think that Analytical Psy-chology could have a political function, that it should and could contribute something to the project of bringing peace to the world, etc. All pious and, to my mind, inflated illusions.

What I insisted on with my comments in *What is Soul?* on this topic is that psychology as the discipline of interiority does not have a mission in and for the real world, cannot offer to it any message worth mentioning, no higher meaning, wisdom, or answers to the great questions of life and of our time. It is not (like religion or philosophy) the bringer of true knowledge to the generality. It is merely the practice of soul-making as psychology-making. As far as impact on and essential contribution to the world *on the empirical or ego level* are concerned, it stays *quantité négligeable*. It is, after all, the discipline of *interiority*. As such, it is in itself "Home Office" pure. But as such, as speaking from the point of view of its commitment to interiority and soul, it claims according to *The Soul's Logical Life* that true knowing can happen.

What needs to be understood is that the one book denies psychology's possibility of knowledge as the I's *possessions* or *contents* that can be offered to the public on the marketplace or be *taught*, while the other book is concerned with *our* upholding, against its present-day deniers, the *notion* of true knowing as the soul's own knowing and as moments of truth. The claim in *The Soul's Logical Life* about true knowing was not an epistemo-logical thesis, but rather my insisting that the (after all uroboric) *soul* can, in principle, indeed come home to *itself.* Likewise, but conversely, the dictum in *What is Soul?* about psychology's having given up[12] the striving for true knowing amounts to the explicit rejection (for psychology) of any *episte-mological* (ego-based) claims to knowing. Psychology is for me the project of *soul-making,* "a methodological *procedere*".

In the same paragraph quoted by Barreto in which the abdication of the striving for true knowing was stated, the counterpart was also clearly expressed, namely, that the (non-epistemological, soul-based) "sense of truth is still vital to" and in psychology.[13] And, conversely, the denial of the true-knowledge claim expressed in *What is Soul?* was also already valid in *The Soul's Logical Life,* although not an important theme there ("The whole idea of 'the truth *of*' contents of consciousness must be dismissed. Truth in our context is nothing positive, not even anything like the so-called 'eternal truths' (which are actually the *frozen* former truths of previous states of the world)", p. 221).[14] This shows: Both seemingly contradictory ideas coexist and exist in both books. In fact, in the Introduction of my German book *Animus-Psychologie,* published five years earlier than *The Soul's Logical Life* (in late 1993), I had already clearly stated the gist of the no-knowing idea:

> In this day and age, a psychological author must be able to provide his answer to the question of why he is adding yet another psychological book or article to the thousands that are published every year. Does he claim to have something to say that the public absolutely needs to know? Does he believe he can offer the answer to the question of "Meaning", or at least one single insight of crucial importance, to the psychologically

---

12 N.B.: "given up" over against Hegel's philosophy. Not with respect to the position taken in *The Soul's Logical Life*!

13 In a footnote (# 31, p. 227), Barreto himself points to another passage in *What is Soul?* that contradicts his interpretation. There I spoke of the "internal not-I" as "the subject of true knowing, the organ of truth" that clearly shows that the idea of true knowing has by no means been given up in that book. But instead of taking this as a sign and a hint to himself that *his interpretation* cannot be adequate, he sees this as an (unnoticed) "conflict" not only between the two books but also within this one and the same book, a conflict that he prefers to interpret as "the neuroticizing betrayal of our psychology's own truth".

14 Wolfgang Giegerich, *The Soul's Logical Life* (Frankurt am Main: Peter Lang, 2001), p. 221.

interested audience searching, if not craving, for Meaning? Already 200
years ago, Goethe's Faust came to the insight, behind which we must
not regress: "I do not pretend to aught worth knowing, / I do not pretend
I could be a teacher / To help or convert a fellow-creature".[15]

It is therefore preposterous to suggest that with my denial of true knowledge in *What is Soul?* I have, many years after *The Soul's Logical Life*,
revoked[16] my original thesis and finally succumbed to the Kantian
position:

> It seems that Jung's "deep-seated fear of appearing as a 'metaphysi-
> cian'", which led him to rule out the question of truth for the sake
> of Kant's "epistemological barrier", almost invisibly instilled itself
> into the veins of our psychology, leading to the giving up of psycho-
> logical true knowing, the very heart of psychology as the discipline
> of interiority as boldly presented in *The Soul's Logical Life*. (Bar-
> reto, p. 223)

My description of what separates Hegel's *philosophy* from *psychology* in
my sense is just that: A *phenomenological* description of an objective historical rupture that separates the two and positions them each in their own
time, the one as philosophy in the time just before the end of metaphysics, the other necessarily as psychology during modernity. To construe this
objective observation as *my* personal *epistemological* (namely "Kantian")
stance is, as I said, preposterous. As psychologist I try to be committed to
the standpoint of soul, for which there simply is no epistemological problem. We are avowedly dealing with the soul's speaking about itself, with
its productions, self-manifestations, symptoms, myths, fantasies, fictions.[17]

---

15 Wolgang Giegerich, *Animus-Psychologie* (Frankfurt am Main: Peter Lang, 1994), p. 11.
    My translation (translation of the lines from *Faust* is by Bayard Taylor).
16 But why could I not also revoke earlier positions? It is quite natural that in the course of
    time there could possibly come a moment when one feels one has to depart from previ-
    ous convictions. I have changed my mind on many individual conceptions of Jung's and
    Hillman's that in my psychological youth I had accepted. But if so, it is ridiculous to
    see in such changes of mind "difficult dilemmas" or "blatant (let alone neuroticizing)
    contradictions".
17 This is why I criticized Jung's adopting, within psychology, the Kantian "barrier through
    the mental world" for the psychological topic of the god image. There cannot be a barrier

Psychological statements do not proclaim *truths*, but are about concrete *phenomena* ("empirical" *appearances, manifestations, events*) of soul truths[18] or *moments* of true knowing, as well as about the *historical phenomenology*, the, to cite Jung, *Wandlungen und Symbole* of the soul's life. Where should, under these conditions, a deep-seated fear of appearing as a metaphysician come from? And where should, on the other hand, any higher truths come from? Psychology has no truths to offer.[19]

The difference between soul truths and true knowing in my sense and Barreto's insistence on truth in the sense of epistemology can also be figuratively expressed in the following way. For me the *moments of truth* and of true knowing *occur (and stay) within* the "alchemical retort" (one has to have entered the retort, have become initiated into what happens in it and *have left* the standpoint of the *alchemist* looking from outside into the retort[20]), whereas for Barreto truth has to be valid outside of it (or rather: *His stance knows of no retort* and *insists* on the elimination of the difference between interiority in it and exteriority in favor of general, all-comprehensive validity). The image of the retort with the two possibilities of within it or outside of it can also serve as a visual aid for psychology's Janus-faced-ness.[21] When I said at the end of the previous paragraph,

---

between psychological phenomena and "the true reality" since for psychology the psychological phenomena (including the idea of "gods" and "God") are all *products* and *manifestations* of the soul and precisely *as such* soul truths, as Jung himself realized and insisted at least in the case of dreams.

18 I often use the phrase "soul truths". When Barreto writes, "If we accept this abdication of true knowing on the part of psychology, talking about soul *truths* becomes just a rhetorical expedient . . ." (p. 219), he misunderstands this phrase. In my usage, the name "soul truths" has nothing whatsoever to do with the topic of "true knowing" and "moments of truth", but is the title or name I use for established mythological, archetypal motifs such as "the virgin birth of the hero", "the union of death and rebirth", etc. and the ideational content of other soul phenomena. "Soul truths" is a purely semantic term. True knowing, by contrast, requires the correspondence of the semantic with the prevailing syntax. See next section.

19 To offer *to the world*.

20 This is the reason for the existence of "Psychology as the discipline of interiority" and for the operation of "absolute-negative interiorization".

21 The thinking and experiencing during ages of mythology, religion, and metaphysics took as a matter of course place, if I may say so, *in* the retort, or better: In what later became the retort. Because for those ages "the retort" did not exist yet, just as there was no place yet for the figure of the alchemist. "The retort" in the sense of this essay—and thus the *explicit* difference between interiority and external reflection (and ultimately also positivistic thought)—came into being only through "the birth of man", which is reflected

"Psychology has no truths to offer", I can now complement this statement by saying, what it—exoterically—does have to offer is the sense of interiority and an invitation into it. This is also why I must contradict Barreto's claim at the end of the quoted passage that "psychological true knowing" is "the very heart of psychology as the discipline of interiority". No, its heart is, as its name suggests, *one's entering*. Everything else that possibly happens in this psychology, such as also an event of truth, is unforeseeable product and result of this entering. But Barreto spares himself the concern about "entering". In his thoughts and actual concern, he has leapt right away to the (imagined) result.

The explanation Barreto gives is twofold: He resorts by way of explanation, on the one hand, to an *emotional* cause, an insinuated personal fear of mine of becoming "metaphysical", and, on the other hand, to a *theoretical* ground, the epistemological "Kantian interdiction". Both are explanations on the ego level and rely on impediments that within a psychology as the discipline of interiority, inasmuch as it understands itself, cannot come up. For the same reason he ends his piece by presenting two (or three) alternatives for psychology. Alternatives stand side by side on the same *horizontal* level and represent options for the ego to choose from according to its rational judgement or personal preference.

Abstract truth versus truth grounded in the psychological earth

But instead of an alleged Kant-inspired personal fear of appearing as a "metaphysician", what in reality made me distinguish psychology *as discipline* from Hegel's philosophy the way I did was a purely psychological reason, the necessity to respect *the objective soul*. And herewith I come to the most essential difference between Barreto and me. At stake is a *vertical* issue: The psychological difference between the ego level and the (objective) soul level, and between the level of semantic contents and the level of syntax or logical form. The real problem I see is that the latter level (in each case) is totally ignored by Barreto. Jung once exemplified this difference

---

in the figure of "the alchemist" or "psychologist" as well as those ordinary persons who are, just as the alchemist/psychologist, outside the retort, but other than the latter *wholly* outside in the sense of being ignorant, completely unaware, of such a thing as the retort/interiority.

between the two levels and its crucial psychological importance perfectly when he said about the Catholic Mass, "I cannot experience the miracle of the Mass . . . I know it is the truth, but it is the truth in a form in which I cannot accept it any more . . . I need a new form" (*CW* 17 § 632). It is undoubtedly the truth, but nevertheless no good, because it is the truth not in the right (historically appropriate) logical *form*. This gives us in a nutshell the modern situation. In my psychology I try to do justice to this the modern *soul's* complication.

What Jung showed in this case is—to consider it for the moment only in *theoretical* regards—that to know, have, and believe in, truths *as such* is not enough because all this only belongs to the ego, the subjective, and above all the semantic, side of the psychological difference. What *formally* and *abstractly* is admittedly *the truth* requires for its being *really* (and thus *truly*) true in addition its authentication by the logic that governs our real mode of being-in-the-world at our historical time. The psychological difference here reveals itself to be also what we could call the *historical difference*. The truth as such must, in order to be truly true, also *correspond* to and be *backed up* by the logical form prevailing in the historical age in which we and in which psychology exists. Without this, psychology becomes an empty ideology. The "truths", which by themselves are nothing but free-floating and abstract semantic contents or ideal forms,[22] have to be rooted, grounded, in the psychological earth: The *autonomous objective soul*.

(On the level of individual and practical life this possible discrepancy is reflected in the problem of "the right means in the hand of the wrong man" [*CW* 13 § 55, cf. §4] or in Lichtenberg's *bon mot*, "S. rarely did anything wrong, but what he did he generally did at the wrong time".[23])

The objective soul is not in us and not at our disposal, but is *antecedently given* as an objective, factual *reality*. It is around us. We find ourselves in it, much the same way that in empirical life we as individual human beings find ourselves born into the hard facts of a certain family, mother tongue, nation, economic and cultural situation, and a specific historical age, all of

22 These ideal forms can of course impress the ego, thereby creating emotions in people that seem to give life to the forms.

23 Georg Christoph Lichtenberg, *Schriften und Briefe I*, ed. by Wolfgang Promies (München: Hanser, 1968), number J803, p. 765, my translation. I discussed this in *What is Soul?* (New Orleans, LA: Spring Publications, 2012), p. 220.

which circumscribe for us certain limits as well as open up certain potentials and affordances. It is the particular phase of the history of the soul's
logical life in which we live that determines the prevailing logical form of
the world and life for us and that has the last word on what is true or not.
Barreto tries to establish his "metaphysical psychology" solely on the ego
level on the basis of his own reasoning, without respect for the soul's history—as a blossoming flower cut off from its roots in the earth. He reckons
without the host.

What Jung showed us in the cited case of the Mass—now describing
it in more practical terms—is that we have to *abide* by what we find as
given; abide in both directions: With respect to the ego level as well as to
the objective soul level. His *psychological-ego* insight forced Jung to admit
without reserve that the Mass was—semantically—the truth. But his loyalty to the objective soul forced him to realize, disappointing as it may have
been for him, that it—syntactically—was not the truth for him and his time.
Barreto's psychological error in presenting his alternatives at the end of his
paper is in my opinion that he thinks that it is *our* decision, *our* choice, that
we have a say[24] in the matter of how psychology should be set up. But we
are not the cooks, we are the guests who have to eat what we find our host
has dished out on our plate.

What creates the for Barreto "disastrous" dilemma that he sees is the
result of his own doing or neglecting to do.

Psychology as no more than a pastime—a fatal fault?

The response to the "blatant contradiction" between the statements about
true knowing in the two books of mine cited by Barreto provides already
the answer to his second dilemma, the problem that he has with the idea that
psychology has no greater significance than that of a pastime or hobby or
that it has its place only in a niche. Again, for me this merely describes the
status that this psychology has with respect to the world around itself at its
historical time. The psychology as the discipline of interiority is something
exclusively for the few who are so minded. The modern world at large is
simply not interested in "soul-making" and "absolute-negative interiorization". It has no real place for it. In fact, not even the majority of the Jungian

24 Jung: "*We* decide, as if we knew" (*Letters 2*, p. 591, to Read, 2 Sep. 1960).

world is attracted to the discipline of interiority. This psychology does not have the dignity of a public status. So, seen from outside, from the realistic "foreign relations" perspective, it is something only for a few, something one can do as a private "hobby". That is all. But from the inside perspective, for him who practices the discipline of interiority, for his own attitude and self-assessment, it is not at all a pastime. Once a psychologist is *in* psychology, doing its work, he should be wholeheartedly committed to it. Within it, you have to be present as *the whole man* (*homo totus*).

But now comes the other side. Even if *we* as persons (therapists or patients) are fully committed, *psychology as discipline*, being a child of the modern world (the world of Nietzsche's "last man"[25]) nevertheless inevitably has the status of a hobby, because it is not backed up by the logic of the age. It is not *psychology* that enters the wilderness and becomes the place of true knowing, it is always *we* who need to do this *in this psychology* (whether we in fact will do it or not is always in the lap of the gods). However, only if we do it, and with full commitment, can psychology as discipline be truly a discipline of interiority. Thus the idea that *psychology* has the status of a hobby is no ground for the kind of disastrous dilemma that Barreto imagines.

The discipline that studies the soul as historical product of this soul

At this point it may be helpful to recall that psychology is itself a psychological *phenomenon*, produced by that very *history* of the soul's logical life that is the object of study (or subject-matter) of psychology.[26] Psychology

25 It is essential to realize that the "last man" (for Nietzsche the most despicable man) is not still coming, as Nietzsche seems to have thought, and not a danger, aberration to be avoided. It is rather simply the title of the logical status of *modern* man as such, of the status in which *we all* inescapably are and have been all along. It is precisely the very institution of psychotherapy that corroborates this: One characteristic of the last man according to Nietzsche is that "whoever feels different goes voluntarily into a madhouse". Millions of people the world over voluntarily having undergone or seeking psychoanalysis or psychotherapy: What is this if not the realized small-scale version of Nietzsche's dictum?

26 Above I called Barreto's "metaphysical psychology" a blossoming flower cut off from its roots in the earth. From the present argument we understand better why he on principle refuses to accept the idea of a historical end (obsolescence) of metaphysics. He obviously cannot allow metaphysics to have its place *in* the soul, to be a soul *phenomenon* and as such be produced by, as well as be *subject to*, the history of the soul. It seems

does not, like the external observer or the atemporal consciousness-as-such in the sciences, perceive its object of study from an Archimedean point. It could, as Jung showed, only become possible (as well as necessary) through the historical loss of a culturally *prevailing* mythological or religious or metaphysical constitution of the world, only because of the "end of Meaning". Psychology is therefore concomitant of and a true child of modernity with its new standpoint of modern subjectivity.[27] Psychology *is* the sublation of the previous world condition(s) of myth, religion, metaphysics, and the sciences, their having been *downgraded* to the state of (psychological!) obsolescence; but at the same time it is also the *elevation* of consciousness to the superior standpoint of the (previously unheard-of concept of the) objective autonomous soul. What this means is that within itself (in its own structure) psychology as discipline is aware of its own being *contained in* its object of study (in the soul, in its historical logical life) and, furthermore, that the emergence of psychology ultimately amounts to, nay, *is* the *objective* becoming-conscious-and-explicit of the psychological difference.

Earlier I pointed out that for mythological consciousness the psychological difference was directly the "ontological" character of the things in

---

that for his thinking, metaphysics, because it is *semantically* the domain OF TIMELESS TRUTHS and changeless principles, must also *logically* AS THIS DOMAIN be set up as being above and outside the historical logical life of the soul; metaphysics must be taken literally, must not be *seen through*. A mutual entwinement with its other, namely, the changes of cultural history (or the history of the soul's logical life)—similar to how the psychological *discipline* and the soul's *phenomenology* are, logically, uroborically contained in each other—has to be prevented.

27 Subjectivity inevitably establishes the subject-object opposition. This is why modern psychology, be it as academic or psychoanalytic and introspective psychologies, can only be concerned with the *psyche* (as "object", with what goes on inside people). They cannot be psychologies *with* soul, because soul is itself the true *subject* and not object. – A psychology that wants to be a psychology *with* soul is therefore necessarily faced with the "No Admission!"-problem discussed in chapter 1 of *The Soul's Logical Life* and has to be a discipline of *interiority*, which, as shown, is qua discipline in the hands of modern subjectivity, but, through the psychologist's having logically died as subject, is able to achieve interiority or to arrive "in the land of the soul". – A "*metaphysical* psychology", as projected by Barreto, manages to escape the necessity of overcoming the entrance hurdle by—in the logical form of what we call a *faith* or *belief*—simply claiming to be, *as* subjectivity and *as* psychological discipline, *a priori* already in possession of the "soul standpoint", and thus, just like that, to be able to go on the "*Great* Hunt" and to attain to higher truths.

the world (including man himself). This means that the difference had not become conscious as *difference*, as opposition. Reality (including man) was both sides at once, without any conflict making itself felt, which in turn was *existentially* tantamount to man's containment in Meaning and, in *practical* life, to the possibility and necessity of initiations. The later emergence of religion and metaphysics with their sense of transcendence (as a first loosening of the direct undivided presence of both sides in the Real) can be seen as a cultural intermediate stage and bridge to modernity as the time of the fully explicit and consciously felt difference. Psychology (in the rigorous sense) is that unique place in modernity at or in which the two sides of the difference touch, which makes psychology in a very remote way reminiscent of the mythological situation. Psychology is (like the alchemical *Mercurius duplex*) *utriusque capax*, a kind of pivot. As already pointed out earlier in different words, it is ego and soul at once: As *discipline* "ego", human-all-too-human, part of the world of the "last man"; but as the discipline *of interiority* "soul". This duality is reflected on the "object-level", the level of psychological phenomenology, in the difference between

7. the *opus parvum* (*our* soul-making work *in* the sublated sphere of the ego-personality's "inner") and
8. the *opus magnum* (the *objective soul's* work, in the *real world*, upon the constitution of the logical form of human existence, consciousness, and culture).

True knowing even in a tamed wilderness

The *opus parvum*, which is above all dealt with in the consulting room, is objectively a fenced-in realm for psychology. No doubt about that. My example earlier of how dreams have to be viewed is taken from this already fenced-in sphere, and one's beginning and dwelling with the *not-understood* in one's working with psychological phenomena is certainly our entering a wilderness that is rather tame. The crucial point here is, nevertheless, that even when in this sphere of the *opus parvum* the psychological work, for example, with a dream truly succeeds, then this is a moment of the soul's true knowing-itself, an event of truth, the momentary opening of a little window to eternity. Such a real happening of knowing is always one of *true knowing*, no matter whether this knowing relates to something in the small private sphere or to public life. This is so because any such moment amounts to a breakthrough from the everyday world or consciousness into another dimension. Truth, for psychology, is truth on the level of eachness and here-and-nowness, the truth of soul phenomena and as events, *moments* of truth, not *the* Truth (the true soul knowledge of the Real) that metaphysics is concerned with and the Great Hunt is hunting for.

Furthermore, *on the personal level* wilderness is not an objective empirical fact, not simply given. Potentially, *any "here and now"* can for a person be the true wilderness in the soul sense—just as conversely it is possible that an empirically given real wilderness will *not* be a wilderness for him who does not unconditionally expose himself to it (or is already familiar with it). What really makes a real situation *be* a wilderness is (in addition to its being radically unknown to us) whether we without reserve enter it with the full sense of "This is it!" It depends on our showing presence, our wholehearted, relentless commitment. This was one main point in the last chapter of *The Soul's Logical Life*. In the myth, as I showed in that book, it is not just Aktaion (or you or me) that moves into the forest. Aktaion is the soul itself *as human psychology* approaching *itself* as truth *if and when*, in all its concrete work, our psychology relentlessly subjects itself, its logic and all its presupposition, to its own inherent necessities and to the complexities of its inner essence. *This* is the *psychological* wilderness. And, with respect to the question of truth, we are only concerned with the wilderness of psychology, only with psychology's coming home to *itself*!

And is not, even in modernity, life itself, the life to be lived by us, a real wilderness for each of us, not fenced-in at all, provided life is seen with the eyes of the soul and as the place where we sense that we *must* ourselves come forward and enter the lists? And can there, during one's going through one's life in this spirit, not also be a moment of truth, in the sense of a moment that forcefully and fatefully places a *télos*, a "circle" or "band", on the head of the person for his whole life?[28]

---

28 As to *télos* see Richard Broxton Onians, *The Origins of European Thought about the Body, the Mind, the Soul, the World, Time, and Fate.* Reprint of the 1951(Cambridge University Press) edition (New York: Arno Press, 1973), pp. 426ff.

The new real wilderness

But above all in the domain of the objective soul's historical *opus magnum*, the wilderness is as wild as ever. Today perhaps even more so than before. The present-day Aktaion—the soul in the form of "modern man as such" (modern man not as the people but as the psychological or archetypal *Anthropos*, the Concept of Man)—has already, against people's intention and without their awareness, entered it and has relentlessly exposed himself to it, still aimlessly wandering through it. This is the objective, the cultural wilderness, the *real* soul wilderness that began with the time of the End of Meaning. It was further described, for example, by Jung with the following words:

> The great problem of our time is that we don't understand what is happening in the world. We are confronted with the darkness of our soul. . . . It hollows out and hacks up the shapes of our culture and its historical dominants. We have no dominants any more. . . . Our hitherto believed values decay accordingly and our only certain[t]y is that the new world will be something different from what we were used to. (*Letters 2*, p. 590, to Read, 2 September 1960)

Meanwhile even more characteristics of the wilderness that has to be wandered through have become visible than could be perceived at Jung's time. We now have witnessed the emergence of the center-less Internet and all the abstract, anonymous networks encompassing everyone, indeed modern life as such, and rendering such a thing as "the individual" and "the subject" logically obsolete; we experience social media, cybercrimes, virtual reality, Artificial Intelligence, deepfakes, etc.; furthermore, a human world to a large degree addicted to drugs, entertainment, excitements, constant noise (music) purposely pulled in by earphones . . .

This objective wilderness is again a situation of the real world without center, aim, direction. To be in the wilderness therefore means confusion, lack of orientation, and even real turmoil. And it *is* completely independently from whether the psychology as discipline of interiority is viewed as a pastime or not.

What Jung wrote about man if and when he has become "completely modern" can just as well be taken by us as a description of the new, present-day Aktaion as the one who enters the new wilderness. Present-day man, Jung wrote,

> is completely modern only when he has come to the very edge of the world, having *behind him* all that has become obsolete and outgrown and *before him* admittedly the Nothing out of which anything and everything may grow. (*CW* 10 § 150, transl. modif. according to the original, my italics)

To be Aktaion he has to be in the no-man's land or rather at zero point exactly *between* the "behind" and the "before him"; he has to have the refined culturally developed and civilized world, the time-honored traditions, and the wealth of all the inherited images and precious symbols behind him and before him the emptiness and total unknownness of the untrodden, untreadable territory of the future. Only as such *is* there wilderness for him in the first place.

My thesis is that the empirical experience *by us* of this special historical situation of fundamental loss of orientation must not be taken at face value by us, not be frozen into, and elevated to the level of, a *theoretical dogma of the impossibility of true knowing*. At least for a psychology with soul this would be a mistake and a betrayal of the notion of soul. When present-day Aktaion, as the explicit soul, is still erring through the wilderness, the implicit soul has from the outset always already been "naked Artemis", ready to appear to him when the time of his being exposed and slowly becoming fully *adapted* to the wilderness has come to its completion. This would be the moment of truth and true knowing with its full Dionysian consequences for Aktaion, in the sense of the *achieved* assimilation of his subjective style of consciousness (i.e., our human mind) to the logical constitution intrinsic to the new real world. But of course, this is a process "taking place 'in Mercurio'" (*Letters 2*, p. 394, to John Trinick, 15 Oct. 1957), in the "archetypal background", "the psyche's hinterland", *not* in the personal psyche and not on the empirical level of events and lived experience.[29]

---

29 Cf. Wolfgang Giegerich, *The Soul's Logical Life* (Frankfurt am Main: Peter Lang, 2001), p. 155.

This means that *our* relentless commitment to it, *our* coming forward and showing presence, are here precisely not needed. The *opus magnum* proceeds behind our backs and over our head and is not in need of our, be it inner or active, participation nor of our conscious awareness. Psychology as discipline is not needed, cannot contribute to it. It is all the objective soul's doing. We only feel, and are changed by, *its* effects. So this is a point where I need to correct my presentation in *The Soul's Logical Life*, in which I emphasized our needing to be present without, however, distinguishing between the *opus parvum* (for which this our commitment is crucial) and the *opus magnum* (for which it is not). In fact, I now believe that an attempt by us (us as people) to enter this process, our thus confusing *ourselves* with the present-day Aktaion, would be an undue interference in the soul's objective process. We must not try to play Aktaion. All *we* can do in this area is to observe what is going on on the level of the external impressions and try to see through to the "other picture that looms up behind the scenes".

By the same token, psychology cannot and should not try to anticipate the future and thus to at least *mentally* try to simply skip the difficult time of passing through the wilderness, thereby cheating itself out of the full impact of the essential experience. We have to let the soul do its thing and patiently wait and see if, when and how the moment of true knowing may appear. But since it is the soul that is at work, some form of indeed making itself explicit to itself in *reality* (through the new "Aktaion") seems likely. Jung at least, using a rather different image than that of the Aktaion myth, envisioned already—precisely on the basis of his description of the signs of our time given in the above-quoted passage—the approach of "the awe-inspiring guest who knocks at our door portentously" and he even intuited his eventual arriving (!): "All his [the modern artist's] love and passion (his 'values') flow towards the coming guest to proclaim his arrival" (*Letters 2*, to Herbert Read, 2 September 1960, pp. 590 and 591). I tend to think this is premature. If at all, his arrival, or, to say it with our myth, the moment of truth, naked Artemis, will probably need centuries to become possible.

I distinguished the myth per se whose logical topic is a single momentary, point-like event (comparable to one beam of white light in physics) from the myth as narrative, which, much like a prism that disperses this *one* beam of white light into its internal constituents, unfolds the internal logical moments of the one event into a narrated succession of happenings. The narrative form of, if I may say so, today's "Aktaion myth" does no longer appear as a story, a mythic tale, to be told in a few minutes. *Today, this narrative appears as history*, "acted out" as the real-time course of events. Because it is the *objective* soul's own[30] story.

---

30 The ancient myths were of course also the objective soul's own stories, the soul's speaking about itself. But in *today's* Aktaion myth as well as in the process of history in general, the objective soul is not *speaking* about itself, merely *manifesting* its inner truths as contents of human consciousness, but *directly living out*, acting out, its own logical life in the *reality* of our human cultural process.

Chapter 6

Love the Questions Themselves

Wolfgang Giegerich at 66, Interviewed
by Rob Henderson[1]

Encountering Jung

(RH): How did you become interested in Jung?

(WG): In the light of my early biography, it is surprising even to me that I became a Jungian psychologist. From what I learned in high school (*Gymnasium*) about depth psychology (practically exclusively Freudian psychoanalysis) I had developed a downright aversion to it. The mechanistic approach of psychoanalysis ("psychic apparatus") and above all its detective-like attempt to get behind the hidden secrets of people were distasteful to me. So I would never have considered becoming a psychoanalyst.

My attitudes toward psychoanalysis at the time were of course mere prejudices because they were based on only very superficial knowledge. Also, the little I knew about academic psychology with its positivistic mentality did not make *it* any more attractive. The type of questions that interested me was different. I was curious about such issues as what art is (the mystery of art), what it is that gives a poem its particularly lyrical quality, what about myth and magic, how education actually works (what the factors are that really influence a child), how ethical norms can be justified, what the nature of Christian faith is and how it happens that a person experiences this faith, to mention only a few topics. From this it would seem to have suggested itself that I turn to philosophy or theology as my field of study (all the more so as I had learned Greek and Hebrew in school). But I had a very clear sense that I would not take up these fields.

---

1 Conducted by email between September 2007 and June 2008, with an addendum of October 2008.

DOI: 10.4324/9781003611400-7

My own theory now about this is that I somehow wanted to keep the questions alive, rather than be confronted with fixed systems that provide ready-made answers. So I turned to languages and literature as my university subject, where one is much closer to the actual living process of the mind. In particular I also wanted to study, in addition to familiar languages, at least one language that was totally different in structure and cultural tradition from our Western (Indo-European or Semitic) ones, but was also characterized by a rich, high-standing literature, because I wondered if and how language and thought influence each other. I chose Chinese.

All this is very far away from psychology. But these studies did not really do for me what I had hoped, so I did not continue them. It was not before I heard lectures and took seminars from Prof. Andrew O. Jászi at Berkeley that I had the sensation that he was speaking about, or himself moved by, questions that were of deepest interest to me. Prof. Jászi taught, e.g., courses on Goethe's *Faust* and German lyric poetry, and had a philosophical mind. He was influenced by Ernst Cassirer, but also occasionally showed familiarity with C.G. Jung and Erich Neumann. During my years as a graduate student I did not find the time to turn to Jung and Neumann myself, but I had made a mental note about them, and after the conclusion of my university education I read all the works of these two authors that I could lay my hands on.

I felt that many of my diverse interests came together in Jungian psychology and that through it I came in contact with a live matrix from which to understand and investigate those questions that I really wanted to know more about. Within a year or so it became clear to me that I would give up my university career and become a Jungian analyst. If I devoted myself to Jungian psychology, I wanted to know it thoroughly also from its practical side. This is the circuitous way in which I ended up professionally where I originally never expected to be. Now, after more than thirty years as a Jungian analyst, I can say that I have not regretted my decision, although I now see many aspects of Jung's work much more critically.

(RH): What are a couple main areas of Jung which you now are much more critical of?

(WG): It is good that you speak of "main areas", because my critical assessment aims at the core of Jung's psychology project as a whole rather than at certain particular details. What I consider one main fault is that Jung hypostatized (substantiated) "the unconscious". This is a mystification.

Often "the unconscious" is treated in his work (a) as a positive fact and (b) as if it were a kind of author, the author of dreams, visions, myths, ideas. This is exactly analogous to some misguided present-day neuro-scientists acting as if the brain were the cause or author of our thoughts. By the same token, Jung more or less reified "the archetypes". He explicitly set them up as timeless "factors" in the literal Latin sense of the word. In this way they, too, are positivized and logically removed from *within* the real psychic process and set up as external "dominants" of this process, in violation of psychology's constitutive principle of interiority.

A second serious problem is for me that Jung tended to see neurosis ultimately as a *morbus sacer*, and addictions, for example, alcoholism, as a kind of religious quest that merely happened to be unsuccessful. In other words, psychic illnesses like the ones mentioned are given out as something basically valuable, noble, even sacred, and what is wrong with them as merely being due to a mishap. This is a neurotic interpretation of neurosis, the doctor riding the same hobby-horse as the neurosis itself.

A third major stance that I find fault with is Jung's insistence that the individual is "the makeweight that tips the scales", indeed, that the salvation of the world consists in the salvation of the individual soul. This zooming in on the individual again expresses Jung's need to positivize. It should be clear, I think, that a psychology that deserves its name cannot take any positive reality, neither the individual nor society (the collective), as fundamental. Everything psychologically important happens in the not-positively-existing "soul", in what Heraclitus called the *logos eôn*, the existing logos, the logic or syntax of consciousness, which is neither something in the individual (the literalized "inner", his "unconscious") nor something "collective".

The unconscious

(RH): If the unconscious is neither a positive fact nor a mystified author of dreams, myths, and ideas, how would you explain or describe the unconscious to a beginning Jungian class?

(WG): I think I would begin by stating that "the unconscious" is a *historical* fact, an idea in the intellectual history of the West and in the history of the soul; that it came up at a particular time, during the nineteenth century, and was adopted by the most influential psychologists of the twentieth century, Freud and Jung, in their own ways. This idea exists for us today as much as, to different degrees, ideas from other ages exist, the idea of a purgatory, of an ether, of a *perpetuum mobile*, or the ideas that Marx and Lenin bestowed on us.

Then I would probably describe in some detail what was meant by "the unconscious" by different schools of thought, i.e., what they claimed the unconscious to be and to consist of. Part of such a description would have to be that the depth-psychologists of the 20th century actually *believed* in the unconscious, and interpreted the fact that this idea had come up only recently as their *discovery* of "the unconscious" (the way America or the sources of the Nile or certain pathogens had been discovered).

In my answer to your previous question I mentioned the analogy between seeing the unconscious as the author of dreams, etc., and seeing the brain as a kind of author of our thoughts. But now I have to qualify this statement by pointing out the fundamental difference between these two ideas of authorship: The brain is at least a demonstrable fact, a positivity, something real, which thus might in principle be a candidate for being an "author", whereas "the unconscious" cannot be demonstrated and is therefore something that could not possibly have been discovered. It is really only an idea or construct in the minds of certain people. There is no such thing as "the unconscious". What indeed exists, however, is unconsciousness. And there is plenty of it and in many different senses of the word, senses which would of course have to be elaborated and differentiated. In other words, "unconscious" should only be used as an adjective, not as a noun. Finally, but this may already be too much for a beginning class, I could go a bit into the psychological reasons for the invention of "the unconscious", the function it had for its time, the purpose it served, the historical-psychological needs that gave rise to it.

Today, being able to see the crazes of the 20th century a bit more from a historical distance, we no longer have to believe in the unconscious. We no longer need to positivize, split off, and project out the one integral moment of the mind's life, which is in itself the dialectical unity of "unconscious" and "conscious", something that began to dawn on Jung in his later years. In understanding such phenomena as dreams, psychological symptoms, or the production processes of great art we can do completely without any substantiated notion of "the unconscious".

Where do dreams come from?

(RH): Where do you feel dreams, fantasies, and symbols come from? Some people believe that dreams are messages from God.

(WG): Aristotle said man is a *zôion logon echon*, a living being endowed with "logos". We have a mind, we speak. Or better: we *are* mind (mindedness). We are not simply, like things (*Dinge*), affected and conditioned (*bedingt*) by what happens, we inevitably apperceive, interpret, "make" something of it.

The mind is productive, nay, is productivity. When I speak of "soul" I often mean this ongoing productivity itself, this "logical life" (where "logical" simply implies the *logos*-nature of this life), rather than some kind of existing entity as the producer of this production. At least this is one of the meanings of "soul". Now, what one has to keep in mind is that this productivity can (a) go on quite different levels (close to the surface, as an "ego" activity, or at various degrees of depth), and (b) be more this particular individual's (private, personal) expression, or express more one of the relationships that the person is in, his family, group, the spirit of the age, the entire culture or even the human race.

The mind or soul is not a kind of fixed organ in each person, his or her private possession. Basically infinite, its limits, when it expresses itself in and through a particular individual, are difficult to define and vary greatly in extent and depth. And (c) we have to keep in mind that this productivity is itself dialectical, the contradictory unity of "making" and "occurrence/happening to . . .", of active and passive, like the uroboros, and always—and in different ways and senses—both "conscious" and "unconscious". This is why I would neither say, without further qualification, that dreams, fantasies, and symbols *come from* somewhere (in the emphatic sense of "come from"), nor that they are messages, because this would undialectically conceive of us as passive recipients, if not victims, of our dreams and fantasies. Jung of course liked to think this way. But I think we are not that innocent of our dreams. We are actively involved in the making of our dreams (*I* dream, when I dream), even if they *also* and *at the same time* truly happen to us. It is similar as with our whole being. I did not create myself, I happened to myself, and yet in living I constantly am, I exist as, my own "making myself".

As to God, this word can have very different meanings in different theologies and at different levels of cultural development and refinement. There might be senses in which, and stages of consciousness at which, the belief about dreams as His messages is perfectly legitimate. However, the idea of dreams as messages from God in modern psychological circles is in my opinion psychologically irresponsible. Epistemologically one would posit an invisible, unknowable agent or author behind the scene, and ethically one would palm responsibility off for the production of one's dream. And with the idea of a "message", especially if it is thought to come directly from God Himself, one would not only try to strut in borrowed plumes (playing, as it were, "Mary and the Annunciation" on a small scale), one would also pretend that dreams have a fixed meaning.

But the way dreams come to us, they are not messages. They are *only* stories, images, texts that *we* have to *make* sense of all on our own responsibility. It is we who construe what *they* are supposed to be saying.

The soul

(RH): What do you mean that Jung had a need to positivize?

(WG): Just like life as such, so also "the soul" (the logical life as which "soul" *is*) is (logically) negative. You can dissect a human being, but you will NOT find his or her life, let alone "soul". Life and soul are not positive facts, although they are powerful realities. They escape any positivistic research. But Jung—this is at least one side of him; he also has a very different, indeed almost opposite side—felt the need to construe psychology as a natural science, to insist that what he presented were simply facts, nothing but facts. This is why he not only invented the Association Experiment, but also hypostatized "the unconscious" and the archetypes. But psychology is not about facts: What it deals with does not have fact nature.

Everything psychological is from the outset and inescapably already *interpreted*, if not the interpretation of an interpretation of an interpretation . . . It has mind nature (which is why I speak of the soul's *logical* life). Take, for example, dreams. They are not facts. They are only my *memory of* and (often fuzzy) *idea about* what I dreamed last night (and that which I try to remember is itself the production of a "poetic" fiction to begin with). In courtrooms, where, after all, one is out to get at the facts, one nevertheless knows full well what to think of eyewitness reports; here the Japanese movie, *Rashomon*, comes to mind. Positivizing is ultimately an attempt to get out of the "uroboros" situation of the mind to some solid ground, cause, or truth which, itself being outside of and exempt from the soul's life, is supposed to explain the soul's life.

(RH): To illustrate what you mean by "the logical life as which 'soul' is", will you give an example from your own life or the life of someone else when the "soul" was experienced?

(WG): I am taken a little by surprise by your question. I have to think a bit. I wonder, is "soul" really something that we experience? I don't think so. It is accessible only on reflection and to our insight (after the fact) and this insight presupposes both some effort (study, so-called "analysis", "seeing through") and a particular eye for things psychological. Experiences are immediate and subjective. But "the soul" is, according to Jung, precisely non-ego, an objective psyche; he spoke of background processes, just as Hillman located the soul, metaphorically speaking, in the underworld. "Soul" is certainly not about us and what we feel or think.

There is no direct access to it. If one wants to learn something about the soul and its logical life it is far better to turn away from us people and instead turn to myth, theology, archaic ritual (like the Roman Catholic Mass), great literature and art, philosophy, or alchemy, on the one hand, and to the course of real history, social changes, the development of technology and the like, on the other hand.

If one wants to see the soul at work in us people, the best and a truly grand, even if twisted, example is neurosis (not this or that person's neurosis, but the modern phenomenon of neurosis as such). But it is essential to realize that a given neurosis is not *experienced as* a manifestation of soul and that what is experienced of it is not the soul; not even most psychologists view neurosis in terms of soul, but rather from an ego perspective: For example, as caused by certain traumatizing conditions. That neurosis is a free creation of "the soul" for its own ends and purposes (not for ours) and a work of freedom cannot be experienced, it can only be comprehended. You need psychology (a psychology with soul) to see "the soul".

(RH): From the standpoint of the "Soul", what would be some ways to understand the Holocaust?

(WG): Much has been written about the Holocaust from an ego point of view (historical descriptions of the facts, moral evaluation, the personal experience of surviving victims, etc.). So it is apt to also give some thought to what the Holocaust means from the standpoint of "soul". But this is also a very difficult question. It is said that when you are wounded by a gunshot you at first don't feel anything. It takes a while for the pain to be allowed into consciousness.

In a similar way, I think, the soul is still dazed by the enormous trauma caused to it by the Holocaust. It will probably take several more decades, if not centuries, before it can truly open itself to the full reality of what happened to it. For the time being the soul is still completely enveloped in and deafened by the buzzing noise of our ego emotions around the topic of the Holocaust. And anyway, whatever one can say about an event of such unheard-of dimensions is probably at the same time too little and too much.

Nevertheless, I will give here two hints about two different directions into which my—preliminary—thoughts, from the standpoint of soul, move. But I first have to point out the difference between the soul standpoint and the ego point of view. The ego perceives things in terms of an external, clear-cut division of doer and victim, cause and effect, subject and object, whereas the soul—the methodological principle of inwardness and absolute-negative interiorization—understands what happens to it "uroborically" in terms of its own self-relation.

The soul is not only something nice and harmless. As the alchemists conceived it, it *also* turns against itself, cuts into its own flesh, and destroys and overcomes its own initial innocence. Occidental history in particular is a progressive series of such self-negations of the soul.

To give a few examples, and only in the briefest and most abstract way, thousands of years ago, the soul first turned against its own innate polytheism, its deep devotion to nature gods; in the 16th and 17th centuries witch-hunts it severed its precious bond with its intuitive knowledge of the spirit of nature; in the Enlightenment it cut itself off from the imaginal *per se* as mere superstition; in the French Revolution it destroyed its sacred sense of majesty; during the age of positivism it emancipated itself from the very idea of a God. All these were and to some extent still are painful wounds inflicted upon the soul by itself for the purpose of overcoming itself and achieving a higher logical status of itself. In the light of the process of this self-negation trend in the history of the Western soul, the Holocaust could be seen as that event in which the soul attacked and ruined for good its own innocent belief in "the Good".

I will only set down my second, complementary idea here, without further comment, as if it were a Zen *kōan* to be meditated: The Holocaust is the soul's initiation into Love.

(RH): "I will only set down my second, complementary idea here, without further comment, as if it were a Zen *kōan* to be meditated: the Holocaust is the soul's initiation into Love." Does this mean you do not want to elaborate further about "the Holocaust is the soul's initiation into Love?"

(WG): That's right. There are times and topics where the ego has to become silent. And whoever would like to understand what could possible be meant by that dictum will never find out if he or she turns to others for an explanation, for example to me. No, for an understanding one has to turn to nothing else but the bewildering notion itself, here the notion of Love (with a capital L) in connection with the Holocaust, and turn to it in the quiet and loneliness of thought, the thought of the heart, with the patience of being able to wait.

(RH): How does a person discover the impact of the soul in their life?

(WG): When you speak of "impact", what in our time first comes to mind is psychopathology, disturbing, interfering symptoms. Maybe also certain dreams. And of course, in the case of the rare great persons, the creative impulse that is frequently felt by them to be an imposed burden. But a person may experience the impact of the severest psychological symptom and nevertheless not *discover* it as an impact *of the soul*. You can just as easily give it an ego interpretation.

The same applies to dreams. It is not enough to *have* dreams or symptoms. The awareness of soul depends on what you make of your experience and who you are, who, in you, experiences. This is also why the greatest impact of the soul in our time, one that affects each of our lives massively and constantly, the impact of the enormous development of our technological and capitalist civilization, is generally not seen as the present form of the soul's *opus magnum* at all.

But we should also not have any illusions about people and the soul as if everyone longed to get in contact with soul. In fact, most people today *have no need for it*. They get along quite well without "soul". This is my one caution. There is a second one. Jung once asserted that the Church serves as a fortress to protect us against God and his Spirit. Analogously I think we could, if we wanted, realize that much of today's "really-existing"

Jungianism—much of the inflationary talk about mythic patterns in our lives or one's personal myth, about the Gods, the sacred, soul-making—while pretending to serve the soul, in truth serves as a distraction from today's real locus of soul and merely functions as ego entertainment.

So much on our age. In former times I think it would have been less a question of the impact, and of a discovery, of the soul than of people's constant living with and in the soul, as a matter of course: Daily religious service, ritual practice, what Jung called "the symbolic life", to which, as he claimed, the Australian Aborigines devoted two thirds of their available time.

The unknown Jung?

(RH): There are people like those with the Philemon Foundation who claim that there is a large amount that is still unknown about Jung; in fact, some claim that if we knew what is still unknown about Jung we would have some radically different understandings of what he was about. Do you agree?

(WG): Since I belong to those who don't know "what is still unknown about Jung", I cannot take a position on this issue. I will have to wait until all the material is on the table. Theoretically, it is of course possible that Jung kept secret an entire dimension of his life and thought ("one must have a good exoterics", Jung once wrote to Hermann Hesse) and that the editors of his writings selected only material that would not disturb a certain image of Jung.

But then, considering that we already have a very rich and variegated œuvre of Jung's before us that comprises in 25 or more volumes his writings as well as such diverse material as seminars, interviews, letters, memories, and that spans most of the time of his adult life, it would be surprising if the new material would really radically change our understanding of what Jung was about.

One would actually have to expect that "what Jung was about" would inevitably have had to reveal itself in this mass of available texts. Also, there have been previous cases where sensational claims or expectations preceded the posthumous publication of unpublished manuscripts (for example, Nietzsche, Heidegger), but where the new revelations were not all that great. This is not to say that we might not get valuable new background information on Jung's early intellectual development, on the origin of certain of his ideas both from out of his inner "visionary" experience and through contact with correspondents or books. But all these reflections are really pointless. We will simply have to be patient and wait to see what is in the new material.

A very different question is what is meant in the first place by "what Jung is about"? What are the criteria and what is the basis for determining the answer to this question, and, no less important, who can judge?

The shadow

(RH): From the standpoint of the Soul, what is the Shadow?

(WG): The Shadow is a *term* in Jungian psychology, a personified *concept*. This is important to remember. We often forget this and act as if the shadow were a given, the *name* for a real fact, the name perhaps for something like a psychic organ, in much the same way that the liver is an organ in the body. But as a personified concept, the shadow is not a name, but a fantasy or interpretation. As a psychological concept, it is at once *our* concept or interpretation *and* the soul's self-interpretation.

"Our concept" means that when we call, for example, a certain dream figure a shadow figure, it is we who are speaking and have to take responsibility for this our interpretation. With respect to the other aspect, we have to avoid misunderstanding the shadow as a personification of certain unconscious personality aspects, *in addition to* the ego, anima, animus, the self as so many other personality aspects. At least on one occasion Jung rightly rejected this compartmentalizing view of the soul, saying that the shadow is simply the *whole* unconscious. That is to say, it is one self-interpretation or self-representation of "the unconscious" (or better: The soul) as a whole, just as the ego, the anima, the self are also, but different, self-interpretations of the soul as a whole. Rather than parts of the personality, each of these personifications is a different guise in which the soul presents itself to itself at different moments of its logical life. (To present itself to itself is the nature of the soul's logical life; soul IS essentially "uroboric" self-relation.)

The shadow is that guise or self-interpretation of the soul that the soul wants or needs to take when it happens to have defined itself as ego (the ego, which is not the I!) and now wants to present itself to itself, i.e., to the ego-form of itself, *as* its own other. But because that on which it wants to impress itself as its own other is itself-*in-the-guise-of*"the ego" and because it is the very nature of "the ego" not to have any sense of soul, this other cannot really show itself as what it actually is (the soul's own other), but only as *the* Other, the wholly Other—absolutely incompatible and thus dark and threatening (namely to the ego-personality).

As the first and still immediate form of the soul as the other of itself, the shadow is the initial or preliminary psychopomp, both on a personal and a cultural-historical level. It attempts to initiate consciousness into "the soul", into "psychology".

Technology

(RH): How do you see healing taking place between the Soul and Technology?

(WG): I'm not sure I understand what exactly your question is aiming at. If by "how healing takes place" you mean how one can become a fairly unneurotic individual I would say that the two most important factors are one's honesty and one's humility. Honesty implies adaptation, that is, owning up to one's truth; humility implies one's coming down to earth, giving up one's insistence on being more than one is, one's understanding that "I am *only* that!" (Jung). Another way of putting it would be to say that humility implies one's emancipation from the soul and from the mystifications that it brings, one's being cured of all the big words, all the inflated concepts, all the myths that one entertains. I think this need for honesty and humility not only applies to the individual, but also to collective consciousness as such.

Of course, your question situated healing "between the soul and technology" from the outset, and I have not touched on this aspect at all. This is mainly because I don't see such a "between". As I argued in numerous publications (see above all volume 2 of my collected English papers, *Technology and the Soul*), technology is precisely one main place in and through which soul manifests. "The soul" is first of all what Jung called "the objective psyche" and *only secondarily* also a subjective and private reality. Our usual claim and tacit assumption that the main place of the soul is in us human beings and that, for example, our personal dreams are the *via regia* to it is one of the main reasons why we are in need of "healing" in the first place—a collective inflation and delusion.

(RH): As you have said that "technology is precisely one main place in and through which soul manifests", what are some of the implications of this for modern day depth therapists and healers?

(WG): Depth therapists usually work with individuals who have psychological problems. These problems are their personal problems. Unless patients happen to be suffering from a kind of addiction to computer games or some such symptoms for example, the topic of technology does not seem to be directly relevant for therapy.

Psychotherapy takes place in a niche, with technological civilization all around it, but relatively separate from it. Psychotherapy is concerned with (comparatively) petty things and people's private development. The soul's *opus magnum* is neither here nor there for it. Therapy can be successful even if the therapist has no interest in or insight into technology as one main place in which soul manifests.

If individual therapy is not involved with technology, one might perhaps get the idea that technology or the soul's *opus magnum* should now become the new "real patient". But it would be megalomaniac to think that we as professional psychotherapists should or could "heal", on a deep or soul level, what is or seems to be wrong with our technological civilization. The best we can do concerning the *magnum opus* is, on the one hand, to leave the soul alone (Jung once said—although not with respect to the soul in technology—that the best one could do was *not to disturb* the psychic process), *but*, on the other hand, also not to ignore it altogether, but to try to see and, with our conscious mind, accompany the process so as to become *aware* of and *comprehend* what is happening in the depth.

Indirectly, however, I think it is beneficial even for therapy if the therapist is psychologically educated, if he has a wider horizon than what is immediately necessary for therapy and thus knows about today's *opus magnum*, instead of only being a psychological repairman for people's problems. If he knows where the soul's present-day battlefield is and what its battle is about, he may better, and earlier, be able to see through the neuroticness of neurotic attitudes and understand what neurosis, as a general, cultural problem of modernity, comes from.

He may be better able not to confuse his patients with an authentic locus of "the soul", but instead be able to help them to become liberated from "the soul", so that they can learn to live their lives as the ordinary human beings that they are and to respect what is larger than they. One of Jung's main concerns, which I share with him, was that we distinguish ourselves from the soul.

Of course, this idea makes sense only if one does not mean by "soul" the life-force or life-principle in man (that which causes a body to be alive), a meaning which also occurs in Jung. However, I think it is obvious that this definition of "soul", known both from ancient popular belief and from Aristotle, belongs rather to biology—the theory of the living organism—than to a psychology with soul. Constitutive for true psychology is the "psychological difference", the difference of soul from man (as entity: Living organism or existing person).

Whereas the life-principle is in each organism (and thus also in each human being), the soul is, metaphorically speaking, all around us. To begin with, we are completely enveloped in it, in all sorts of archetypal, mythic ideas and other, more personal fantasies, collective prejudices and so on. And this is the reason why the need for our distinguishing ourselves from the soul arises in the first place. Individuation is a descent; essential to it is one's emancipation from the "suggestive power of unconscious images" (Jung), so that one may slowly learn to be "only that!", i.e., only what one really is. I already touched on this earlier when I spoke of humility.

(RH): What are some guides as a person tries to distinguish themselves from the soul?

(WG): If a person is in therapy, it would of course be the job of the analyst to guide him or her in this process of distinguishing himself/herself from the soul. But such a literal guide is probably not what you have in mind with your question.

I think the real guide is truth. Just as we have an inner voice ("conscience") in us that tells us when we are about to stray from or have strayed from the morally right path (*our own* right path), so we also each carry in ourselves the measure for what is truly "me or rather what is NOT really "me". And just as the work of conscience is not a one-time act, but an ongoing lifetime process, so also is our having to listen to the voice of our own truth.

What about god?

(RH): From the standpoint of the Soul, how do you understand God?

(WG): Animals are totally identical with their nature. They *are* their instinctual reactions. In man this oneness has been broken open into his *ek-sistence*, with the consequence that the innermost truths of lived life are experienced by him as if coming from outside and that there are for the human race such things as "truths" in the first place whereas for animals there are only "innate release mechanisms". This state in which one's inmost truths appear from "outside" in the form of representations, images, and concepts we call consciousness. Man IS (exists as) mindedness, soul (rather than as purely physical being) and inevitably has to *relate to* the truths of the inner logic of his (essentially social) existence and being-in-the-world. Since those truths and the necessity of relating to them are fundamentally communal, social, we get what we call culture.

It is in this context that I think about the topic of God. Gods are the crystallization and articulation before consciousness of the deepest or highest soul truths, of particular moments of the inner logic of a concrete social group's or people's actually lived life. All the soul's love and fear flow towards them as to its highest values. The concrete type and form of the gods, as expression of the inner truths of actually lived life, reflect the specific level of consciousness reached and, of course, also the more practical, socio-economical particulars of the culture.

Gods are fundamentally historical and thus relative to the specific epoch in the soul's logical life in which they emerge. Jung spoke, with Leopold Ziegler, of "the metamorphosis of the gods" and meant by this, for example, the historical change from polytheistic gods to the ONE high God as well as the change from gods to Platonic ideas and further to abstract concepts. This development is the sign of an increasing self-consciousness of consciousness. In the course of this development, there ultimately comes a point when it becomes impossible for the soul to still be upward-looking to its highest soul value as a semantic content of consciousness because it now has integrated it into the very form or "syntax" of consciousness. What used to be viewed as some numinous Other has *objectively* been seen through by the soul as part of its own self-relation.

This is why for the modern soul God has become impossible—which, however, does not preclude that now what we call *the ego* may take over instead and say, in one way or another, "gimme that old time religion, it's good enough for me". When this happens, we get religious fundamentalisms as well as all sorts of (more playful or frivolous) theoretical "revivals" of "the gods", or also the reduction of the former *God* (i.e., a Truth) to, and his withdrawal into, no more than a mere subjective "feeling". In these three ways, consciousness tries to retain as semantic content what has objectively long been alchemically distilled into logical form (into the syntax of consciousness).

The phenomenon of fundamentalism *malgré lui* openly demonstrates that *for it* the God it preaches has become psychologically obsolete, because it is only on account of the experienced obsolescence of "God" that fundamentalism's stubborn ego insistence, at time even fanaticism, is needed to prop him up, against the soul's better knowledge.

The ego clings to God (or to former gods in the plural) in order to delude itself about consciousness's already having irrevocably dropped from the level of semantics to the deeper level of syntactical form, alchemically speaking from the level of "the *physical* in the matter" to that of distilled or mercurial matter. The rescue of "God" is so important for this purpose because the notion of God is the linchpin and utmost principle of psychological semanticism as such (the epitome of our objectifying, reifying, personifying—of the whole "physicalism" inherent in the belief of psychologists in "*the* imaginal").

(RH): What do you say to those who say "I cannot understand what Wolfgang is saying. Why doesn't he write in a simpler way so it is easier to understand him?"

(WG): One possibility would be to answer them by quoting what Jung said about his own works, "As a matter of fact it was my intention to write in such a way that fools get scared and only true scholars and seekers can enjoy its reading . . .", but that would not be true at all, because I try to write as clearly as I can, without, however, flattening the issues to be discussed and losing their inner complexities. The problem is precisely not one of articulation.

Rather, the problem is that those people you have in mind seem to expect that what they read should be immediately understandable to them. How weird! An expectation characteristic of the age of fast food and one-minute sound bites. People without stamina. Their demand for immediate gratification

means psychologically two things. First, that what they want from a reading experience is confirmation and stabilization of their ordinary mind-set or,
expressed negatively, that there will not have to be a stretching of the mind,
nor any hard work, any continued circumambulation, any labor of the concept.
But in psychology we are in the field of inwardness, where it cannot be a matter merely of getting new input, new wine into the same old bottles, a mere
downloading of information. Psychological reading essentially involves *oneself* and one's self. It aims primarily for a transformation of the old bottles, that
is, a lifting of the very frame of one's mind to higher levels of differentiation.

Secondly, their demand means that their theory about understanding is
that *they* (as ego) should be the ones who understand. But in psychology it
is not a question of *our* understanding at all. What counts is only that the
soul understands.

In my voluntary reading I read only books that I don't understand. Why
should I bother with texts that I understand at first sight? What they would
bring to me would have to be so close to how I already think that it could
hardly be worth wasting my time on them. But when reading those difficult
books, I harbor the *un*understood within myself and live with it, go pregnant with it, often for many years, until perhaps, at long last, its meaning
discloses itself to me of its own accord.

In this context two quotations are very precious to me. The one is from
The New Testament. "But Mary kept all these things [that had been said]
and pondered them in her heart" (Luke 2:19). "Keep" in this sentence
means preserve, enclose, keep safe, like a treasure. This statement could
almost be considered a recipe for soulful reading. The other quote is from
Rilke who in *Letters to a Young Poet* wrote: "One must have patience
towards the unresolved things in one's heart and try to love *the questions
themselves,* as if they were locked rooms or books written in a very foreign language. . . . *Live* the questions now. Perhaps you will then gradually, without noticing it, live along some distant day into the answer" (July
16, 1903).[2] There is no rush. One's understanding can wait. It has all the
time in the world. The alchemists said: "In your patience you will gain your
soul" (Luke 21:19). So the issue here is: Immediate understanding—*or*:

---

2 Rainer Maria Rilke, *Letters to a Young Poet*, trans. M.D. Herter Norton (New York: W.W.
   Norton & Co., 1934), p. 35.

Carrying the ununderstood to full term and thus, possibly, *living* into the answer, into an understanding.

Behind this difference there is of course another, deeper one. Has, underneath *my* not understanding, *the soul in me* already caught fire by what I read, but do not understand—or has it not? Only if a kind of passion is kindled about what is in the ununderstood, in other words, only if the soul has already understood that *this* is something precious that simply needs to be understood, can I "keep all these things and ponder them in my heart" in the first place.

The point here is that for a psychological approach, the question or the ununderstood is known to have everything it needs within itself, even the solution to it. It *is* already the solution from the outset (or else we are not dealing with a soul question in the first place, but rather with a technical one). The solution or answer is not a second thing, a new addition.

At first we merely cannot see the question as the solution because we still look at it from outside (whereas the soul has already comprehended). To live into the answer therefore would mean nothing else and no more than our own being fully inwardized into the question.

Soul in today's world

(RH): What do you sense are some of the questions the Soul is living today?

(WG): I would of course say that what for us are questions are not so much questions for the soul, but rather the purposes or goals, the *telos*, of its *opus*. The soul always knows from the outset where empirically it still wants to go because in the last analysis, that is, logically, it always is already where it wants to go. This is so because it is uroboric. The "uroboros" includes, among all the contradictions that constitute it, also the one of "process" (still having to become or having to get to; the soul's *opus*) and "being" (always already having arrived, or being at home with itself, dwelling in its truth). "Process" is the empirical, historical aspect, "being" is the aspect of its inner logical truth. "Being", however, is dynamic movement, too. It is not static but dynamic as logical movement ("simultaneity of beginning and end"), not movement in time.

Kant introduced the notion of "transcendental appearance (or illusion)". In a similar way, but in a very different sense, I speak of a "psychological appearance" or "psychological delusion", because this is one that seems to come with, indeed, be built into, the very field of psychology as a modern science.

It is, as I already pointed out earlier, the self-indulgent, inflated modern mind's illusion that what psychologically counts is allegedly what goes on inside people—our private feeling, thinking, dreaming, and pathologizing (all of which is only material for ego-psychology). (By saying it is the modern mind's illusion, I want to distinguish it from subjective, personal illusions and inflations.)

The soul's process has never been inside people, it has always been in the culture at large, in how for each given culture reality was objectively constituted: In the mythology of heaven and earth, sun and moon, trees and rivers, birth and death, etc., or in the metaphysics of the world, in what later Kant and still later Heidegger would call ontotheology.

Jung said the soul is all around us. And so also today, when the soul has long left metaphysics (let alone mythology) behind as a valid expression of its truth, we have to look around us at the condition of the world that we find ourselves in, at our scientific and technological civilization, the economy (with its money market, consumerism, throw-away products, and advertising), the World-Wide-Web, the world of the media in general with its flooding people from outside with and enveloping them in information and images—in order perhaps to become aware of where the soul's process is today. And of course we would have to do so *with soul* and not only with our habitual positive-factual, scientific, or moralistic mentality if what we want to get aware of is really the soul, logical life, animating in the depths the enormous transformation of our world. Furthermore, it would be necessary not to approach these phenomena with an innocent, "child"-governed expectation that soul is something harmless, nice, beneficial, as if the soul had not always been a "tremendous" reality, demanding for example in ancient times blood-sacrifices and imagining gods of often downright brutal character.

After this long introduction I finally come to the core of your question. Looking *with* such an attitude and *at* the right places, we can perceive that the process we are in today, expressed in alchemical terms, seems to be one of *solutio, evaporatio, distillatio.* "All that is solid melts into air", Karl Marx had already observed 150 years ago. The issues that the soul is living today seem to be the overcoming of otherness in favor of self, the transformation of "entity" or "substance" into relation, functionality, mobility, and fluidity, of "semantics" into "syntax", as well as the substitution of an endless "futurity" (a fundamental openness and a centrifugal forward orientation, constant innovation) for any ground, center, home, and tradition.

As to the overcoming of otherness let me just point to the fact that in all previous ages the soul had made man look up and out to gods, in other words, to itself in the form of otherness and externality, which in the modern world is no longer possible for the soul. Only "the ego" can, by way of superstition and by means of voluntary self-stultification, pretend to still have an Other (examples are all kinds of fundamentalism as well as the idle talk in psychology of "the gods" and "the sacred", etc.). The soul has already objectively interiorized itself into itself (a fact born witness to—albeit, of course, only in literalistic, positivized form—precisely by the emergence of modern psychology itself with its "psychological illusion").

As to the dissolution of entity or substance and of our rootedness in a "metaphysical" ground and in tradition, one of the most obvious examples is to be found in an area immediately relevant for conventional psychology: The obsolescence, in the soul, of the concept of the human individual as a self with a clear and more or less constant identity. The present-day individual is *logically* a center-less "surfer" and has to reinvent himself or herself ever anew and maybe even lives simultaneously several imaginary identities ("second life", "web 2.0").

Jungian analysis

(RH): You have spent over thirty years as a Jungian analyst. How would you describe a Jungian analyst?

(WG): The world's Jungian analysts present a picture of the greatest diversity. Your question must therefore be conceived as referring to the "ideal type". But even then there cannot be a uniform description. One cannot present a list of articles of faith, theoretical convictions, and technical approaches that constitute the essence of being a Jungian analyst. I can only give a *formal* "description", and one that entails a contradiction.

A Jungian analyst is a person who is truly himself or herself, but who precisely inasmuch as he or she is himself or herself nevertheless feels committed to the "same" task that is the *spiritus rector* of Jung's psychology. Being oneself, honestly oneself, has priority in the description of a Jungian. Jungians are the "school of individuation", as Rudolf Blomeyer said, and this also means individuality. Jung rightly remarked that he alone can be a Jungian.

This means: To be a Jungian, you cannot be a Jungian, you have to be yourself. Any *imitation* of how Jung thought, any dogmatic *adoption* of his ideas, any *application* of techniques developed by him would disqualify you as a Jungian analyst.

The notion of "Jungian analyst" is thus inevitably a plural and not, as its linguistic form seems to suggest, a singular. The description of the ideal type of Jungian analyst unavoidably itself entails diversity. And as an aside I may mention that I think that here, in the area of real human individuals, we have the place where the important topic of pluralism in psychology really belongs. Jung referred to it under the label of the "personal equation". To locate it in the soul ("the plural psyche") or with the archetypes or gods ("polytheistic psychology") seems to me a misplacement. Now the question arises what makes all these diverse individuals, who are truly themselves, nevertheless "Jungians"? The distinguishing mark cannot be anything else in addition ("oneself plus Jung"), but it must already be intrinsic to the very notion of "being truly oneself".

If we were to define "Jungian analyst" along the lines of "oneself plus Jung" by means of a set of certain theoretical convictions, i.e., positive-factual features, this could be called a horizontal description, a move from oneself to some other. By contrast, the move to what one truly is oneself, to one's wanting to be *only* oneself, is vertical, a move from surface to core or inner essence. This commitment to *verticality*, if it is not restricted to oneself but extended to whatever shows itself, is in my opinion the distin-guishing mark of the Jungian analyst.

On the one hand, it is a commitment to the eachness of each phenome-non, the nowness of *this* patient's situation today, the my-ness of my under-standing of, and my answer to, whatever presented itself (instead of any subsumption of it under already given abstract-universal concepts, diagno-ses, or mythic images, or of any application to it of ready-made techniques). On the other hand, it is in all these regards the commitment to something that doesn't meet the eye, something beneath the level of positive facts, to the "soul" in the real, to the logical life or "alchemical opus" at work in what shows itself, to the historical depth of each present.

It is in keeping with this orientation that a Jungian analyst, although he may spend most of his time in the consulting room, in his perception and understanding does not start out from the experience gained in the treatment of patients, always remaining mindful of Jung's insight that it is only "the smallest part of the psyche . . . that presents itself in the medical consulting room" (*Letters 2*, p. 307, to Nelson, 17 June 1956). His starting point is the soul's life at large as it is displayed in the whole of cultural history. He appreciates the consulting room phenomena as no more than this "smallest part", and so he tries to see even them in the light of the larger horizon of the soul's *opus magnum* rather than conversely interpreting great cultural phenomena on the basis of his narrow consulting room experience.

One further implication of this orientation that deserves to be mentioned separately is that the Jungian analyst will not practice a personalistic psychology (which confuses empirical person and soul). "Rendering unto Caesar the things which are Caesar's and unto God the things that are God's" (Matthew 22:21), he meets his patients eye to eye, on a strictly human, personal level, *but* his *psychological* focus does precisely not go to the person. It goes to the Concept.

(RH): What is it like for a person to be truly themselves?

(WG): You should ask this of a person who is, or at least believes to be, truly himself or herself. I imagine that if one is truly oneself, one does not feel all that differently from other persons. Life and the difficulties it brings and *la condition humaine* would still be the same. But at least one would be relieved of all the contortions that come from being dissociated from oneself and having to fight against one's own truth.

Another point to be kept in mind is that how it is like to be truly oneself must greatly depend on who one is. If one is Mozart, being truly oneself is probably something quite different from being truly oneself as Napoleon, or as a sales clerk, or as an analyst, not to mention all the personality differences between individuals in temperament and character traits.

Sacrificial killings

(RH): In your book, *Killings. Violence from the Soul: An essay on the origin and history of consciousness*, you elaborate the importance of killing in the development of consciousness. You state: "The soul first made itself through killing. It killed itself into being". Given that, how do you think the Soul considers all the wars, genocides, murders, animal killings, and suicides?

(WG): Your question makes it necessary for me to introduce four differentiations on four levels. (1) There is a radical difference between acts in the service of the primordial *autopoiêsis* of the soul *in empirical, historical reality* on the one hand and acts performed on the basis of an already established or even highly developed soul on the other. In my book I interpreted the killing of the prehistoric hunters and that of the sacrificial slaughters in archaic cultures as killings of the former class, whereas all the phenomena you mention in your question belong rather to the latter class. (2) The kinds of killings that you mention are distinct phenomena and each kind needs to be looked at as a psychic phenomenon in its own right. (3) Each *instance* of war, of genocide, of animal killing, etc. needs to be looked at in its individuality (singularity) and in its own specific context. Not all real murders, to take only this example, are psychologically the same phenomenon.

In (2) it was a question of psychic phenomena as abstractions, as types (either "ideal type" or archetype, e.g., "war as such", "suicide as such"). It is clear that each type could again be divided into subtypes (for example, different types of murder: Out of jealousy, out of revenge, out of greed, for ideological or religious reasons, a sex crime, to get rid of a witness, calculated or spontaneous murder, etc. Many distinctions are possible.). Under (3) the focus is on concrete deeds happening at a specific time and place. So we always have to try to be clear about what exactly we are speaking, on what level and about what side of the distinctions on each level. But this also means that things become very complex and complicated, which is a good moment to remember that Jung called his psychology *"komplexe Psychologie"*.

With the last distinction (4) I come directly to your question. It is the distinction between phenomena of soul significance and phenomena of seemingly the "same" kind but without soul significance. Many, probably most, murders nowadays do not mean anything to the soul. They mean something to the ego, to our emotions and complexes, to the sensational press, and of course also to the police and judges, the perpetrators and the victims. They are human, all-too-human. Beware of those psychologists who try to inflate banal human experiences and biographies with mythic significance: They are "archetypal hysterics".

But if, for example, we recall that in ancient times the succession of the priesthood at a certain sanctuary was regulated in such a way that only he could become the new priest who had killed the incumbent priest, we immediately understand that here we are confronted with a murder of soul importance. The same applies to headhunting. But even today in very special, unlikely cases, an outrageous act of murder might have the soul significance of a transgression beyond the limits of the human, all-too-human into the region of the untread, and as such be the beginning of an initiation, who knows? Genocides are probably in all cases pathological events without soul dignity, just born out of human passions, prejudices, and complexes as well as ideological fixations; in other words, they have to be located on the level of the ego, however of the collective or mass ego, not of all the separate subjective egos.

Many questions come up in connection with wars. From which point of view does one want to look at a war? From the point of view of the politicians, of the nation, of the combat units, of the individual soldiers, of civilian victims? A war can mean very different things. Dictators may begin a war as a mere ego-trip or to distract attention from internal conflicts. There are imperialistic wars. Wars may be the result of economic necessities. We have Hillman's magnificent analyses of how the heat of battle can lead to the most extraordinary experience of soul depth for *individual* fighters. Sometimes war is psychologically (from a soul point of view) the indispensable and best answer to a situation of conflict. In such cases war means that one is willing to stake one's life for one's cause and to expose what one stands for to the acid test in material reality.

Now people often think that war should be avoided at all cost (which is the view of the ego solely interested in its own safety and comfort), and that conflicts could be resolved up in the air, merely through negotiations, that is, on the abstract-intellectual level of mere *talking*, not on the *real* level. But wars can also be irresponsible and stupid mistakes. So many possibilities . . . one could go on and on.

As I am speaking I have become aware of a necessary additional distinction. Let's take the French Revolution as an example. If you look at it sort of with a magnifying glass, in other words, at all its details, each single action and event, you will probably have to say that it is psychologically insignificant, a sum of many individual ego happenings. For those immediately involved in it, it will have ego character because they will inevitably be too close to it. As participating agents they are driven either from below by passions or from on top by pigheaded ideology, and for its victims it means just ordinary human misery and/or strategic effort to survive, all of which is "ego". The soul takes no interest in that. One needs distance to be able to see the French Revolution with the cold, sober glance of the soul (we must never forget that Greek *psychê* is related to *psychros*, cold).

From a distance, the French Revolution can be seen as a phenomenon in its entirety and with the place it has in the context of history at large. As such it speaks to the soul and is of great soul importance, because, *as* an empirical historical fact or *as* a semantic event, it is at the same time *also* symbolic or syntactical—the soul's killing once and for all its own age-old highfalutin notion of majesty, its ridding itself of the whole "*ancien régime*" (in the widest sense of the word: The whole system of numinosity), and its bringing itself down to a merely pragmatic, human level.

The soul is interested only in changes on the level of the logical constitution of consciousness or of the world. This distinction between individual actions or events in their positivity and empirical-factualness on the one hand, and the logic or syntax of the total phenomenon on the other hand, probably applies also to such a phenomenon as headhunting, indeed to rituals in general.

I imagine that each individual act of murder in a headhunting context is psychologically not all that significant. It is probably just one of those things a man has to do in such a society; it is executed pretty much on the ego level, and may thus even be "routine". The individual act of headhunting can only have soul importance, too, if and to the extent that it is, *as* this standard event, also immediately an instance of the *general institution* of headhunting and in fact authorized by it. Headhunting has a soul meaning or soul truth on the level of the cultic institution of headhunting, that is, the level of syntax, not on the empirical level of the (always contingent and human, all-too-human) performance of each individual instance of headhunting per se.

The precondition for the empirical act's immediately being an instance of the cultic institution, that is, for the possibility that *as* "semantic" event it is also immediately "syntactical", is that it occurs prior to the emancipation of the ego from the soul. The moment the ego has emancipated itself from its containment in the soul, rituals have become impossible, or "possible" only as simulation and pretense. What is left of them are hollow, lifeless, soulless semantic forms. This is why Jung, as a modern person, said, "I cannot return to the Catholic Church, I can no longer experience the miracle of the Mass" (*CW* 18 § 632). Modern man is irrevocably *extra ecclesiam*, which is of course a metonymy, a metonymy for *extra animam*, outside the soul (in the traditional sense of soul).

Working with dreams

(RH): How important are dreams to you and what are some of the ways that you work with your own dreams?

(WG): There is the view that dreams have a message (you already mentioned this earlier). They are the voice of "the unconscious". When one wants to go on a journey or has to decide for or against a project one has to consult one's dreams and listen to their message. Sometimes one hears people say something like "My dream told me that I should not go on this journey". I don't believe in this message idea.

Decades ago, Patricia Berry presented one dream to seven different analysts and got seven different interpretations. It has also happened that when I went back to a dream that I myself had interpreted a few days or a few years ago I saw it quite differently. The so-called message is always our subjective and situation-bound interpretation. It is a naive assumption that dreams have a fixed meaning. It greatly depends on what mind is hearing the dream and in what situation. So the idea that there is such a thing as "*the* dream" is already fallacious. For Berry's seven analysts her dream was seven different dreams.

This is why I shift "the importance of dreams" away from the dream itself as naked fact to our work (*opus*) with the dream. By itself the dream is not precious. It must not be inflated and mystified, as if it were something quasi holy. On the contrary, like the alchemical *lapis* it is *exilis* (uncomely), *vilissimus* (the cheapest because the commonest thing—anybody can have dreams), and of course in itself *occultus*. But it can *become* precious *when* it is worked and only *through* its being worked intelligently, with a certain depth of feeling and an antenna for soul. Working means: Decomposing, cooking, distilling, with a view to freeing the spirit Mercurius imprisoned in the dream's "matter".

It is deeply moving to see what *can* happen when one gives oneself over to an innocent little dream devotedly for a couple of hours, with diligent attention to each detail, each word, and with an attitude of simplicity and humility that does not want to "interpret" ("get its message"), but allows the words and phrases themselves to speak, without a will of one's own, with no pressure and lots of time. What first appeared to be a weird or banal text slowly comes alive. New horizons open themselves. One gets into deeper waters and becomes aware of a rich mesh of relations and meanings. It is a process. But of course, this happens only when one lucks out. There is no guarantee.

And it can happen only if one truly focuses on the dream rather than abusing the dream as a mere means to understand the person who had the dream, which is the *prôton pseydos* ("the basic error") of dream interpretation. The goal of the work has to be soul-making, the process and event of soul-making (here and now) as an end unto itself, not the cure or improvement of the *person* who dreamed. No ulterior motives. No wish for efficacy and results. The dream has to be enclosed and hermetically sealed in the retort. Everything that is not intrinsically part of the dream has to be kept out.

In the way of working, there is no difference between working with my own dreams and—in therapies or in the many dream seminars that I have held or supervision sessions I give—working with the dreams of others. But for some time now I have not kept a dream diary anymore, and it is rare that I really devote myself to some dream I had. There are enough other and better starting points ("prime matters") for the *opus* of soul-making than my personal stuff. I'm not interested in myself. I find other things interesting.

Also, I do my thinking openly and on my own responsibility; I do not have the need, as Jung apparently did, to push my insights down into unconsciousness so that they could only pop up, surprise, surprise, "from out of the unconscious" in the form of "spontaneous" dream revelations and as "objective natural facts".

(RH): It surprises and interests me that say that you are not interested in yourself. How then do you react to a statement Jung once made:

> If things go wrong in the world, this is because something is wrong with the individual, because something is wrong with me. Therefore, if I am sensible, I shall put myself right first. For this I need—because outside authority no longer means anything to me—a knowledge of the innermost foundations of my being, in order that I may base myself firmly on the eternal facts of the human psyche. (*CW* 10 § 329)

(WG): I find this quote pretty awful. It is full of fallacies—one-sidednesses and half-truths. How does Jung know that there are *eternal* facts of the human psyche? This is a "metaphysical" assumption. To be sure, I take it for granted that all human beings at all times existed as mind or soul, but it in no way follows from this that this mind or soul as which we all exist was constituted the same way. Are the "facts" of the human psyche the same in me as in an Aztec or a prehistoric hunter, or even a medieval European? The "facts" of the human psyche change. What they are always remains to be seen, to be found out. The soul is essentially historical. It is not like human biology, which strictly speaking is of course also not eternally the same, but concerning which we can, for all practical ends and purposes and in comparison with the malleable and adaptable soul, speak of its eternal facts.

Another point: It is certainly a good idea to put oneself right. But first of all, I consider this to be one's general responsibility throughout life, independently from whether things go wrong in the world or not. It's one's duty toward oneself and toward one's neighbor and simply part of being fully human.

Secondly, this task of self-reflection and work on oneself must not be abstractly dissociated as one's navel gazing in isolation from the world. We have to see the dialectic of self-relation and world-relation. I can only hope to put myself right (in the sense of this permanent task) if I stay in contact with the world and the people around me. My interaction with others and my involvement in the world must in themselves be self-reflective. No split: First the one and then the other. Let's take speaking as an example. When I speak, I speak to others, but at the same time I listen to myself and reflect whether what I said really makes sense or not. And if I become aware that it was stupid, I try to correct what said. Living in the world and self-correction go hand in hand. This is the normal situation: "Ad hoc engineering".

There are of course exceptional situations, like situations of psychic illness when one has become trapped within oneself. In that case it would be helpful to be, as it were, dry-docked, taken out of circulation for a general rebooting, in other words, given the opportunity to devote one-self abstractly to oneself in the *temenos* of a consulting room. And I also think that a time of analysis especially in young adult years would be good for everybody (except maybe for born politicians and leaders in the world of action, in the economy, etc., and perhaps great artists and thinkers) to give one's capacity of self-reflection a boost. But what I find detestable would be to live with the feeling that I am for myself "problem no. 1".

This takes me directly to Jung's assertion that "if things go wrong in the world, this is because something is wrong with the individual, because something is wrong with me". What an inflation! Both the inflation of the notion of the importance of the individual, of myself with my petty psychic problems (am I to be likened to "the lamb who taketh away the sin of the world"?) and, indirectly, the inflation of the significance of psychology, psychotherapy.

Psychology is not all that important. It has nothing to do with the improvement of the world or, as Jung once even said, the rescue of the world. Hillman rightly attacked the idea that psychotherapy could bring about a bettering of the world and suggested that there should be a shift "from mirror to window". But by saying "We've had a hundred years of psychotherapy and the world is getting worse" he shows his disappointment, and inasmuch as a disappointment is the disappointment of a hope or wish he shows that he, too, wants to be in the business of world-improvement, and that ultimately he has a deep longing for a rescue of the world. For me, this is the hope of a prophet, not the job of a psychotherapist. That in the perception of its contemporaries the world is getting worse is normal. It applies to all times. One must not literalize it.

There is nothing wrong with the world's getting worse. It is simply how the world *is*. No need for a rescue. Nothing to make a fuss about. What is really needed, and all that is needed, is that *we* prove ourselves in our life in this world. Let me call Jung to witness against the Jung of your quote: We "want to see the world as it is and leave things in peace. We do not want to change anything. The world is good as it is" (*CW* 18 § 278).

Jung's statement that you cited is also very unfair. Many things go wrong in the world that have nothing to do with my psyche. I may have gotten my house in order, but it may not make any difference in the world at large. And things can be really wrong with me internally, and the world outside is not getting any worse.

Above all, Jung's view operates with a fiction, the fiction of an abstract, isolated individual, that is to say, with the idea that the individual is a fixed natural entity (in analogy to the biological organism). But, if I may use a term from physics, the human individual *is in itself* the *resultant* of itself and the world, the resultant of individual and collective. It is a dialectical reality.

It is not that here there is the individual as a positive fact and over there, vis-à-vis it, the world as another positive fact. Just as the world is always (the unity of the world itself *and*) the world as it is *seen* by people at a given historical time, so the individual has always already been formed and continues to be informed by the world. Is what I personally think really my personal thought? Or is it not, *as* my thought, an expression of the *Zeitgeist*, even if what I think should be, as in Nietzsche's case, *untimely* meditations? This is why, although the focus on the individual is at times helpful and necessary for a person, the individual is certainly not the locus where the wrongs of the world are rooted and could be tackled.

This is a positivistic fallacy of Jung's. The "wrongs" of the world are not psychic, but psychological, that is to say, they are located in the logic of the situation at each historical locus, a logic that permeates the world just as much as it does each individual.

The future of Jungian analysis

(**RH**): In the western world of psychotherapy and mental health, attention is now given to short-term and solution-focused work. More and more people have an assortment of medications they regularly use, often without any end in sight. More parents are asking that their children be on medications and more and more children are given mental diagnosis. People often want to feel good quick and long-term healing and transformation work involved in depth approaches usually takes and is not paid for by insurance companies. Some people today feel they are "in therapy" by seeing their psychiatrist monthly for a medication check up. Given this what do you see as the future for the work of depth psychotherapy such as Jungian analysis?

(**WG**): What you described is indeed a very powerful, and also a very deplorable development. I think it is one aspect of a large-scale historical development towards the redefinition of man as an apparatus (cf. La Metrie, *L'homme machine*, 1748) and toward a fundamental systematic repression of the mind. Even Jungian analysts nowadays often participate in this movement by trying to interpret the findings of the new neurosciences as "support" for, or even proof for the correctness of, what psychoanalysis has said all along, thereby projecting mind into matter, that is, burying it there.

Another rather different aspect of the same movement is the strong desire of many people to benumb themselves by means of roaring music, drugs, mass sports events, etc. This is a love of mindlessness, consciousness wanting to become unconscious. I discussed some aspects of this once under the title of the soul's "self-immurement in Plato's Cave". All this is of course absolutely counter to what Jungian analysis aims at, but then one must also see that Jungian psychology is itself in some ways a counter-movement against the stream of modernity, a defensive attempt to rescue something that it *knows* to be over.

What do I think about the future for the work of Jungian depth psychotherapy? Let me mention a number of different options and considerations.

1. In a diversified society such as ours, there will always be a market for all sorts of things, no matter whether they are crazy or respectable. There are so many different people with different needs that one can be sure that some people will also have a need for Jungian analysis in all the different ways that it is and will be practiced by all the numerous different persuasions in Jungianism. Conversely, as the demand gets smaller, analytical psychology may also adapt to the changes in society and accommodate the public tastes, becoming more and more a pop psychology. One aspect of modernity is, for example, the search for meaning, and many Jungians already today cater to this longing, about which one must not have any illusions: It, too, is a mode of drugging the mind, of making consciousness more unconscious. The more complex and technical life gets, the stronger this longing might possibly become, at least with some people.
2. There will always be people with psychological problems, and some will find that medication and "quick techniques" do not work for them. For them Jungian analysis really has something to offer, at least if it is practiced, for example, along the lines that Marco Heleno Barreto ("It is something like antique philosophy", in *Spring 77*) showed to be Jung's approach to therapy.
3. Jung did not conceive his psychology as being something for the masses anyway. He aimed at an elite. In this sense the general trend of society away from analysis might not hurt Jungian analytical psychology and practice at all. Considering the development toward pop psychology that I mentioned, an enforced shrinking of its presence in society, a lack of public recognition (both financially, by health insurances, and intellectually), might even be good for Jungian analysis. It could perhaps work upon it as a kind of *sal sapientiae*, and represent a new chance for it, the chance to become aware again of what is really significant.

4. A final thought. Everything has its time. It is not unthinkable that the time of Jungian analysis is nearing its end, by which I mean that it has served its historical purpose, that the life that once has been its internal motor has gone out of it, so that all it can still do only amounts to a kind of rehash. I mention this only as a possibility. If so, maybe truth will find completely new forms of expression in the future. Jung once said that the middle of life is the birth of death. In this sense psychotherapy, especially during the second half of life, sometimes attempts, as one of its aims, to help consciousness to integrate death into life. Hillman reminded us in his *Suicide and the Soul* that for Plato and others, philosophy is the pursuit of death and dying. Jungian psychotherapy must not fear its own death.

(RH): What would make consciousness want to be unconscious?

(WG): In one or a couple of hundred years from now we might be in a better position to answer this important question, because the outcome of a development tells us something about its telos. But we are still at the beginning of this development, so all I can offer is a provisional answer in the nature of hypotheses and hunches.

It would be easiest to view this tendency as a defensive reaction to the fundamental, revolutionary changes that we are confronted with and thus ascribe it to "the ego". On the one hand we have lost most of our values, established customs and traditions; we are deprived of all our accustomed and cherished certainties; on the other hand, modern life is becoming increasingly complex and thus makes ever higher, for most of us probably overtaxing, demands on us, intellectually and emotionally.

The extraordinary abstractness and sublimatedness of the level reached in modernity makes the plight that is deeply felt nearly invisible and intangible. It is not like war-time, for example, where you know what dangers you are up against. Closing one's (psychological) eyes to this situation even when factually inevitably having to go through it with one's literal eyes still open may seem to be a relief—much like undergoing surgery under local anaesthesia.

But such a personalistic interpretation in terms of an ego defense is probably too easy. This development is too powerful, too "big" not to also have a certain soul dignity. It is of course possible that the personalistic ego perspective and the soul perspective both apply at the same time: The ego may, unbeknownst to itself, be in the service of the soul and do the soul's bidding; that is, the defense described may be an instrument of the soul for its own, very different purposes. This is all the more likely when we consider that "the ego" *is* in itself unconscious(ness) anyway and from the outset. But that leaves us with the question what those soul purposes might be.

I have tried to think about them along the lines of the Christian idea of *kenôsis* (Phil. 2:7), an emptying or self-divestiture. We seem to be in the process of the soul's radically working-off all remnants of its previous commitment to myth and metaphysics, its notions of substance and subject, the inner and the individual. Man becomes (psychologically) redundant, obsolete. And this may be the way in which the soul moves from the hitherto prevailing subjective psychology to a truly objective psychology.

The soul's logical life, so one might think, wants to give up and come down from its lofty place in the human mind (mythic imagination and metaphysical ideas) and realize itself as in fact independent, objective life, that is, to *incarnate* in objective reality "out there", all around us. Formerly, it was the nature of the real that it was natural life—the *natural* sequence of day and night and the seasons, the *natural* forces and events of birth and death, growth and decay, illness, earthquakes, volcanos, floods, famine, wars—and the soul was merely the *mind's* mythic or metaphysical in-depth *apperception, reflection,* and ritual accompaniment of these natural forces.

But now the real is no longer simply natural life. It is decidedly postnatural. Now it is precisely the real that is in itself intellectual or soul life, governed, as it is, by obviously not natural forces—the self-propelled development of industry, technology, science, capitalism, advertising—and what is imagined and thought about all this by the human mind is merely "ego" (personal opinions, "feelings", hypotheses, ideologies).

(RH): Viktor Frankl and others have highlighted the search for meaning. You feel such a focus contributes to consciousness becoming unconscious?

(WG): Definitely. While not wishing to deny that Frankl was an intelligent man with valuable insights into many important issues, I do think that the search for meaning (meaning per se) is ideological and as such self-stultifying because it is a *petitio principii,* a begging of the question. One then approaches reality and life with an ego agenda, an idiosyncratic prejudice. One is ultimately motivated by a striving for wish-fulfillment and not for truth. And this search is positivistic in the sense that it makes out of "meaning" an entity, a commodity that is supposed to be available somewhere and only has not yet been found.

There is a difference between two types of searches. It sometimes happens that I have to look for my keys or my glasses. I know they must be somewhere because I had them in my hands an hour ago, I just don't know where. When during the 19th century people searched for the sources of the Nile, they were not searching for something already known and merely lost; nevertheless it was a legitimate search because it is inherent in the concept of a river that it must have a source in positive reality. This is not a subjective, ideological presupposition. It, too, is a search for something positive-factual known to exist, even if nobody had ever before set eyes on them.

These are examples from the sphere of positive fact. Now I come to the sphere of meaning. If an ancient inscription in unknown characters is discovered and scholars try to "search" for its meaning, or if we are confronted with works of art or with our dreams and try to get their meaning, this is a legitimate search. It is the inscription, the work of art, the dream themselves (and not us) that make the presupposition that they have a meaning inasmuch as they are products of the mind and not facts of nature, that is to say they are produced to express a meaning. In those cases, a "search for meaning" would be hermeneutic, an attempt at interpretation, deciphering, a search for the (still unknown) meaning *of a text*.

The search for Meaning absolute is totally different because it is neither hermeneutic nor an empirical search. *This* Meaning refers to the *omnitudo realitatis* and to life as a whole. As such it can neither be discovered *in* reality like the sources of the Nile nor can mortal man fancy himself to be in a position to decipher the meaning of the world and life, because this would imply that he claims to have the world and life before him as a well-circumscribed "text" or a "sign", as if he were the Creator God. We are *in* the world and *in* life and thus cannot have an overview of it. For the Creator the world as a whole may be a "text" or artwork that has a meaning.

For "unborn" man, e.g. medieval man, whose psychological unbornness precisely consisted in his still being identified with the standpoint of God and in his consequent viewing life *sub specie aeternitatis*, the meaning of life was a legitimate idea. But for this very reason he could not and did not need to search for meaning, did not speak of meaning—meaning absolute was simply no topic—because being identical with the viewpoint of God he always already lived in the self-evident presupposition of meaning. For "born" man, however, this Meaning is illegitimate, and that it is illegitimate is betrayed in the very phrase "search for meaning", which is a contradiction in terms.

To come back to your question, inasmuch as the search for meaning amounts to one's cocooning oneself in an inflationary phantasm, it is part of the modern striving for becoming more unconscious.

The internet

(RH): Many people spend a good portion of everyday on the internet. Creative minds devise clever ways to devise viruses that do severe damage to computer servers and data systems. Pornography, cyber sex, doing business, meeting others for dating and support groups help drive online life. One person told me she has found God in the "Google". What is it about the internet that has captured us?

(WG): It might perhaps be better to say that a door to an absolutely new realm, a new world, has been pushed open for us rather than that something has captured us. This new realm is at first like a vacuum into which quite spontaneously stream all sorts of energies that had before been packed into, contained in, and restricted by, our tight natural world. And inasmuch as it is a decentralized, deregulated, to some extent even lawless realm, in a limited way comparable to the Wild West of the 19th century, you find not only useful and valuable things in it, but also all sorts of stupid or despicable things as well. You mention the malicious or criminal activities of creators of computer viruses or pornography, we could also add hate and defamation blogs. It appears, for the time being, to be a realm of unlimited possibilities.

Having mentioned the Wild West as somehow comparable, I now have to point to the fundamental difference. The Wild West was a new realm on the same reality level, the same earthly plane, as the already inhabited civilized world, simply "west" of it. But the new world of the internet is "above" the old world and categorically (logically, syntactically) different. It represents a totally new reality level. With or in it, the new logical status of consciousness or the new logical constitution of being-in-the-world has at long last come home to itself, I mean that status of consciousness or logic that in fact, but only implicitly has prevailed ever since the final collapse of myth and metaphysics at the beginning of the 19th century. The internet is the objective representation or concretization of that new reality level.

Myth and metaphysics had been the mental reflection *of the life in the naturally given world*. In the latter, they had their ground. This is why one of the central notions of philosophy had been that of Being. But the time of Being and with it that of nature, of the physical world as the unsurpassable logical, psychological *basis* of human existence has been over for two hundred years. With the emergence of the internet this has become obvious, visible. With the internet, the substrate of the real itself has become intellectual. It is no longer natural, substantial; it is logical form: programs, algorithms, and its contents no longer come with the old sense of the seriousness and dignity of a truth-claim, but are much more playful, for the moment, for show.

Along with the sense of nature as the absolute base, the notion of truth itself has evaporated. How could there be truth as the *adaequatio rei et intellectus*, if the *res* has (logically, not literally) dissolved into thin air? Truth has been replaced by self-referentiality.

The physical that the internet still cannot do without has been reduced to the absolute minimum of a combination of two states, 0 and 1. We have now *in practical reality* entered the new definition of the world as a thoroughly virtual reality. The world as "mediality". This is what the internet is the objective self-display or symbolic expression of. The post-natural character of the new world as visibly displayed by the internet also shows in the fact that the internet has, for all practical ends and purposes, made itself independent of the limits of time and space. It is global and instantaneous. It has no place. As such it is, to be sure, not a social utopia in the sense of a fiction, the dream of a better world, but an ontological and *real* utopia (*oy topos*: "No place").

Healing

(RH): What have you found that heals people?

(WG): This is a highly complex question, first, because "healing" can mean many different things, secondly, because it is also part of *my* experience that all sorts of other therapists working with entirely different techniques (including even charlatans) can have healing successes, and thirdly, because people and their needs are very different, so that what may have a healing effect in one case may not work at all in another.

Instead of going into the diversity of the topic of "what are the factors that heal?" (I wrote and lectured on this; a short version of the text has been published, but only in Japanese and in German), let me here merely give a few hints about three general factors or aspects that in my estimation are both helpful for healing and required by my sense of psychotherapeutic ethics.

(1) I agree with the characteristically Jungian insight that it is the person of the therapist and not his techniques that is one main factor for healing. I have an effect on a patient first of all through *who* I am (through my truth) and not so much through what I say or do, my appearance—or through what I say and do only to the extent that it is really me. This means ethically that I have to try to *be* who I am and face my patients on that basis. Honesty with respect to myself and simplicity (no airs). And: *Oportet me adesse*; I have to be fully present, as myself, and not be merely a functionary.

(2) My next point is indirectness. Although therapy ultimately is of course usually undertaken for the purpose of healing, in whatever sense of the word, as a therapist, in my actual working with patients, I have no interest in healing and I try to get my patients to forget their concern about getting healed, too. The interest in healing would place the whole therapeutic endeavor under an ego intentionality. But the therapeutic purpose is to work without a purpose of one's own and to *devote* oneself instead to each topic at hand, trying to do justice to it at best one can. Therapy as liberation in action from ego willing, a liberation in and as a continued practice. For this reason I do not think about therapy in terms of the "healer archetype" or any such highfalutin ideas.

I know that I am not a healer, not *the* healer (I am only me), and that it is not my job to heal. If anybody or anything, it is the soul that does the healing. By standing back from any interest in *my* having a healing effect and success, I let the soul do its work, letting the soul cure itself (if it wants to), while I do my work of diligently attending to what *is* at each point. The indirectness described is in itself a main healing factor because psychic illness means that the soul's logical life has become stuck at some point and healing, the way I understand it, means nothing else but its becoming fluid again.

(3) "The truth shall make you free" (John 8:32). Leaving aside what it is intended to mean in its own religious context, this statement can also be considered a motto for therapy. The soul wants, the soul needs truth. But what is truth here? In a first preliminary sense, it of course includes what Jung discussed under the heading of one's "confession" of one's (conscious)

dark secrets ("confession" in therapy after "its prototype, the institution of the confessional") as well as the lifting of any repression and denial, i.e., the integration of one's (unconscious) shadow into one's self-definition. But both of these are still truth projects only in a strictly subjective and ego sense. Even more important, deeper, and more soulful is the task of *releasing* each phenomenon, whatever *is*, into its truth, that is to say, both into its *being* true and into the disclosedness (*alêtheia*) of its inner essence, its soul.

This latter aspect could imaginally be described in alchemical terms as the liberation of the spirit Mercurius from his imprisonment in the opaqueness of the matter. But with both these aspects we are approaching a sensitive terrain where something Jung once said, albeit in a different context, applies. "Naturally these things can hardly be made clear to unintelligent people. An adequate capacity to understand is essential, for without a considerable degree of *subtler* intelligence they will only be misunderstood" (*Letters 2*, p. 410, to L. King, 14 January 1958, my emphasis). One of the relatively common misunderstandings of a cruder, less soulful intelligence is to read the phenomena back into ready-made myths from the property room of antiquity and to cloak, enwrap, them in those myths: Mystification by "mythologizing" instead of unconcealment.

Giegerich vs. Jung

(RH): How do you suspect Jung would react to all your challenging ideas about his psychology?

(WG): Let me preface my response with the following general comment about a point I feel strongly about. I do not think it appropriate to trespass into somebody else's mental territory and his freedom of thought by anticipating what his possible answer to what I said might be. I feel it best to stay on my side, that is, to merely state my case and, stopping there, leave it to the other person to react any way he or she sees fit. The reaction must, I think, *logically* always come as a "surprise" to me (even if in its content it may be conventional or in tune with my previous experience of the person concerned). In this sense, I think that Jung's reaction, too, to my ideas must be left open. He might react in a completely unforeseen way, or he might react as is to be expected from what we know about him. Therefore, in order to stay on my side of the dividing line in the encounter between him and me, I take your question to be about how *I assess* the position in which my thoughts stand to Jung's ideas. And I will only consider what you call my "challenging" ideas about his psychology, not the many areas and points in which I concur with him.

Jung, who is usually seen as a defector from Freud, once made the perhaps surprising statement that he, Jung, was the only one of Freud's followers who developed further those themes that were closest to Freud's heart. In other words, he felt that in the deepest sense he was true to Freud despite the radical disagreement between them. I view my relation to Jung in a similar way. I think I have been true to Jung, to his deepest concern, however in a way that also (yes!) violates him. And by "violate" I do not only refer to the one-sidedness with which I concentrate on the *psychological* Jung and ignore or reject the other, the naturalistic, scientistic Jung; I also think that with some of my ideas I do not even do full justice to the psychological Jung. For to do full justice to him would mean to accept Jung's teachings in the very way that *he* presented them and that he passionately stood up for. His *central* views were not merely opinions he held, opinions that might be up for discussion, but they were Jung himself, the unique person he was.

But by in this way doing justice to him one would paradoxically not be really true to him, that is, true to the soul of his life-work. We see, for example, from his stubborn, complex-ridden reaction to some of his critics like Martin Buber and from the venom with which he rejected Hegel (without having any intimate knowledge, let alone understanding, of the latter's philosophy) that not everything was above board with his theorizing. Because, on the one hand, he was a child of his time, a member of a generation born during the second half of the positivistic 19th century, but because, on the other hand, what he saw as being absolutely at stake at his time and which he was deeply committed to was utterly contrary to the positivistic spirit prevailing to some extent also in him, he was unable to give to the soul (the deeper Mercurial spirit and essence) of his psychology a convincing and coherent conceptual formulation.

The concept of "the unconscious", to take only this one obvious example, is a compromise formation, a compromise between Jung's need to rescue the notion of soul as a truth and reality (truly soul in its logical *negativity*: *Un*-conscious) and the character of the age he lived in, Industrial Modernity, which was basically *positivistic*, materialistic, atheistic. I already critiqued "the unconscious" earlier in our discussion. Its problem, with respect to the present context, is at least threefold.

First, the way Jung conceived it, it manages indeed to save the *notion of soul* in its negativity, but only for the dear price that what soul now meant was restricted to "symbol", "myth" and "mythic image", "the divine", "meaning", in other words, to a *former*, long obsolete figuration (form of manifestation) of soul that was no longer how and where the soul in fact showed itself in modernity. This makes it regressive.

Second, the *validity* and *truth* of the contents of the unconscious was positivistically claimed to be already fully given with, and guaranteed by, no more than the bare positive fact of their occurrence, the mere event of their experience (plus, of course, their amplification, which, however, amounted to no more than the gathering of other earlier, *likewise* merely positive-factual occurrences of the same). The notion of the unconscious is conceived on the basis of a naive and again positivistic belief in the possibility of immediacy or directness and primordiality (the notion of *Urerfahrung*). The indispensable topic of mediation, of the syllogism (or *coniunctio*) nature of psychic truth, was expelled from the level of the syntax of experience and theory and reductively relegated to the semantic level of the contents of experience (the images from the unconscious).

And third, the *negativity* of the notion of soul was literalistically acted out in the form of the establishment of the idea of the *un*-conscious, that is, of a segregated, independently existing psychic realm systematically dissociated (split off) from consciousness and actually lived life. It *had to* be dissociated for two reasons, because what was to be experienced from out of the unconscious (in Jung's sense) was from the outset obsolete and therefore had to be a fundamentally alien element in modern life, and because, being in the status of flat positive-factual events (experiences), it was cut off from the syntax of really lived life. But of course, precisely on account of both these features what came from "the unconscious" could for some people's consciousness hold a powerful attraction, the fascination of the exotic (usually uncritically called "numinosity"; for much the same phenomenon, although in the different area of economic life, Karl Marx had critically used the term "fetishism").

Jung did not see these severe shortcomings of the concept of "the unconscious" and so it was, as we know, absolutely non-negotiable for him.

Coming back to your question, at least I would not have to fear that particular standard charge from him that he leveled at Buber and many theologians and other theoreticians, the charge that I lack the practical therapeutic experience to know what he was talking about.

(RH): What is a favorite poem and selection of music for you?

(WG): I have numerous favorite poems from different epochs and poets (e.g., Andreas Gryphius, Matthias Claudius, Goethe, Hölderlin, Mörike, Hugo von Hofmannsthal . . .), quite a few of which I know by heart. It would be unfair of me to single out one of them. There is a great variety of topics, styles, moods that have their own place and importance in or for different life situations. As to music, my favorite composers are Bach, Händel, Haydn, Mozart, examples of favorite works: the St. Matthew Passion, the Nelson Mass, *Così fan tutte* . . .

(RH): It has been an honor for me to share this interview with you. Your ideas give my thinking function a true work out. I look forward to keeping up with your work.

(WG): Thank you for so patiently bearing with me and for your openness to my (as you say) challenging ideas.

* * *

(Addendum, October 2008)

Worries about the future

(RH): At the time of our interview the United States and the whole world are experiencing the shaking of our financial foundations and people are frightened and very worried about the future. From a depth standpoint what is a helpful approach to understand and approach such enormous concerns?

(WG): Worries about the future may well be justified under the present conditions. But I think that such worries and fears are emotions that belong to the sphere of the ego, its "survival" interests, its needs "to cope". For the soul those worries are not significant. It is not really affected or involved, so I would not want to introduce a depth standpoint here. I rather think what is really needed is common sense and a kind of "philosophical" attitude. World War I rudely awakened people from their illusions that there would be a constant progress of humanity toward ever higher rationality and more refined civilization. The current crisis may shatter some of our illusions that we have a vested right to financial security and happiness and remind us again of the ancient insight that we are in the hands of fate that may bring to us good as well as bad times.

We don't *own* our good fortune, and so also not our fortunes (just as we do not even own our life, for that matter). Former ages lived with the idea of the Wheel of Fortuna that can take you to the top but also drop you down into misery. Homer's *Iliad* has a passage about the two vats of Zeus, one filled with good things, the other full of evils, from which Zeus is said to mete out to each person his personal share. And we learn there that to most people he gives a bit from both barrels, but to a few only from the one filled with evils, whereas the third possibility, that he allots to a person only good things, has never been heard of. Homer's advice is: *Anscheo*, take it in your stride. Religious people might say: "the LORD gave, and the LORD hath taken away; blessed be the name of the LORD". The main thing today is not to get hysterical about the situation (the way people got hysterical about "September 11"), not to inflate this ego issue and ordinary life event with soul importance, but to lick one's wounds and to think about one's next best moves. And maybe one can even learn something from the mistakes that were made and become a bit wiser than before.

Index

For Product Safety Concerns and Information please contact our EU
representative GPSR@taylorandfrancis.com
Taylor & Francis Verlag GmbH, Kaufingerstraße 24, 80331 München, Germany